AF323816

DISCOURSE, IDENTITY AND THE QUESTION OF TURKISH ACCESSION TO THE EU

For Martha, Gabriel and Daniel MacMillan

Discourse, Identity and the Question of Turkish Accession to the EU
Through the Looking Glass

CATHERINE MACMILLAN
Yeditepe University, Turkey

ASHGATE

Published by
Ashgate Publishing Limited
Wey Court East
Union Road
Farnham
Surrey, GU9 7PT
England

Ashgate Publishing Company
110 Cherry Street
Suite 3-1
Burlington, VT 05401-3818
USA

www.ashgate.com

British Library Cataloguing in Publication Data
A catalogue record for this book is available from the British Library

The Library of Congress has cataloged the printed edition as follows:
Macmillan, Catherine, author.
  Discourse, identity and the question of Turkish accession to the EU : through the looking glass / by Catherine MacMillan.
      pages cm
  Includes bibliographical references and index.
  ISBN 978-1-4094-5559-2 (hardback) – ISBN 978-1-4094-5560-8 (ebook) – ISBN 978-1-4724-0743-6 (epub) 1. European Union–Turkey–Membership. I. Title.
  HC241.25.T9M32 2013
  341.242'209561–dc23

2013005981

ISBN   9781409455592 (hbk)
ISBN   9781409455608 (ebk-PDF)
ISBN   9781472407436 (ebk-ePUB)

Printed in the United Kingdom by Henry Ling Limited, at the Dorset Press, Dorchester, DT1 1HD

Contents

Acknowledgements

This book would not have been possible without many discussions with friends and colleagues at different stages in its preparation, including Dr Adriana Raducanu and other colleagues at Yeditepe University, Dr. Armağan Emre Çakır and participants at the various conferences where the ideas of this book were presented, especially the Workshop on Europe and Islam at the 13th Mediterranean Research Meeting at Montecatini Terme in March 2013. Other friends and colleagues whose work over the years has been a particular inspiration for this book include Professor Nedret Kuran-Burçoğlu, Dr. Çiğdem Nas and Dr. Selcen Öner.

I also wish to thank the staff at Ashgate for their support of the project and for all their hard work, in particular Social Sciences editor Rob Sorsby. Thanks are also due to the anonymous reviewer who suggested chapter 2 of this book. I would also like to thank the editors of the *Journal of Contemporary European Studies,* and Dr. Clara Sarmento who edited articles where some of the ideas included in this book were first developed.

Although there are too many of them to thank individually, I also wish to thank all those friends and colleagues who have provided much needed moral support during the writing of this book. Special thanks are due to my family, in particular to my parents Ian and Susanne MacMillan, for their support over the years and their enthusiasm for this project.

Istanbul, December 2012

Introduction

Turkey's accession process, the longest in the history of the European Union (EU), has been likened to the myth of Sisyphus, condemned to the torture of repeatedly rolling a boulder up a hill only to watch it roll back down again (Çakır 2011: 166). Despite making its first application for associate membership in 1959, Turkey remains in the waiting room for accession, although in the meantime at least 21 other countries have 'jumped the queue' for membership. In this context, Paul describes Turkey's accession process as 'a story of misperceptions, misunderstandings, prejudices, and irrational expectations' (Paul 2012: 25).

According to the 1963 Ankara Agreement signed between Turkey and the EU, a customs union would be set up in three stages: a preparatory stage, a transitional stage and a final stage (Yılmaz 2009: 2). The Ankara agreement was potentially seen as a step towards full membership: in fact, both the preamble and article 28 of this agreement clearly mention the prospect of Turkey eventually becoming a member of the European Community (EC), although no commitment is made in this respect (Diez 2011: 170). In this context, Turkey's intention to accede to the European Economic Community (EEC) at an unspecified later date was officially recognised, with then Commission President Walter Hallstein declaring that 'Turkey is part of Europe' (Dorronsoro 2004: 49).

The Turkish military coup of 12 September 1980 naturally postponed both the development of the customs union and Turkey's bid for full membership still further. In effect, European Community (EC)–Turkey relations were frozen[1]. The military regime in Turkey lasted for two years, during which the political system was completely redesigned, curbing freedom of speech and political participation (Yılmaz 2009: 3). This regime formally ended in November 1983, when elections took place and a new civilian government led by Turgut Özal was elected. Following the restoration of democracy, the EC's suspension of its relations with Turkey, which had come into force in January 1982, was eventually lifted in September 1986 when the EC-Turkey Association Council resumed meetings (Yılmaz 2009: 3).

In 1987, following the reestablishment of relations with the EC, Turkey submitted another application for full membership. While only Greece opposed Turkish accession from the outset (Sümer 2009: 127), its application was eventually

---

1 Other factors which contributed to delaying the implementation of the Ankara Agreement include Greece's veto of a financial aid packet of 600 ECU and the German government's blocking of the provisions of the Agreement related to the free movement of persons (Sümer 2009 :126).

rejected in 1990 on the grounds that neither Turkey nor the EC were yet ready to begin accession talks. The Commission pointed to continuing political and economic instability in Turkey, and also argued that the EC, whose finances and institutions had already been strained following the Mediterranean enlargements of the 1980s, would have to complete the Single European Act before contemplating further enlargement (Yılmaz 2009: 3–4) (Asbeek Busse and Griffiths 2004: 22–3). However, it was at least established that Turkey was considered a European country from the point of view of EC accession, and was potentially eligible for membership[2]. Although there was no promise of accession, it was nevertheless decided to revive the Customs Union between Turkey and the EU, resulting in the phasing in of a Customs Union for industrial goods between 1996 and 2001 (Togan 2002: 2). In addition, both sides agreed on an improved and intensified political dialogue on foreign policy issues of mutual interest (Sümer 2009: 128).

In spite of these developments, the prospect of enlargement to the Central and Eastern European Countries (CEECs), many of which were not notably more economically or politically developed than Turkey, made it difficult to keep the Turkish application for membership on hold any longer (Togan 2002: 2). However, the 1997 Luxembourg Council, at which Greece and Germany in particular were against Turkey's being given candidate status, did not grant Turkey official candidate status although it was granted to several CEECs. This resulted in a crisis in Turkey–EU relations, with Turkey announcing that it would cut off political dialogue with the EU (Sümer 2009: 128–9).

Turkey was finally granted formal candidate status in the 1999 Helsinki Council and, after an intensive period of reform, was invited to open accession negotiations in October 2005. The decision to open negotiations was based on the conclusions of the 2004 Commission Progress Report on Turkey, which stated that, 'in view of the overall progress of reforms, and provided that Turkey brings into force the outstanding legislation mentioned above, the Commission considers that Turkey sufficiently fulfils the political criteria and recommends that accession negotiations be opened' (European Commission 2004a).

However, the opening of accession negotiations with Turkey was certainly not without its controversy. Austria, for instance, proposed a so-called 'privileged partnership' with Turkey, while even the Commission was divided on the issue. The result was a significantly tougher set of accession conditions for Turkey when compared to those that had been imposed on the CEECs. The negotiations were described as 'open-ended', there was a new emphasis on the EU's 'absorption capacity', the negotiations could be suspended with a significant breach of the political criteria on Turkey's part, and Turkey was required to sign customs agreements with all new members, including Cyprus (Casanova 2006: 234–5).

---

2   This is in contrast to the case of Morocco, which also applied for EC membership in 1987, and was rejected on the grounds that it was geographically not part of Europe (Rumelili 2004: 42).

Accession talks have indeed since been held back due to a set of external and domestic problems. Notably, in December 2006 the Council of Ministers decided to freeze 8 out of 35 of the negotiation chapters in response for Turkey's refusal to open its ports to Cyprus. Turkey's progress in the negotiations has therefore been much slower than that of Croatia, for instance, which began talks at the same time as Turkey. By 2012, Turkey had opened 13 of the 35 chapters and closed just one, while 18 chapters remain frozen because of vetoes by Cyprus, France, Germany or the European Council as a whole (Paul 2012: 26). In contrast Croatia signed the Treaty of Accession in December 2011 and, following its ratification, is expected to accede in July 2013 (European Commission 2012).

Thus, although no country which has started the accession process has yet failed to become a member (Bogdani 2011: 24), whether Turkey will eventually accede to the EU as a full member or not is still unclear given the large amount of Turkoscepticism among large parts of both the EU public and elite, as well as increasing Euroscepticism within Turkey. Indeed, Turkey's accession process appears to be in danger of a 'train crash' or, at the very least, a temporary breakdown.

On the Turkish side, the pace of reform has slowed notably since the opening of negotiations, with Turkey increasingly 'cherry-picking' reforms, with backsliding in certain areas including fundamental rights and freedoms, particularly freedom of the press (Paul 2012: 26). Moreover, support for EU accession among the Turkish population has plummeted. According to a survey carried out in eight Turkish cities in June 2012, a mere 17 per cent of respondents supported their country's accession to the EU, a huge drop from the 78 per cent support recorded in 2004 (*Milliyet* 2012: 13). This can be attributed to increasing self-confidence in a Turkey 'rolling in successes and emerging as a global winner' (Paul 2012: 27), in the context of the economic crisis in the EU which contrasts with Turkey's still vibrant economy, and the negative attitude of some EU countries towards Turkish accession (Milliyet 2012: 13). The lack of a clear membership perspective also appears to be a vital factor in the loss of Turkish enthusiasm for reform and accession (Aktar 2012: 36). On the EU side, the political right in many EU countries, including France and Germany, has increasingly called for Turkey to be granted a more limited 'privileged partnership' in lieu of full membership, while the majority of the EU population is against Turkish accession. A further problem is that EU interest in the question of Turkish accession has waned in the context of the current economic crisis and concerns over the fate of the Eurozone (Aktar 2012: 35).

There have been some attempts to break the impasse, most notably the 'New Positive Agenda' launched by the Commission, the brainchild of Štefan Füle, the European Commissioner for Enlargement and Neighbourhood Policy, and Egemen Bağış, Turkey's Minister for EU Integration. The 'New Positive Agenda' is supposed to be complementary to, rather than a replacement for, the accession process, and is intended to speed up Turkey's compliance with eight chapters of the *aquis communitaire*[3]. In order to achieve this, it introduces new mechanisms for communication, including eight working groups where Turkish and EU officials will work together. In addition to the working groups, special dossiers will be tackled, including political reforms, anti-terror co-operation, energy, and visa issues, as well as the prospect of training for Turkish bureaucrats in the Commission (Paul 2012: 29) (Aktar 2012: 37). However, negative reactions, particularly on the part of Austria and Germany, to Ankara's handling of recent anti-government protests across Turkey have also resulted in the postponement of negotiations on Chapter 22 by four months (*Today's Zaman* 2013). It therefore remains unclear whether the Positive Agenda will be enough to secure Turkish accession. The replacement of Nicolas Sarkozy, a proponent of 'privileged partnership', as French President with Socialist François Hollande appears to be a positive step as far as Turkish accession is concerned, although Hollande's views on Turkish membership are rather ambiguous, as is discussed further in the final chapter of this book. Similarly, the outcome of the German elections in 2013 will also be important in this regard.

Despite this, even with a supportive German Chancellor Turkish accession is far from a certainty, particularly as the accession of a new member state has to be accepted unanimously in the Council, as opposition to Turkish accession has also been prevalent in other EU countries, including Austria, Belgium, Luxembourg and Cyprus. Another issue is the question of public opposition in referenda on Turkish membership. In this context, the current book argues that the issue of Turkish accession has caused an 'identity crisis' in the EU; in other words, it has provoked a considerable amount of soul-searching and discussion among EU elites as to the EU's ideal identity and eventual borders. The main focus of the book, discussed in more detail below, is on a two part discourse analysis of EU elites. By examining the arguments they use regarding Turkey's EU accession, the aim is to get a better idea of which visions they have for the future development of the EU. The second part aims to put these arguments in a national context, and argues that national discourses on Turkey's EU accession are shaped by discourses on state and nation and on European integration. The work, then, aims to answer the following research questions:

- How can the different arguments used in favour/against Turkey's EU accession be classified?
- What do these arguments tell us about how the EU itself is conceived?
- How might differing national discourses on state and nation lead to differing discourses on Turkish EU accession?

---

3   The chapters concerned are the 'Right of Establishment and Freedom to Provide Services', 'Company Law', 'Information Society and the Media', 'Statistics', 'Consumer and Health Protection', 'Financial Control', 'Judiciary and Fundamental Rights' and 'Justice, Freedom and Security'.

Thus, Chapter 1 aims to set out the wider theoretical framework within which the discourse analysis is set. The study is a broadly constructivist one, in that it begins from the premises that identities matter and that identities are socially constructed, usually on the basis of elite discourse. Moreover, this study accepts that identities tend to be constructed *vis-à-vis* an Other (or Others), which may be perceived in many ways; as threatening, inferior, simply different, as not upholding universal values, as an internal Other, or even as superior. The limits between Self and Other may be pliable or fixed, either enabling or preventing the potential inclusion of the Other into the Self.

Beginning from the framework discussed in Chapter 1, Chapter 2 provides a historical overview of European images of 'the Turk' in order to put contemporary EU discourse on Turkey in a historical context. Arguing that European images of the Ottomans were themselves influenced by older images of the East, the chapter begins by discussing ancient Greek images of the Persians and medieval images of the 'Saracen'. Following this, the various images of the Ottoman Turks from the beginning of the Empire to its collapse are discussed and put in context. It is argued that most of the forms of Othering discussed in the previous chapter have been in evidence at various times in European views of the Ottoman Turk.

Chapter 3 moves to a discussion of contemporary attitudes to Turkish accession. Despite the fact that the main focus of the book is on elite discourse, Chapter 3 discusses questions of EU identity and attitudes towards enlargement, particularly Turkish accession, among the EU public as well as the Turkish public. This perspective is important as elite discourse does not, of course, take place in a vacuum; it affects, and to a certain extent may be influenced by, public opinion. This chapter, therefore, aims to evaluate the existence and nature of a European identity among the European public. The analysis is carried out mainly on the basis of survey results, although these are illustrated by examples taken from Internet discussions on Turkey's EU accession. In the second part of the chapter, public opinion on enlargement in general is examined, before a more specific analysis of attitudes towards Turkish accession. Another aim of this chapter, then, is to compare and contrast attitudes to enlargement to CEE and to Turkey.

The following two extended chapters focus on elite discourse regarding Turkish accession to the EU. The first section of the discourse analysis, used in Chapter 4, has been derived, primarily by scholars associated with the ARENA centre in Oslo, from the theories of Jürgen Habermas. Here, the arguments that political elites use in favour of or against enlargement are examined in order to shed light on how they envisage the EU; as primarily a problem-solving entity, a rights-based postnational union or a value-based community. In the first case, the legitimacy of the EU is viewed as primarily based on its ability to secure pragmatic benefits, notably security and economic advantages. In this vision, it is potentially without borders as enlargement is seen as a question of efficiency and utility, and often linked to arguments about extending the free market or reinforcing security. In the second, the EU is based primarily on a set of legally entrenched fundamental rights and democratic procedures. In the context of enlargement, a candidate country should be allowed to accede to the EU if it is considered to fulfill conditions based on 'universal' liberal democratic norms such as respect for human and minority rights, democracy and the rule of law. Finally, in the third example, the EU is viewed as based on a 'thicker' identity rooted in, perhaps, a shared culture, history and/or religion. From this perspective, enlargement is encouraged only into spaces which are considered to have a similar cultural heritage.

The final chapter offers a national perspective. Here, Foreign Policy Discourse Analysis (FPDA) is used to analyse different national discourses regarding Turkish EU accession. FPDA is a three-level discourse analysis approach which argues that discursive constructions of state and nation constrain discourse on the EU, which, in turn, constrain concrete policies towards the EU, including those connected to enlargement. While discourses do not *a priori* have clear borders beyond which they do not apply the concepts of nation and state, themselves constructed discursively, have an important effect on a country's foreign policy as they define national identity and have a constraining effect on which discourses are possible at the level of foreign policy, including those concerning European integration. An advantage of this approach is, then, that it can help to shed light on the way that views may be shared across national political parties. While competing national discourses may certainly exist, then, they do not necessarily contradict each other at every level; they may, for instance, differ only on a single point while sharing codes at a deeper level. This chapter, then, attempts to apply FPDA in order to shed greater light on national discourses regarding Turkish EU accession by focusing on three case studies; France, Britain and Turkey itself. These fundamentally Foucauldian and Habermasian forms of discourse analysis may appear to make unlikely, even quarrelsome, bedmates. However, the logic behind this combination is that, while national discourses on enlargement are relatively constrained, ultimately by the way that state and nation are constructed in each member state, there is a need for the different member states, with their various discursive baggages, to come to a consensus through argument at the EU level if enlargement is to go ahead.

Chapter 1
The Construction of Self and Other: A Conceptual Framework

The approach taken towards identity formation in this book is a broadly constructivist one; that is, identities are understood to be socially constructed and reconstructed rather than given, and political elites, through their discourse, have a particularly important role in identity construction. For this reason, then, the current work focuses on elite constructions of EU identity in the context of the debate on Turkish accession to the EU. It is also important to point out that identities are constructed against an Other. While the Other is normally viewed in a comparatively negative light, conceptions of the Other vary considerably; the Other may, for instance, be seen as threatening or inferior, but also as equal or superior. Thus, it may be expected that different elite visions of the EU also come with the baggage of their respective Others.

Elite discourse on European identity in the context of enlargement to Turkey is analysed on two levels; the national and EU levels. It is argued here that, at national level, attitudes towards the EU and visions of its *finalité* are closely linked to national discourse on state and nation; these constructions of nation-state identity and of Europe thus constrain national policies towards the EU, in this case towards Turkish accession. At the second level, these national visions of the EU and of Turkey's place in (or out of) it are debated at the European level together with political actors from other member states and from the EU institutions, in an attempt to come to a consensus.

The purpose of this chapter, then, is to explore these theoretical concepts in more detail. The chapter begins by discussing the basic principles of constructivism in International Relations (IR) and European Studies, and proceeds with an exploration of how identities are constructed, and how they are interlinked with alterity in IR. In this way, the chapter aims to build the theoretical foundation for the rest of the study.

The Constructivist Turn in European Studies

While constructivism can perhaps be traced back to the writings of the eighteenth century Italian philosopher Giambattista Vico, who argued that the natural world was made by God but the historical world was made by people (Öner 2011: 31–2), it is only in the last two decades or so that it has become a widely used approach in IR and European Studies.

As Rosamond argues, 'Constructivism has become hard to ignore in contemporary International Relations scholarship, certainly since the 1990s' (2000: 171); it has thus provided an alternative approach to the rational choice based approaches, notably realism and liberalism (and their 'neo' forms) which have traditionally dominated IR. In contrast to rational choice approaches, constructivism is based on the premise that 'human agents do not exist independently from their social environment and its collectively shared systems of meaning' (Risse 2004: 167). The differences between constructivist and rational choice approaches can be defined as follows;

> Constructivists hold the view that the building blocks of international reality are ideational as well as material; that ideational factors have normative as well as instrumental dimensions; that they express not only individual but also collective intentionality; and that the meaning and significance of ideational factors are not independent of time and place. (Ruggie 1998: 33)

Thus, constructivism represents the connection of international theory with important strands of social theory. However, there are important divisions within constructivism; as Rosamond points out, 'rather than there being a single constructivist approach, there are many constructivisms'. These differences tend to focus on whether we can use conventional rational research methods to investigate a world that is socially constructed (Rosamond 2000: 171–2). Constructivists can also be divided according to the scale of the society on which they focus. As Reus-Smit points out, *systemic* constructivists focus on interstate relations, *unit-level* constructivists focus on the relationship between domestic social and legal norms and the identities and interests of states, while *holistic* constructivists seek to bridge the international and domestic domains (2009: 224–5). Checkel, in turn, distinguishes three constructivist approaches to European integration in particular. *Conventional* constructivists focus on the role of norms and identity in shaping international outcome, *interpretive* constructivists analyse the ways in which social reality is constructed through discourse analysis, and *radical* constructivists, while also interested in linguistic analysis, focus on the role of the researcher in affecting the reproduction of identities (Checkel 2006: 4–6).

While there are important differences within constructivism, there are also important common points. As Knutsen argues, among constructivists;

> All agree that the structures of international politics are outcomes of social interactions, that states are not static subjects, but dynamic agents, that state identities are not given, but (re)constituted through complex, historical overlapping (often contradictory) practices – and therefore variable, unstable, constantly changing; that the distinction between domestic politics and international relations are tenuous. (1997: 281–2)

In a similar vein, Reus-Smit points out that all constructivists base their work on three ontological propositions about social life. Firstly, normative and ideational structures are just as important as material structures in shaping the behaviour of social and political actors, both individuals and states. Therefore, constructivists pay attention to such normative and ideational structures as they are thought to shape the social identities of political actors. Secondly, understanding how non-material structures condition actors' identities is important because identities inform interests and, in turn, action. Such an understanding can, then, be helpful in exploring many aspects and instances of international policy formation. Thus, 'to explain interest formation constructivists focus on the social identities of individuals and states' (Reus-Smit 2009: 221). These normative and ideational structures are seen as shaping actors' identities through three mechanisms; imagination, communication and constraint. Thirdly, constructivists argue that agents and structures are mutually constitutive. While normative and ideational structures may condition the identities and interests of actors, those structures would not exist if it were not for the knowledgeable practices of those actors (Reus-Smit 2009: 220–23). As Christiansen argues, for instance;

> A constructivist epistemology … must conceive of territorial units on all levels as social constructs [and must] view the political significance of [these] in the processes for which they provide containers, and such research must address the agency/structure problem, meaning that no level in the studied process must, ex ante, be assumed to be primary. (1997: 54)

Thus, while rationalists assume that actors are atomistic egoists, constructivists treat them as deeply social. In this way, then, constructivists differ from rationalists in that, instead of treating actors' interests as exogenously determined as they are 'given' prior to social interaction, they treat them as endogenous to such interactions as a consequence of identity acquisition. In other words, while rationalists view society as a strategic realm, constructivists see it as a constitutive realm (Reus-Smit 2009: 222) (Rosamond 2000: 172). However, this does not imply that constructivists focus on identity construction to the detriment of interests; instead these are seen as intertwined;

> We do not promote an 'interest vs. identity' account, but try to figure out the precise way in which both interact. On the one hand, embedded identity constructions, mentioned above, define the boundaries of what elites consider to be legitimate ideas – thereby constituting their perceived interests. On the other hand, perceived interests define which ideas political elites select in their struggle for power among those available to actors. The precise relationship remains a matter of empirical study. (Marcussen et al. 2001: 103–4)

As Risse argues, the difference between rationalist and constructivist approaches can also be understood in terms of March and Olsen's distinction between a 'logic of consequentialism' and a 'logic of appropriateness'.[1] The 'logic of consequentialism', linked to rational choice approaches, treats the interests and preferences of actors as mostly fixed during the process of interaction; thus they try to realise their interests and preferences through strategic behaviour, including collaboration and co-ordination with others.

In contrast, social constructivists tend to prioritise the 'logic of appropriateness', according to which actors try to 'do the right thing' rather than maximise or optimise their given preferences. This also implies the constitutive effects of social norms and institutions, in that these rules define social identities as well as regulating behaviour. Thus, in social constructivists' view 'collective norms and understandings' constitute the social identities of actors and also define the basic 'rules of the game' in which actors find themselves in their interactions.

As Sjursen notes, however, the logic of appropriateness may cause some confusion in that it may imply both rule-following as a result of habit or a particular identity and rule-following based on a rational assessment of morally valid arguments. For the sake of clarity, then, a third logic may be added here, the 'logic of justification' which specifically pertains to a rational assessment of morally valid arguments (Sjursen 2006: 9).

According to Christiansen, Jorgensen and Wiener, a constructivist approach may be particularly well-suited to studies of European integration, as it is reasonable to assume that European integration has had a transformative effect on the European state system and its constituent units. It is thus likely that this change has affected agents' identity and, consequently, their interests and behaviour (2001:2). Constructivist approaches therefore differ from the other prevailing theories of European integration, including neofunctionalism, liberal intergovernmentalism and multi-level governance in that the latter are committed to a rationalist ontology which is agency-centred by definition. However, a constructivist approach may actually be complementary to, rather than in competition with, these theories (Risse 2004: 161).

A Constructivist View of Identity Formation

Constructivism is relevant to the study of identities in two ways. Firstly, as has already been pointed out, social identities are useful in explaining the interests of actors, which were taken for granted in rational choice approaches. Second, constructivism is itself directly relevant to the study of identities as social constructions (Risse 2010: 20). In this way, according to the constructivist approach to identity formation, identity is continuously constructed, negotiated

---

1   Serboş neatly explains the difference between the logic of consequentiality and the logic of appropriateness as follows: if the former can be defined as 'do X because you will get Y', the latter is 'do X because it is the right thing to do' (2008: 11). The logic of justification can perhaps best be defined as 'do X because it is the best argument'.

and contested between political actors (Rumelili 2008: 2). Thus, according to constructivism, while there is a relation between cultural variables (including ethnic belonging or religious or political affiliation) and collective identity this connection is much less fixed than in the primordialist version[2] and is subject to construction and reconstruction. However, as Risse points out(2010: 21) a social constructivist approach does not imply that identities are always contested and/ or permanently in flux. Despite the fact that identities may be relatively stable, though, if they are taken to be discursively constructed, as is argued below, there are always alternative constructions against which the dominant identity construction has to be defended, and which offers the opportunity for change (Laclau and Mouffe 1985: 41–2).

Insights from social psychology, particularly social identity,and self-categorisation theories, can shed light on how collective identities are formed. Social identities link individuals to social groups with which they identify. Thus, 'social identities are not about "I" or "Me", but about that part of "me" which belongs to a larger "we", a social group and/or a community. This implies that "I cannot have a social identity on my own, but share it with a larger group"' (Risse 2010: 22). Tajfel, for instance, defines social identities as 'that part of the individual's self-concept which derives from his knowledge of his membership of a social group (or groups) together with the value and social significance attached to that membership' (1982: 255). In addition, social identities have a specific substantive content consisting of 'the constitutive norms and rules that define the social group and its membership, as well as the collective worldviews shared by the group'. This content includes narratives of a common fate, a common history and a common culture,as well as a sense of common purpose in terms of the ultimate goals of the group and visions of what are regarded as good and just political and social orders (Risse 2010: 25).

Moreover, our identities are made up of various attributes, and group affiliations, which can be 'downplayed, emphasized or politicized depending on the context in which they are expressed' (Demossier 2007: 59–60). Regarding territorial identities, then, an individual may regard themselves, for instance, as simultaneously a resident of Barcelona, a Catalan, a Spanish citizen and a European.[3] Which of

---

2   Essentialist or primordialist concepts of collective identities argue that cultural variables are givens which then develop into national identities during the process of nation building. These 'givens' include roots, heritage, language and religion (Demossier 2007: 59). Thus, in this view, identities are fixed and the creation of supranational or postnational identities is impossible (Risse 2004: 166). Thus, while, in the essentialist view identities are fixed and unchanged, they are actively constructed, and therefore more fluid, from the constructivist position (Demossier 2007: 61). Thus, essentialists are generally rather pessimistic about the possibility of constructing a European identity, unless the EU becomes a replica of the nation state (Demossier 2007: 59).

3   Of course, territorial identities only form a part of the various, perhaps myriad, identities which make us who we are. This same hypothetical individual, for instance, may

these identities is emphasised is likely to depend on the context; this individual is perhaps likely to emphasise their Catalan identity when in Madrid (or perhaps Scotland), their Spanish identity in London and their European identity in New York. Thus, as Laffan points out, 'social identities allow us to say who we are and what makes sense to us in different situations' (2004: 82–3).

It is important to emphasise at this point that a constructivist approach to social identities does not necessarily imply a particular theoretical stance; rather constructivism is 'more an approach than a theory' (Smith 2001: 189). Indeed, as Risse argues, identities can be studied using a variety of qualitative and quantitative methods, including survey data, discourse analyses and psychological experiments (2010: 21). In the constructivist view *discourse,* particularly that of elites and epistemic communities, is an important factor in social learning and, ultimately, identity construction. As Fearon and Laitin argue, for instance, 'discourses define identities and shape or determine actions' (2000: 853). While epistemic communities tend to have an impact on policy learning, the discourse of political elites tends to have more of an impact in framing particular issues (Milliken 1999: 233).

Active efforts to construct a territorial identity, then, usually constitute an elite driven, top-down process. As Öner, among many others, has noted, elites have always played an important role in the construction of European identity, even before the establishment of the European integration project (2011: 191). According to social constructivists, elite attempts to construct identity are more likely to result in social learning on the part of the general population during a time of perceived crisis (Checkel 2001, 2005), also known as *critical junctures* (Marcusen et al. 1999: 5). As Checkel argues, when 'the target of the socialization attempt is in a novel and uncertain environment … [it is] cognitively motivated to analyse new information' (2005: 9). Risse points out that the Second World War provided just such a critical juncture for German identity in particular, resulting in an almost complete change, including the subsequent Europeanisation, of German national identity (2010: 32). In contrast, in the absence of such a crisis, discourse, and therefore identity, is likely to remain relatively stable; it is, for instance, probable that Britain's World War II experiences actually served to strengthen rather than change its existing national identity, perhaps explaining the relative lack of Europeanisation of British identity. It is argued here, in line with Müftüler Baç and Taşkın (2007: 41) that the prospect of Turkish accession to the EU has provided a critical juncture for the development of European identity.

Secondly, the public is more open to elite attempts at identity construction when the elite in question is viewed as legitimate and credible; in other words it must be part of the audience's 'in-group' (Checkel 2001: 59). Moreover, from a constructivist view, this tends to be more successful when the ideas promoted by the elites in question do not significantly clash with those held by the public; the

---

identify herself, among many other things as a woman, a mother, a dentist, a supporter of Barcelona football team, a natural redhead, a Catholic and a keen runner.

audience should have 'few prior, ingrained beliefs inconsistent with the socializing agency's message' (Checkel 2001: 59). Thus, ideas about European identity and European political order are transferred to national discourses;

> to the extent that they resonate with pre-existing and consensual identity constructions and concepts of political order embedded in a country's institutions and political culture (*resonance* assumption). Only those ideas that resonate are considered legitimate in a political struggle. (Marcussen et al. 2001: 117–18)

For these reasons, priority will be given to analysis of elite discourse throughout this book; however, given that a certain degree of compatibility between elite discourse and public opinion is necessary, public opinion, particularly in the form of survey data, will also be explored especially in the following chapter. It is argued here that, to a significant extent, elite discourses take place in and are observed by the various public spheres; thus collective identities and public spheres are connected in that they provide communicative space where identities are constructed and reified (Risse 2010: 107). As McNair argues, public spheres in a democracy are supposed to inform citizens about the political process, to monitor and critically evaluate governance, and to enable public debate. Thus, they must allow for meaningful communication and exchange of views, thereby satisfying certain normative criteria (2000: 108). Similarly, Diez Medrano defines public spheres as follows;

> The public sphere is a deliberative political space in which both government and civil society participate. It provides political information to the citizens and a channel of communication that citizens can use to influence government. In contemporary societies, a public sphere exists when a minimum of free speech allows for political debate through the media. The geographic scope of this public sphere corresponds to the space covered by political or governmental institutions, be they municipal, regional, national, European and so on. (2009: 91)

However, as Diez Medrano argues, the 'public sphere is only one factor shaping the citizens' attitudes to the European Union'; other actors, such as far-right groups, Eurosceptic groups or anti-globalisation groups may also be influential while remaining relatively invisible in the debate on European integration in the public sphere (2009: 83).There has been considerable discussion in the academic literature over whether a European public sphere exists, or can exist, or whether public spheres remain exclusively at the national level. Earlier research on the European public sphere argued that, given the lack of both a common language and a European press a European public sphere was an impossibility (Diez Medrano 2009: 90).

Later research, however, argues that these are not preconditions for a European public sphere. Indeed, 'we should not conceptualise a European public sphere as a separate entity above and beyond other public spheres' (Risse 2010: 11); instead a Europeanised public sphere can be said to exist when the same topics are being discussed across the national press and media, and when the frames of reference, meaning structures and patterns of interpretation that are used are similar across national public spheres and media (Eder and Kanter 2000; cited in Risse 2010: 116–20). In addition, Risse argues that a European public sphere exists when European or national speakers regularly participate in cross-border debates, when speakers and listeners recognise each other as legitimate participants in transnational discourses, and when particular issues are framed as common European problems. In this way, then, Europeanised identities and public spheres reinforce each other (Risse 2010: 125).

There appears to be a close connection between the Europeanisation of identities and public spheres; just as the Europeanisation of identities is uneven, so is that of public spheres. Overall, however, research suggests that in Western Europe during the 1990s and 2000s, there has been an increasing visibility of the EU and a greater similarity of issue cycles in the media resulting, to a certain extent, the Europeanisation of public spheres (Risse 2010: 154–5) (Kaelble 2009: 195) although the scale of this Europeanised public sphere remains small (Diez Medrano 2009: 90). The main exception to the Europeanisation of Western European public spheres is the British one, which appears to be less Europeanised than its counterparts in continental Western Europe. Thus, as Risse suggests;

> I tentatively conclude that we can disconfirm the notion that Europeans talk past each other because of different languages or different orientations towards European integration. On the contrary, the findings seem to suggest that polarization and controversies lead to similar interpretations and frames of reference rather than driving communication apart. (Risse 2010: 154–5)

However, in Diez Medrano's view, as elites have tended to put forward a republican rather than a cultural political identity for the EU in recent years this has resulted in the alienation of a large minority of the European public. His research suggests that 'there is a current mismatch between the national leaders' conceptions of the EU and those of a significant minority of citizens and, at the same time, a strong disagreement among the elites about Europe's political identity' (2009: 82). As Risse argues, most studies of the European public sphere focus on quality newspapers, likely to be read by better educated citizens with a relatively high socio-economic status – indeed just those citizens who, as discussed below, are more likely to already identify with Europe and the EU. Opinion polls, in contrast, suggest that most European citizens get the majority of their information about the EU from television, a medium which has been studied comparatively little in this context. Habermas, however, argues that quality newspapers have a particularly important role to play in the public sphere;

> At least in the domain of political communication – in other words for the readers as citizens – the quality press plays the role of 'leading media'. Even

radio and television, as well as the remainder of the press, depend to a large extent on the issues and reports fed to them by the 'reasoning' newspapers in their political reporting and commentary. (Habermas 2009: 134)

Taking this into account, then, while the main focus of this study is on national and European-level political elites, particularly political leaders, members of national parliaments and the European parliament, editorials from quality newspapers and magazines will also be taken into account.

As has been argued above, elite discourse appears to have a particularly powerful effect on identity construction. Agents make sense of the world and attribute meaning to their activities through discourse (Risse 2004: 164). Thus, as Christiansen, Jorgensen and Wiener argue, 'If the study of identity formation is accepted as a key component of constructivist research, the role of language and of discourses becomes crucial' (2001: 15). As Diez points out, 'To talk about a European identity that somehow needs to find a political expression is therefore not an innocent statement but a political act that inscribes the notion of a political identity into the political debate' (Diez 2004: 321).

As Risse argues, the study of communicative practices has been applied to IR in two ways. The first is the application of the Habermasian theory of communicative action to IR. This theory focuses on argumentation and reason giving among actors. According to this approach, actors seek to justify the principles and norms guiding their action, while the goal is to seek a reasoned consensus (Risse 2004: 164–5). While communicative action is as goal-oriented as strategic action, then, the goal here is to seek a reasoned consensus; therefore actors' interests and perceptions of the situation are no longer fixed but subject to discursive challenges.

Thus, communicative action presupposes that actors not only try to persuade others but they are themselves prepared to be persuaded by the 'better argument' (Risse 2000: 8–9);

> Where argumentative rationality prevails, actors do not seek to maximise or to satisfy their given interests and preferences, but to challenge and to justify the validity claims inherent in them and they are prepared to change their views of the world or even their interests in light of the better argument. (Risse 2000: 7)

This situation is more common when actors are 'uncertain about their own identities, interests and views of the world and/or if rhetorical arguments are subject to scrutiny and counterchallenges leading to a process of 'argumentative entrapment' (Risse 2000: 7). Moreover, a communicative approach also implies that relationships of power and social hierarchies recede into the background. Thus, as Eriksen argues, the EU, due to its lack of power structures is conducive to attempts to reach consensus via deliberation (2003: 170).

Similarly, in the view of Sjursen (2002) (2006) (2008) and of Piedrafita and Torreblanca (2007), this approach can provide important insights into the EU's decisions regarding enlargement, as is discussed further in Chapter 4.

The second discursive approach, which deals less with arguing and reason-giving, focuses on discourse 'as a construction of meaning allowing for certain interpretations while excluding others' (Risse 2004: 165). As Wæver points out, this approach is dominated by French conceptions of discourse – 'Foucault and all that' (Wæver 2004: 198). Thus, this approach examines discourse as a way of establishing power relations; it therefore not only asks who can speak in a discursive arena but also what makes a good argument, and which discourses become so entrenched that they become almost taken for granted (Risse 2004: 165). In this view, then, discourses delimit what can, and cannot, be said (Wæver 2002: 29).

The discursive approach used in this book is a two-step one based on a combination of both broad approaches described above. The first level of analysis, adapted by Sjursen, Eriksen, Torreblanca and Piedrafita, among others, from Habermas' theory of communicative action, examines how political elites in the EU argue about Turkish accession. Following Sjursen, it is put forward here that such arguments can also reveal attitudes to EU identity itself. The second level, using Foreign Policy Discourse Analysis (FPDA), which takes place at the level of the nation state, is based on Foucaultian concepts of discourse. Here, it is argued that national attitudes to the EU, and specific policies such as enlargement, are constrained by the national discursive construction of state and nation.

Identity and Alterity: Self and Other in the European Context

Importantly, social identities also describe the boundaries of the group; therefore, they imply that social identities have their Others (Neumann 1999: 7–9). As Mayer and Palmowski argue, 'Identity is essentially Janus faced: it is as much about differentiation and individuality as it is about commonality' (2004: 577). It is also argued that, as social identities are context-dependent, so are their Others. In particular, social identity theory puts forward that membership in a group can lead people to view their in-group, no matter how random, as more favourable than the out-group, which tends to raise self-esteem, and that individuals tend to categorise more people as outsiders than as members of their in-group. Moreover, according to social identity theory, the stronger an individual identifies with the in-group, the less likely they are to support the inclusion of an outsider, and the stricter their criteria will be for entry into the group. As Curley notes, this has important ramifications for the issue of EU enlargement; 'The stronger a decision-maker identifies with Europe the stricter he/she will be when deciding which country should be allowed entry into the EU' (2009: 657).

Thus, identities imply limits; if some people are included in a particular identity group there must be others who are not. Borders, then, are an important part of territorial identities; they define not only who is 'in' but also who is 'out' (Risse 2004: 257). As Diez, for instance, argues, an identity which is not constructed against an Other is unthinkable; 'It would make no sense to say "I am European" if this did not imply a difference from being "Asian", "African" or

"American"' (2004: 321). Thus, the Self is entirely interdependent with the Other (Adib-Moghaddam 2011: 8). In this way, contact with an Other may either result in a reaffirmation of the existing identity construct or may provoke it to change and evolve in response to the new social environment (Johansson-Nogues and Jonasson 2011: 114).

Moreover, it should be taken into consideration that, just as identities appear to be multiple in nature, it follows that the Others which define those identities can also differ (Risse and Engelmann-Martin 2007: 292–3). As Rumelili argues, then, 'The logic of identity allows for a great deal of variation in self/other relationships' (2004: 36). Thus, an examination of Othering can help to shed light on the various ways in which identities are constructed;

> Unstated in these narratives representing the Other are counternarratives of the self. Thus, if the Other is an 'infidel', then 'we' are 'the faithful'. If the Other is a 'barbarian' then we must be 'civilized'. If the Other is a 'sick man', then we have 'healthy' and 'robust' regimes and societies. If the Other is 'backward', 'despotic', or a 'laggard', then we are 'modern', 'liberal' and 'progressive'. If the Other is 'Asiatic' and 'Eastern' then we are 'European' and 'Western'. (Hall 2002: 104)

Indeed, it has frequently been put forward that Europe has several Others.[4] Among these, in Neumann's view (1999), Europe's primary Other has been 'the East', notably Turkey and Russia but at times also 'Eastern' Europe; he argues that, while the way that the East is constructed as Europe's Other may change, European identity is likely to continue to be constructed *vis à vis* the East in some shape or form;

> The use of 'the East' as the other is a general practice in European identity formation. 'The East' is indeed Europe's other, and it is continuously being recycled in order to represent European identities. Since the 'Eastern absence' is a defining trait of 'European' identities, there is no use talking about the end of an East/West divide in European history after the end of the Cold War. The question is not *whether* the East will be used in the forging of new European identities but *how* this is being done. (Neumann 1999: 207)

Other authors, including Wæver (1998) and Diez (2004), argue that the EU's principal Other has been its own past. Risse, in turn, argues that these Others should be seen in the context of two contrasting European identity constructions.

---

4   As Hall argues (2002: 105) it is important to note that those who are Othered do not take it lying down; instead they respond to it in their own discourse, which may, in turn, affect national identity constructions. As will be discussed later in this book, it is particularly notable how Turkey has responded to instances of Othering on the part of EU elites during its accession period.

The first is based on European integration as a modernisation project based on 'universal values' and a market economy, while the second aims to construct an antimodern, traditional European identity based on religious values. In the first case, the Others are Europe's own past and racism and xenophobia, while the Others in the second case are Islam and immigrants from outside Europe (Risse 2010: 53–4). Finally, as is discussed further below it has been proposed that the EU's identity, particularly the concept of the EU as a 'normative power', has been principally constructed in opposition to the USA.

In addition, the type and degree of Othering may vary. It is important in this context to consider whether an identity is inclusive or exclusive. In an inclusive identity, the possibility exists that the Other may eventually become part of the Self; in an exclusive identity this possibility does not exist. Thus in an inclusive identity formation, the Other is considered different on the basis of *acquired* characteristics; in an exclusive identity formation, on the other hand, it is considered different on the basis of *inherent* characteristics, such as geographical boundaries.[5]

In the case of an inclusive identity, then, it is perfectly conceivable that the Other may eventually disappear, and be absorbed into the Self. Rumelili argues that, during the enlargement process, the CEECs were constructed as similar in terms of inherent identity characteristics, such as culture and geography, but different in terms of acquired characteristics like democracy and capitalism. In contrast, in relation to Morocco, while the EU has pointed out acquired identity differences, it has, critically, invoked perceived inherent identity differences, most notably arguing that it is not geographically European (2004: 41–3).

It is important to note in this case that the construction of inherent identity differences precludes EU accession while that of acquired differences does not providing that the candidate country in question is willing and able to make the required reforms. As will be discussed later in this study, this point has extremely important implications for Turkey's prospects of becoming a full member of the EU. However, the variation in types of Othering is certainly not confined to the difference between inclusive and exclusive identities. As Rumelili points out;

> Some of this variation is in the substantive, emotive, and normative contents of representational practices. The differences of the other may be represented through various, more or less favourable predicates, metaphors and binaries, which are often very culturally specific. Through these representational practices,

---

5   A classic example to illustrate the difference between inclusive and exclusive identities is the controversy between the philosopher Sepulvedra and the Dominican bishop Las Casas during the Spanish conquest of the Americas. While Sepulvedra constructed Indians as different on a civilized/barbarian dichotomy, Las Casas argued that they were different on the basis of a Christian/pagan dichotomy. The former identity construction is exclusive in that it represents fixed characteristics, while the latter is inclusive as it entails the possibility of conversion (Todorov 1984: 146–7) (Rumelili 2004: 33).

the constructed other may be idealized or completely denigrated, affirmed or negated, or even eroticised and exoticised. (2004: 36)

Diez defines four main forms of Othering in international politics (2005: 628–9):

- The Other may be represented as an existential threat. Thus, it may be *securitised*, in the sense used by the Copenhagen school, through a speech act of securitisation, legitimising extraordinary measures outside the 'normal realm' of politics.
- The Other may be represented as inferior. In this case the self is constructed as superior to the Other as, for instance, in the case of Orientalism which views the 'Orient' as exotic but ultimately inferior to the West.
- The Other may be represented as violating universal principles. Here the standards of the Self are not only seen as superior, but as universally valid. In this view, then, the Other should be brought to accept the principles of the Self.
- The Other may simply be represented as different. In this case there is no obvious value judgement placed on the Other; while not being completely innocent it is thus the least harmful form of Othering.

Ian Manners proposes a fifth category; that of the 'self as Other'. In this context he argues that, 'the projection of otherness onto individuals and the social groups they represent is so strong precisely because they are also an abjected and disturbing part of ourselves' (2006: 177–8). In addition, the work of Zarakol (2011), for instance, suggests that the Other may sometimes be perceived as superior. These six concepts are discussed in more detail below, and are illustrated with examples from various periods of the history of relations between Europe and Turkey/the Ottoman Empire from the Middle Ages to the present.

Securitisation: The Other as Existential Threat

The construction of the Other as threatening may be better understood by examining the Copenhagen School's concept of *securitisation*. The Copenhagen School views securitisation primarily as a *speech act*; the act of naming a certain development or issue as a security problem. In order to be meaningful, however, such a speech act must be carried out by a security actor, or *functional actor*, that is one (or more) of the actors who affect the dynamics of a sector and significantly influence the decisions in the field of security (Wæver 1995: 54). Thus, security is viewed as subjective and socially constructed rather than objectively absent or present (Huysmans 1998: 57). However, for a securitising speech act to lead to a successful securitisation, a certain audience that accepts the issue as a threat should also exist. This, in turn, grants authority to the security actor to put the issue in question in a primary position, by positing it as a threat to the survival of certain things or values, termed the *referent object* (Williams 2003: 513). This, then, gives the security actor licence to use extraordinary means, such as levying extra taxes or using military means; in other words to break the normal political rules (Buzan et al. 1998: 25).

Therefore, the Copenhagen School does not argue that more security is better. In contrast, it tends to view security as negative as it represents a failure to deal with issues as normal politics (Buzan et al. 1998: 29). As Wæver argues, 'the act of securitization may lead to over-securitization so that securitizing the issues is not a good thing' (1995: 64). For the Copenhagen school, the concept of security is not limited to military security. Instead, from this point of view the referent object may be anything that is seen to be existentially threatened and that has a legitimate claim for survival. The Copenhagen School focuses on five security sectors, namely the military, environmental, economic, political and societal sectors. These, in other words, constitute the potential referent objects of security. However, these sectors are not merely viewed in isolation; instead they are interconnected as a threat in one sector may affect another (Wæver 1999: 335). Thus, the state is no longer viewed as the only referent object of securitisation; firms, for instance, may be the referent object of economic securitisation, or a group of islands threatened by rising sea levels may be that of environmental security (Buzan et al. 1998: 38–9).

Moreover, according to the Copenhagen School, securitisation may be *ad hoc* or institutionalised. Responses tend to be institutionalised if the threat is perceived to be permanent in nature. This is particularly true in the military sector, where the threats are more visible and long standing and where the armed forces are the institutionalised response. In cases of institutionalised securitisation the authorities do not need to convince the audience each time they need to take emergency measures; thus issues in sectors where securitisation is institutionalised are not normally expected to provoke public debate. However, in other security sectors the response is normally *ad hoc*, requiring the authorities to convince the audience of the existence of the threat (Williams 2003: 28).

In the societal sector, the referent object of security is society as a whole rather than particular groups within society. Therefore, the focus is on large scale collective identities that can function independently from the state (Wæver et al. 1998), such as religious or ethno-national identities. Societal security, then, neither refers to the security of the state, although it does have some effect on state security, nor to the security of the individual (Wæver et al. 1993: 23). Thus, in Wæver's view state security and societal security may coincide, but they are not necessarily defined by one another. This is increasingly so as factors such as globalisation or European integration mean that nations or political communities are less defined by state borders.

The Copenhagen School's definition of society is guided by Anthony Giddens, who defines society as follows: 'a clustering of institutions combined with a feeling of common identity' (cited in Wæver et al. 1993: 21). Members of a society may have disagreements, but will bind together to defend themselves against outside threats (Wæver et al. 1993: 21–2). A society can thus be described as a group of people who share a feeling of constituting an entity and having a common sense of 'we'. In this case, a threat to society implies that this 'we feeling' will be altered, along with the way of life and/or beliefs (Buzan et al. 1998: 23). As Waever et al. put it;

> Societal security concerns the ability of a society to persist in its essential character under changing conditions and possible and actual threats ..More specifically it is about the sustainability, within acceptable conditions, for evolution of traditional patterns of language, culture, association, and religious and national identity and custom. (1993: 23)

Thus, identity is a crucial factor in societal security; as Wæver et al. propose, 'societal security is about situations when societies perceive a threat in identity terms' (1993: 23). Moreover, each society has its own criteria to determine what it perceives as a threat (Buzanet al. 1998: 124). It is, however, quite difficult to distinguish existential threats to society from lesser threats as, from the social constructivist view, identity is an evolving, not a given notion. What does turn change into a threat is the general feeling in the society that the change is heretical or invasive, and will thus violate the main components of the identity concerned, rather than being incorporated into the existing identity (Buzan et al. 1998: 23). Moreover, identities and securitisation are viewed as interdependent in this approach, with securitisation tending to reinforce rather than change identities.

Islam, the Ottoman Empire and 'the Turk' have been perceived as a threat to European society since the early Middle Ages. Indeed, it can be argued that the calling of the First Crusade by Pope Urban II was an early example of securitisation as a speech act (MacMillan 2010a: 455). His speech at the Church council of Clermont in France depicts the Turks, 'a race from Persia', as a threat to Byzantium and, by extension, to all Christendom and thus exhorts Christians to take up arms against them. As the monk Robert, an eyewitness, observed 'When Pope Urban had said these and very many similar things ... he so influenced to one purpose the desires of all who were present, that they cried out: "It is the will of God"' (cited in Rietbergen 1998: 115–16). In this case, although the proposed acts are violent the referent object is societal security. This also indicates how securitisation and identity formation may be mutually constitutive. Thus, the European view of Muslims evolved from that of simple 'heretics' to 'the enemies of Christianity'(Kuran-Burçoğlu 2007: 157).

More contemporary examples of societal securitisation may include the securitisation of Turkey's EU accession process by the Franco–German right (MacMillan 2010a), according to which right-wing politicians such as Nicolas Sarkozy argue that Turkey's full membership of the EU must be avoided as it belongs to a different civilization and its entry would, thus, mean the end of the European integration process. In Turkey itself, traditional Kemalists and, especially, nationalists have securitised Western countries as well as national minorities as a result of the Sèvres and Tanzimat syndromes, thus provoking distrust of the EU and the reforms related to accession (Bardakçı 2010: 27) (Yılmaz 2006).

The 'Inferior' Other: An Orientalist View

It has been argued that traditionally one of Europe's most important Others have been the Muslim countries of the Middle or Near East; the 'Orient'. As Said argues, 'The Orient was almost a European invention, and had been since antiquity a place of romance, exotic beings, haunting memories and landscapes, remarkable experiences' (1995: 1). The East has had a pivotal place in the construction of European identities;

> the Orient is not only adjacent to Europe; it is also the place of Europe's oldest and richest colonies, the source of its civilizations and languages, its cultural contestant and one of its oldest and most recurring images of the Other. In addition, the Orient has helped to define Europe (or the West) as its contrasting image, idea, personality, experience. (Said1995: 1)

In European discourse, then the Oriental can be defined in opposition to the European: if the European is powerful, masculine, rational, virtuous and mature the Oriental is by necessity powerless, feminine, depraved and childlike (Yeh 2000). In this way, using an insight from social identity theory, the self-esteem of the European in-group is strengthened as a result of comparison with an Oriental Other perceived as inferior. As Said notes, this depiction of the East as inferior has also been used in order to justify its colonisation by the West; Orientalism is thus a Western discourse for dominating, restructuring and having authority over the Orient (1995: 3).[6]

The European idea of the Orient as Other is said to date from at least as early as the Ancient Greeks. Thus, the expansion of the Persian Empire compared to their own, enabled the Greeks to deliminate 'Europe' and 'Asia': to Greek eyes the latter represented despotism, its inhabitants viewed as weak and cowardly beings in contrast to the brave, passionate, free Greeks. They even provided an explanation for these perceived negative features of the Other. According to Hippocrates, in addition to the passivity encouraged by the political system, climate was responsible: the relatively monotonous Asiatic climate did not provide the stimulus necessary for its inhabitants to develop an active mind and spirit (Den Boer 1995: 16–17).

However, it was the spread of Christianity in Europe and the subsequent threat posed by Islam that developed and consolidated the image of the Near and Middle East as Europe's principal Other. At first, due to the expansion of Islam into Europe in the Middle Ages, notably the Moorish domination of Spain followed by the rise of the Ottoman Empire meant that, as discussed above, the Muslim East was

---

6   It is important to consider, however, that Orientalist-type discourse may not be confined to the Orient. Lilley, for instance, argues that Orientalist-type Othered relations have also existed within Europe itself, and over a much longer period of time than Orientalism (2002: 21).

constructed principally as a military and societal threat to 'Christendom'. With the defeat of the Ottomans at the gates of Vienna and the battle of Lepanto, however, 'the Turk' became increasingly viewed as inferior rather than threatening. Notably, with increased diplomatic contact between the Ottomans and west Europeans, the predominant image of 'the Turk' was the lascivious and deceitful 'Lustful Turk', in contrast to the upright, sober European. Thus, the Ottoman Empire began to be perceived as;

> a focus of exotic pleasure, lust and duplicity ... Soon mendacity, dissimulation and rapacity were also being presented as characteristically *Ottoman* vices. Add to these the all-too-easily imagined scarlet lusts and violent passions of the Harem, and the old stereotypes of the Lusty Moor and the Ensanguined Turks were reinforced, not displaced by the contact with reality. (Wheatcroft 1993: 209–210)

However, by the nineteenth century, the Ottoman Empire was in decline. Not only had it increasingly come under the financial control of the European powers, its territory had also been seriously reduced by a series of wars, leading to the independence from the Ottoman Empire of many Balkan nations, including the Greeks, Albanians, Yugoslavs and Bulgarians. This led to the Ottoman Empire being increasingly depicted as the pathetic, dependent 'Sick Man of Europe'. Here, then, the decline of the Ottoman Empire was explained in European discourse by a combination of inherent tyranny and moral weakness and corruption in the Turkish character.[7] Such stereotypes were, however, certainly not new in European discourse; as early as 1622 Sir Thomas Roe, English ambassador to the Sublime Porte, described it as being 'like an old body, crazed through many vices, which remain when the youth and strength is decayed' (Wheatcroft 1993: 205).

As MacMillan (2010b), among others, has argued elsewhere, along with the perception of Turkey as a threat to 'European society', these Orientalist stereotypes of 'the Turk' are alive and well in discourse on Turkey's EU accession process in EU countries. Turkey is frequently depicted as an inferior, poverty-stricken country that would be economically at the mercy of the EU. Newspaper cartoons, for instance, often uphold the Orientalist tradition of using binary oppositions to emphasise Turkey's lack of development; where the EU is represented as a fast car, for instance, Turkey appears as a horse and cart, or where the EU member states are represented by modern toilets Turkey is represented by a hole in the ground (Erensu and Adanalı 2004: 8–9).

Similarly, as will be discussed further in later chapters of this book, the EU is, in a reversal of the 'Sick Man of Europe' stereotype,sometimes portrayed as inferior to Turkey, 'the robust man of Europe', in economic, demographic and

---

7   Wheatcroft (1993), Kumrular (2008) and Çırakman (2002), among others provide detailed historical examinations of the development and evolution of these stereotypes throughout the Ottoman era.

security terms in Turkish discourse, particularly in that of the currently governing AKP (*Adalet ve Kalınma Partisi* – Justice and Development Party).

The Other as Violating Universal Principles: The EU as Normative Power?

This form of Othering is closely connected to the idea of the EU as a 'normative power'. According to Manners the notion of a 'normative power' involves an understanding of power as power over opinion, or ideological power (2002: 239); he defines a normative power as 'a power that is able to shape conceptions of the normal' (2002: 239). Thus, a normative power can be identified by the impact it has on what is seen as appropriate behaviour by others (Manners 2006: 168).

As Diez argues, the discursive construction of the EU as 'normative power' is widespread among EU politicians, at both national and EU institutional levels, unless they are committed Eurosceptics (2005: 620). In his view;

> There may well be disagreement about the development of the EU's military capacities between Council and Commission, and between different member states and different directorate generals, yet the representation of Europe as a force for peace and well-being is nearly consensual. (Diez 2005: 620)

Therefore, it can be argued that the emergence of the EU's ideological power and EU identity construction are interconnected. Thus, 'the EU's external relations and specifically transatlantic relations form a venue for identity building' (Scheipers and Sicurelli 2007: 453). However, as Rumelili points out, such an identity is also constructed in opposition to Others;

> [critical constructivists argue that] the discourses on international norms, such as democracy and human rights, are intertwined with such oppositional structuring. This is because democracy, to be a meaningful identity category, presupposes the existence of its logical opposite, non-democracy. Therefore, the discourses on the promotion of democracy and human rights are inevitably productive of two identity categories, a morally superior identity of democratic juxtaposed to the inferior identity of non- (or less) democratic. (2004: 31)

In particular, the EU has constructed its identity as a normative power in contrast to the US. According to Scheipers and Sicurelli, this difference is basically focused on four features. Firstly, the EU argues that the principles it aims to institutionalise are universal in nature. Secondly, it views itself as a vanguard in political issues with a global reach such as global warming and human rights, while the USA is perceived as a laggard in these areas. Thirdly, the EU argues that, because it uses non-military, diplomatic and multi-lateral measures, the means it uses to achieve its objectives are superior to those used by the USA. Finally, the EU represents itself as strongly committed to international law (Scheipers and Sicurelli 2007: 455).

In Diez' view (2005), it is primarily this depiction of the Other as violating universal principles that the EU engages in. However, as he argues, the Self/Other articulations of the 'normative power Europe' concept have their origins in the construction of Europe's own past as its Other. Thus, in common with the 'normative power Europe' discourse it constructs an identity of post-Second World War Europe as one 'in which peace and respect for human rights prevail over the use of force and pure power politics' (2005: 634).

To give another example, during the accession process candidate countries are also subjected to this kind of Othering. During their process of accession to the EU, then, as the candidate countries are required to fulfill the accession criteria, based on 'universal norms', a relation of superior/inferior is constructed between the EU member states and the candidates (Rumelili 2004: 41). In addition, the EU itself is sometimes accused of not living up to the universal values on which it claims to be based. Nicolaidis and Howse (2002), for instance, argue that the picture which the EU presents in the international arena does not represent what Europe actually is but presents an idealised picture, or *EUtopia,* while Smismans (2010: 48) also notes that 'the EU has been repeatedly criticised that its human rights standards and scrutiny in external policy and in conditions for accession are considerably more severe than the control it exerts in relation to its own Member states'. Moreover, as is discussed in more detail later in this book, the EU has often been criticised in Turkish discourse for not living up to the universal values on which it claims to be based.

The 'Superior' Other

While the Other is often depicted as inferior, it may also be perceived as superior. This form of Othering may go together with, for instance, images of the Other as threatening. In the case of Turkey, for example, the Kemalist elite has traditionally viewed Europe (and, by extension the EU) as simultaneously threatening and superior, a model of development to be emulated. Zarakol argues that the perception of Europe as simultaneously superior and threatening in Kemalist discourse is a consequence of the internalisation of Turkey's stigmatisation by the West, and of its insider/outsider status in international society. In this view, as Turkey (or the Ottoman Empire) was not part of the original Westphalian state system it has found itself on the inferior side of the established/outsider organising principle of international society, leading to auto-Orientalism, or a self-perception of inferiority and a desire to 'catch up with' the West (Zarakol 2011: 29–30).

Another example, discussed further in Chapter 2, may be European views of the Ottoman Empire during the years of the expansion of the latter. Here, then, while the Ottoman Empire was generally regarded as a threat to Europe, it was also frequently perceived as superior in military and even political terms. Here, then, the absolute rule of the Sultan was seen as forming the basis for the unity, discipline and might of the Ottoman Empire.

The Simply 'Different' Other

In this case, the Other is not represented as threatening, nor is it regarded as inferior. It is merely different. While this strategy of Othering is certainly not innocent, as it still imposes identities on others, it is, in Diez's view, preferable to the others as it 'reduces the possibility to legitimise harmful interference with the other' (2005: 629). As Rumelili argues, for instance, 'the discursive dependence of identity on difference does not necessarily entail a relationship of Othering' between self and other' (2004:36). Risse associates this form of Othering with what he terms a *civic* identity construction (2010: 28).

Here, some examples will be given from the history of Europe's relations with and attitudes towards the Ottoman Empire. Although negative images predominated, there were also some instances where the Ottoman Turk was perceived as different, but not necessarily inferior. Kuran-Burçoğlu draws attention, for instance, to the medieval German Carnival plays, which were designed as popular entertainment for ordinary people. Here, a strikingly different image of 'the Turk' is constructed compared to the negative perceptions of the clergy and upper classes. Staged just a year after the fall of Constantinople, the 'Great Turk' was portrayed as a 'just and brave Emperor' whose 'subjects are treated well' and do not have to pay tribute to their Emperor. Thus, the plays can be seen in the context of an implied popular criticism of European rulers, who were in this case perceived as harsher and more cruel than their Ottoman equivalent (Kuran-Burçoğlu 2007: 157–8).

In addition, the fashion for all things Turkish that was prevalent in European 'high society' in the late seventeenth to eighteenth centuries perhaps falls into this category. This movement spread from France to other parts of Europe following the appearance of Ottoman emissaries in Western courts. It was known as *Turchomania* or *Turcophilie,* and was known as *Turquerie* when it was manifested in art, music or literature (Kuran-Burçoğlu 2007: 159) (Wheatcroft 1993: 209–10). Finally, Kuran-Burçoğlu also argues that the German Enlightenment, which emerged in the eighteenth century based on the ideas of Immanuel Kant, favoured the emergence of a more positive image of 'the Turk', as well as of Jews, through its focus on religious tolerance (2007: 160).

Similarly, in contemporary discourse, both in the EU and in Turkey, which argues that a Turkey anchored in the EU could serve as a 'bridge between civilizations' and could help to prevent a 'clash of civilizations' Europe and Turkey are actually viewed as civilizational Others, albeit friendly and potentially compatible ones. A 'bridge' between civilizations, for instance, fully belongs to neither of the civilizations that it bridges (Yanık 2009: 545).

The Self as Other: The EU and its Historical and Contemporary Ghosts

In Manners' view, the Other is always a part of the Self. His basis for this is work by Habermas and Derrida and, in particular, Kristeva's concept of the 'abject' (Manners 2006: 177). As Kristeva argues, for instance,

> The foreigner is within us. And when we flee from or struggle against the
> foreigner, we are fighting our unconsciousness – that 'improper' facet of our
> impossible 'own and proper' … To discover our disturbing otherness, for that
> indeed is what bursts in to confront that 'demon', that threat, that apprehension
> generated by the projective apparition of the other at the heart of what we persist
> in maintaining as a proper, solid 'us'. (Kristeva 1991: 191–2)

Derrida also stresses that, in common with other cultures, there is no defining
essence on which European culture is based. In his view, then;

> What is proper to a culture is not to be identical to itself. Not to not have an
> identity, but not to be able to identify with itself, to be able to say 'we' or 'me', to
> be able to take the form of the subject only in the non-identity to itself or, if you
> prefer, only in the difference with itself. There is no culture or cultural identity
> without this difference *with itself.*[8] (1994: 8–9)

As Manners argues, 'the projection of otherness onto individuals and the social
groups they represent is so strong precisely because they are also an abjected and
disturbing part of ourselves' (2006: 177–8). It has frequently been put forward,
for instance, that Europe's own past is an important Other for the EU, particularly,
but certainly not exclusively in German discourse. As Hobsbawm notes, 'to be
a member of any human community is to situate oneself with regard to one's
past, if only by rejecting it' (1997: 27). In fact, as Diez (2004: 325) and Wæver
(1998: 90) have argued, such 'temporal Othering' has, at least until recently been
particularly pervasive in EU discourse.[9] As Tony Blair, for instance, noted in a
2003 speech in Glasgow;

> For hundreds of years, Europe was at war, the boundaries of many nations shifting
> with each passing army, small countries occupied and re-occupied, their people
> never at peace. Large countries fought each other literally for decades at a time
> with only the briefest respite to draw breath before the resumption of hostilities.
> For my father's generation that was the Europe they were brought up in. Today
> in Europe former enemies are friends, at one, if not always diplomatically. The
> EU is a massive achievement of peace and prosperity. (Blair 2003)

As Diez argues, following the end of the Cold War, 'Central and Eastern
Europe now became the incarnation of Europe's past, a past that the West had
overcome, and a zone of war and nationalism that was stuck in history' (2004:
326). However, certain aspects of contemporary European society have also been
projected as important Others for an EU seen as based on 'universal norms' and

---

8   Emphasis in original.

9   Interestingly, however, as Diez points out (2004:322) an important aspect of Europe's
past – its colonial past – has largely been absent from European 'past as other' discourse

'unity in diversity'; particularly the rise of xenophobia, racism and the far right. As Manners, for instance, suggests;

> The reactions to Jörg Haider, Pia Kjærsgaard, Rocco Butiglione, George W. Bush, and the hatred they attract are interesting exactly because of the ambiguity between abject-foreignness in questions of immigration, European integration, Christian fundamentalism, homophobia, and imperialism. (2006: 178)

From this point of view it is interesting, as Laffan points out (2004: 83) that many of the Austrians who took to the streets of Vienna in 2000 to protest against the presence of Haider's Freedom Party in power carried EU flags. In Turkish discourse, too, various groups have often been Othered. In traditional Kemalist discourse, for example, the Ottoman past and political Islam are often portrayed as internal Others, as are ethnic and religious minorities (Parlak and Kılıçarslan 2006: 131–2) (Yılmaz 2006: 29).

Chapter 2

Images of the Turk in Europe:
A Historical Overview

This chapter attempts a historical overview of the developing image of the Ottoman Turk, and of the East in general, in Europe from the ancient Greeks to the collapse of the Ottoman Empire. In particular, based on the theoretical framework discussed in the previous chapter, it focuses on the construction of the East as Europe's Other. Moreover, in the broader context of this book, this chapter aims to shed further light on the contemporary debates on Turkish accession to the EU by putting them into a historical context.

Ancient Greek Images of East and West

The concept of the East as Europe's primary Other predates both Christianity and Islam; in fact, its roots can be traced as far back as ancient Greece. The Greeks, as evidenced in the writings of the historian Herodotus, for instance, considered that the world was divided into three continents; Asia, Africa and Europe. In Herodotus' time, while the Eastern borders of Europe were debatable, it was accepted that the Mediterranean separated Europe from Africa, and that the Pillars of Hercules marked its Western limits (den Boer 1993: 14–15). However, it is likely that Europe referred specifically to the Greek sphere of influence; as Rietbergen notes, the first mention of Europe in the seventh century BC refers to 'the Peleponnese, Europe and the islands whose shores are lapped by the sea' (1998: 32).

Europe, previously a neutral, geographical expression, became increasingly defined in contrast to Asia following the wars between the Greeks and the Persians. These wars were provoked by the expansion of the Persian Empire into Anatolia which resulted in the rebellion of the Ionian city states on the Eastern Aegean coast. The Ionian Greeks sought the support of their Greek motherland, notably Athens and Sparta, which were in turn invaded by the Persians. It is in this context that the term 'barbarians', previously a relatively neutral term used to describe non-Greeks who, to Greek ears, could only make an unintelligible 'bar-bar' sound, began to take on much more negative connotations when applied to the Persians. From the fifth century BC, then, Greek authors began to depict Greece and Persia as representing freedom and despotism respectively (den Boer 1993: 16).

In Herodotus' account of the battle at Thermopylae, for example, the heroism and steadfastness of the Greeks is juxtaposed to the cruelty and disorganisation of the Persians (Adib-Moghaddam 2011: 32). Similar negative depictions of the

Persians can be found in ancient Greek literature. In Aeschylus' play *The Persians*, for instance, the Greeks are represented as 'free, emancipated and chivalrous in contrast to the Persian king, who is shown to be hubristic, decadent, a totalitarian master of slaves' (Adib-Moghaddam 2011: 33).[1]

For the Greeks, the contrast between the behaviour of the European Greeks and that of the Asian Persians, resulting in a despotic form of government for the Persians and freedom for the Greeks, could be explained by climatic differences; the variations of the seasons in Europe kept people physically and mentally active and flexible, while the warmer, monotonous Asiatic climate encouraged sluggishness, inflexibility and passivity in the face of despotic rulers (Rietbergen 1998: 33) (den Boer 1993: 16–17). In the words of Hippocrates, for instance, writing in around 400 BC;

> The deficiency of spirit and courage observable in the human inhabitants of Asia has for its principal cause the low margin of seasonal variability in the temperature of that continent, which is approximately stable throughout the year. Such a climate does not produce those mental shocks and violent bodily dislocations which would naturally render the temperament ferocious and introduce a stronger current of irrationality and passion than would be the case under stable conditions. It is invariably changes that stimulate the human mind and that prevent it from remaining passive. (cited in den Boer 1993: 16).

The Middle Ages: Christendom, Crusades and Saracens

In the seventh century, the unity of the Mediterranean was disrupted, in large part as a consequence of the enormous Arab expansion which commenced in that century. Syria, Palestine and Persia were conquered, as was Egypt and the entire north coast of Africa. It was from North Africa that Muslims made their first incursions into present-day Europe, beginning with the 711 crossing of Tariq ibn Ziyard and his forces into Spain via Jebel-al-Tariq (Gibraltar), eventually resulting in the formation of the state of Al-Andalus in 756. In 723 the Moors attempted an incursion into France but were defeated at Poitiers by Charles Martel (den Boer 1993: 26). However, Gül (2009: 58–9), for instance, argues that this defeat was due to the small size of the Moorish invading force, itself a reflection of their limited interest in this then backward part of Europe.

During the Middle Ages, the terms 'Europe' and 'Europeans' were far less widely used than 'Christendom'. The principal Other of Christendom was the Saracen; it

---

1   As Adib-Moghaddam notes, however, the Persians themselves were certainly not immune to 'Othering' their neighbours. For them, anyone who did not believe in the vice regency of the Persian King of Kings on behalf of the Zoroastrian God Ahura Mazda was deemed 'barbarous' or wicked. The distinction was thus drawn between *arya* ('pertaining to ourselves') and *anarya* ('Other') (Adib-Moghaddam 2011: 35–6).

was primarily a religious Other. In the East (the Levant and Byzantine empire) Saracens were framed as the followers of the Antichrist or as God's Scourge, while high medieval images prevalent in Latin Christendom also tended to cast Muslims in the familiar roles of pagans and heretics. This imagery, in turn, had the function of constituting a more inclusive collective Christian identity, associated with a more aggressive and expansive posture towards the Other (Levin 2011: 53).

Christendom was, however, not associated specifically with Europe until the late Middle Ages, as the Latin church still emphasised its universal mission, and because not all of Europe was yet Christian (Levin 2011: 82). As Neumann notes, the term Christendom as used in the eleventh century implied a 'Stoic, universalist belief in the essential unity of humankind with a missionary dynamic to convert the infidel' (1999: 42). In this sense, there was a change from the pacifism of early Christians to the active promulgation of war by the powerful medieval popes, a development that had been influenced by Augustine of Hippo's concept of a 'just war', granting papal sanction for holy wars of conquest against unbelievers (Levin 2011:75) (Neumann 1999: 42). It is in this context that the image of 'the Turk' first emerged, in a provocative letter sent in 1088 by the Byzantine Emperor Alexius Comnenus to Robert 1, Earl of Flandern in which 'the Turk' was depicted as a 'cruel' 'barbaric' and 'devastating' enemy which threatened Christianity, and the wealth, security and even the existence of Byzantium (Kuran-Burçoğlu 2003: 23).[2] As has already been noted, the calling of the First Crusade in 1095 by Pope Urban II is perhaps the single greatest medieval example of the attempt to construct an anti-Muslim identity from above (Reitbergen 1998: 114). Urban II's speech indicates an acceptance of the global mission of Christianity, and highlights the fact that, despite the schism between the Latin and Orthodox churches, the Greek church was considered by the Roman Catholic to form part of the community of Christians. However, Urban emphasises that Christendom has been relegated to Europe, a small continent which, on its periphery, continued to be inhabited by unbelievers; thus the only proper response for a good Christian was to retake the lost territory. Following the speech of Urban II, the resulting religious hysteria provided popular support and finance for the Crusades, and even resulted in several spontaneous popular crusades, including the Children's Crusade and the Peasants' Crusade (Levin 2011: 83–4).

The Crusades also had the function of diffusing knowledge of the existence of Islam and the name of Mohammed, and, following the Crusades, the term 'Saracen' began to be used more specifically to denote Muslims rather than unbelievers in general (Neumann 1999: 42). However, the lack of accurate information about the

---

2   As Adib-Moghaddam argues, the appearance of the Crusaders in the Muslim lands resulted in similar views of Christians as cruel and barbaric. Usamah Ibn Munqidh, a Syrian Muslim writing in the twelfth century, for instance, refers to 'the kind of rule the Franks have' when describing a vicious duel between a blacksmith and an old man, which ended with the former 'trying to stick his fingers into the eyes of his adversary' which he failed to do so 'because of the great quantity of blood flowing out' (Adib-Moghaddam 2011: 53).

Islamic religion meant that Islam was completely misunderstood and demonized in medieval Europe. As Said, for instance, points out, the role that Mohammed played in Islam was frequently misconceived by Christians as paralleling Christ's role in Christianity. Christians, then, believed that Muslims had been duped into worshipping a false god. Thus, the prophet became seen as 'the epitome of lechery, debauchery, sodomy, and a whole battery of assorted treacheries, all of which derived 'logically' from his doctrinal impostures' (Said 1995: 62). Similarly, Christians considered that the Koran was full of lies, and believed that Muslims did not want it translated from Arabic because it was false (Kumrular 2008: 103–7). Hence, as Neumann notes, the two processes of the Crusades – of strengthening Christian identity and firmly establishing Islam as Christendom's primary Other – fed off each other as the increasing solidarity of Christendom gave greater power to the crusade against the Other which, in turn, further increased solidarity among the members of Christendom (1999: 43).

By the fourteenth century, three major developments had contributed to an increasingly territorially defined notion of Christendom. Firstly, Europe became more uniformly Christian, as the pagan peoples of northern Europe converted to Christianity, a process that was completed with the conversion of Lithuania/ Poland in 1387 and, as the Spanish *Reconquista* progressed, with the eventual expulsion of the last Moors from Granada in 1492. Secondly, even greater areas of Eastern Christendom were being lost to the Muslim 'foe' as the Crusaders proved unsuccessful in adding to or even maintaining control of the Byzantine lands. Finally, the greater contact that the Crusades had provided between the Latin and Orthodox Christians only served to heighten awareness of the differences between them on both sides, illustrated in particular by the spectacle of the Fourth Crusade in which Latin crusaders sacked Orthodox Constantinople (Levin 2011: 87–8).

Renaissance and Reformation: 'The Ottoman Turk' as 'Europe's' Other

Following the divisions caused by the Reformation and the resulting religious wars, and, eventually, the principles of sovereignty enshrined in the Treaty of Westphalia which put an end to the fighting, the centre of power shifted from the Church to secular rulers (Levin 2011: 80). In this context, the concept of Christendom gradually gave way to that of Europe, which took on a political as well as religious importance (Neumann 1999: 43–4). After the foundation of the Ottoman Empire in the fourteenth century and the resulting increase of military pressure on Christendom the Saracen gave way to the Ottoman Turk as Europe's principal Other, a process which, naturally, accelerated with the Ottoman conquest of Constantinople in 1453.

As Kumrular argues, during this period in Europe 'the Turk' was 'the most discussed and written about, the most feared, wondered about and, without a doubt, the most envied' (2008: 33). In addition to their victories on the battlefield, the Ottomans were feared for their rumoured aggression off the battlefield; wherever they went they were said according to European reports to rape and pillage, with clergy, women and even unborn children among their victims (Kumrular 2008: 179–82).[3,4] Indeed, some of the first image creators of the Ottoman Turks in Europe were those Byzantine expatriates who had fled from Anatolia and took refuge in Italy, including Theodoro Spandugno and Cardinal Bessarion of Trebizond (Soykut 2003: 47–8).

In the fifteenth–sixteenth centuries, then, the Ottomans represented the greatest challenge – and danger – to Europe, and the Ottoman threat provoked increased discussion of alliances, unification, confederation and coalition in Europe (İnalcık 2010: 217). During this period, then, 'the Ottoman Turk' was seen as a *generalized* challenger to the European self, in terms of its military prowess, its political organisation and its religion which, like Christianity, combined a universalist faith with a proselytizing zeal (Neumann 1999: 49).

Thus, 'the Turk' is transformed from a primarily religious to a primarily military, political Other (Neumann 1999: 46) although the religious element remained important; as a result of their military predominance, the Ottoman Turks were considered capable not only of increasing geographical expansion but also of converting large numbers of Christians to their own religion (Kumrular 2008: 33).[5] Therefore, although the Ottomans also represented a military and political threat, Islam continued to occupy a central position in Renaissance European discourse on the Ottomans and, perhaps surprisingly, continued to be framed in terms of the images elaborated during the Middle Ages; the Turkish peril was often viewed as the latest phase in the centuries-old assault of Islam on Christianity (Neumann 1999: 44) (Levin 2011: 80). King Christian I of Denmark, for example, declared that 'the grand Turk was the beast rising out of the sea described in the Apocalypse' (cited in Neumann 1999: 45).

As den Boer argues, it is specifically in the context of the Turkish threat in the East that Europe becomes a synonym for the Christian world. In the work of Pope Pius II (1458–64), who tried to organise the defence of the Christian world against the Ottomans, the terms 'Respublica christiana' and 'Europe' are used

---

3   However, while this image almost certainly contained more than a grain of truth, Ottoman violence in this period should also be placed in its context; these were, after all, the years of the Catholic Inquisition and the witch hunts in Europe (Wheatcroft 1993: 231)

4   As Kuran-Burçoğlu notes, however, popular images of the Turk in the 15th century were not exclusively negative. Notably, in some of the popular German Carnival plays of the time, 'the Turk' was sometimes portrayed in a positive light. The Sultan, 'the great Turk' was depicted as a just and generous ruler whose subjects lived in peace and were not required to pay tribute to the State. This, then, implies a criticism of the German public of their own rulers in comparison as unjust and demanding tribute from their subjects (2003: 25).

5   As Kumrular puts forward, however, the fearsome image of the Ottoman Turk as violent and haughty was not merely a European perception; it was also the result of a conscious, and highly effective, strategy on the part of the Ottoman state (Kumrular 2005: 112); thus, they chiefly used violence as a shock tactic in Europe in order to gain a psychological advantage in battle

interchangeably; he refers to 'our Europe, our Christian Europe'.[6] He was also the first to use the word *europeus* to indicate an inhabitant of Europe. Similarly, Europe is used in the sense of the home of Christendom, as opposed to the Ottoman Empire, in the works of the Renaissance humanist Erasmus (den Boer 1993: 35–7).

Moreover, with the renewed Renaissance interest in classical cultures, Ancient Greek frames of reference, based on writers including Hesiod, Xenophon and Herodotus, were (re)introduced in discourse regarding the Ottomans (Neumann 1999: 44). Most notably, Bessarion is one of the first men of the Renaissance to identify the ancient Greeks and Romans with the Renaissance idea of 'civilization' and Christendom and to equate the Turks with the Persian enemies of the ancient Greeks (Soykut 2003: 52). Another Renaissance humanist, Juan Luis Vives, also saw the struggle against the Ottoman Turks in terms of the classical Greek distinction between Europe and Asia, arguing that every Asiatic invasion of Europe since the Persian invasions of classical Greece had ended with the complete defeat of the invading forces (den Boer 1993: 37).

Similarly, the Renaissance political theorist Niccolo Machiavelli also alluded to the rivalry between the Greeks and the Persians in his comparison of contemporary Europeans and the Ottoman Empire. In *The Prince*, then, Machiavelli discusses the conquest of the 'kingdom of Darius' by Alexander the Great, who could 'take his country from him' because the Persians did not revolt against his rule in order to suggest how the Ottoman Empire could be conquered. As Machiavelli argues,

> Once the Turk has been conquered, and routed in the field in such a way that he cannot replace his armies, there is nothing to fear but the family of the prince, and, this being exterminated, there remains no-one to fear, the others having no credit with the people, and as the conqueror did not rely on them before his victory, so he ought not to fear them after it. (1952: 7)

For Machiavelli, this is due to a weakness in the 'Oriental' style of rule. In Machiavelli's view, a prince can rule in one of two manners, the first typical of the West, the second of the East. Thus he can either rule by exercising absolute power, with all other persons in the state being subject to him, or he can surround himself with relatively independent lords, whose power is derived not from his favour but from their birth. In the first case, then, the prince's ministers are, in effect, slaves. In the second, the lords control and rule their own territory and subjects. In consequence, then, a prince such as Alexander who chooses to invade an Asian state will find it a difficult task as they are confronted with the whole of the state. However, if the invasion is successful, the state will fall as a whole. In contrast, in Machiavelli's view a Western state is more difficult to dominate in the long

---

6   Pius II is also the author of the famous *Epistula ad Mahumetem* (Letter to Mohammed) in which he invited Mehmed II to convert to Christianity and to rule the world together with the ruler of Rome proper. While the letter was never sent, it remains a classic of fifteenth century political rhetoric (Soykut 2003: 55).

term as the invader will be faced with uprisings due to the large number of small princedoms (den Boer 1993: 39)

In general, then, the ancient Greek concept of the *barbarian* Other was perhaps the most widely resurrected to refer to the Ottoman Turks following the fall of Constantinople. Although the Turks now controlled the birthplace of Greek culture and had taken over the second city of the Roman Empire, they were viewed as vandals and barbarians who were unworthy and incapable of taking on the responsibility of this classical heritage. Instead, then, they were seen as the destroyers of civilization, and their language, religion and traditions all seen as barbarian (Kumrular 2008: 171). This image is reflected, for instance, in the sixteenth century Spanish dictionary prepared by Orozco Covarrubias, who defined the word 'Turk' as 'a low people with dirty habits who live through cheating and mistreating others' (cited in Kumrular 2005: 115).[7] Negative stereotypes of the Ottomans, as well as allusions to the threat of a Turkish incursion into Europe, can also be found in the literature of the time. As Kumrular notes, the similarities between Cervantes and Shakespeare, the literary giants of the time, goes beyond the fact that they both died on the same day (23 April 1616); both eternalised the negative image of 'the Turk' (Kumrular 2008: 47). In Shakespeare's *Othello*, for instance, the Turks are represented as 'a powerful enemy that is dangerous not only through force of arms and large numbers, but also because of its military efficiency and political foresight' (Artemel 2003: 161–2). Examples of similar negative depictions can also be found in other English Renaissance literature of the time, although, as Aksoy notes, not all Turkish characters are evil or base[8] (Aksoy 2003: 207). Cervantes' work also contains negative stereotypes of Turks and Moors, unsurprisingly given the fact that Cervantes himself spent five years as a prisoner in Algeria. This experience is reflected in *El Baño de Argel* and *El Trato de Argel*, in which the Moorish and Turkish characters are portrayed as violent and unjust, while their Christian prisoners are depicted as virtuous and proud (Kumrular 2008: 383). Moreover, negative images of 'the Turk' were also used in Renaissance literature as a metaphor for 'despotism' and 'barbarism' at home. Thomas More, for instance, in his *A Dialogue of Comfort Agaynst Trybulacion* also used the negative image of the Turk as a veiled criticism of the despotism of Henry VIII's regime (Artemel 2003: 163).[9] During the Renaissance period, the

---

7   Ottoman images of Europeans at the time were scarcely more flattering. Kumrular notes that Europeans were often represented as pigs. In the palace festivals in Istanbul it was customary for a lion, representing the Ottomans to fight a pig, symbolising the Europeans (2005: 111).

8   Aksoy points out that the Turkish characters in the plays of Christopher Marlowe, for instance, are often noble and virtuous (2003: 207–8).

9   At a deeper level, More associates the external evil personified by the Turks with the evil in man himself. A similar internalisation of the external evil represented by the Turkish forces in *Othello* takes place at the end of the play, when the hero, at the moment of his death, identifies with his enemy, 'a malignant and a turban'd Turk' (Artemel 2003: 163).

Ottoman Empire was also frequently described as a *tyranny,* although this term was not applied consistently. This inconsistency reflects the fact that sixteenth and seventeenth century writers on the Ottoman Empire tended to focus on specific features of the Ottoman regime, and displayed a wide variety of views on and images of the Ottomans,in contrast to the broad theoretical analyses and comparisons of political structures and belief systems which would become commonplace in the eighteenth century (Çırakman 2001: 51).

Thus, unlike the concept of *despotism,* which was frequently applied to the Ottoman Empire during the eighteenth century, a tyranny could have positive, as well as negative features. In fact the term itself was ambiguous when applied to the Ottoman Empire. On the one hand, it could refer to an unlawful, arbitrary and coercive regime, illegitimate in nature and held together by an excess of cruelty. In this context, tyrannical rule implied 'endless wars, sedition, assassinations, pillage and desolation, cruelty, corruption and excess' (Çırakman 2001: 50). On the other hand, the term tyranny was also used, more generally and neutrally, to mean absolute rule (Çırakman 2001: 50–55).

While, as has been discussed above, images of the Turk as bloody, cruel barbarians certainly abounded, so did more positive ones, often based on an admiration of Turkish military superiority. From this point of view tyranny, understood as absolute rule, was seen as the basis of the unity, success and might of the Ottoman Empire, and the absolute power of the Emperor and the loyalty of his subjects was frequently viewed with admiration (Çırakman 2001: 50–52). This positive image of the Turks can be seen, for instance, in the account of a journey through the Ottoman Empire by the English adventurer Sir Henry Blount (Tomkinson 2003: 211–25). Although negative images are certainly not absent from Blount's account, they are also mixed with admiration for the mixture of love and fear with which the Ottomans ruled their subjects. In particular, he praised the Turkish talent for enforcing law by fear and 'necessary' cruelty as he considered that this could, in the broader view, result in a decrease in delinquency and thus less injustice to innocent parties (Tomkinson 2003: 216–17).

Images of the Turk in the Reformation

At least until the death of Mehmet II, alliances and pacts against the Ottomans had been a prominent feature of European international relations. However, at around this time, the Ottomans begin to become involved in European conflicts, playing an important part in the European balance of power in the sixteenth century (Kumrular 2008: 96). Most notably, the Ottomans played a role in the struggle for the Holy Roman Empire between Charles of Spain and Francis 1 of France when the latter signed a treaty with the Ottomans for an attack against the Italian states. Other examples include Ottoman involvement in wars among the Italian city states, and an attempt on the part of Queen Elizabeth I to form an alliance of 'monotheists' with Sultan Murad II against the 'idolatrous' Philip II of Spain (Neumann 1999: 48). Indeed, the Ottomans themselves, under Sultan Süleyman, declared their support of Protestants in a document sent to Protestant princes through his consul Muharrem Çavuş, arguing that Islam and Protestantism had much in common, most notably due to the Protestants' rejection of 'idols' in their churches (Kumrular 2008: 96). This was reflected, for instance, in a 'Turco-Calvinist' alliance project between the Ottomans and the Calvinist Dutch, based upon the Ottomans being granted a trading post at Anvers in return for their support of the Protestant Dutch against Catholic Spain (Kumrular 2008: 97).

With the Reformation, the Ottoman Turks began to be used as a discursive tool for both Protestants and Catholics. It is important to remember that Martin Luther was writing at the height of Ottoman power, at a time of Ottoman incursions into the Balkans and into the Holy Roman Empire, including the siege of Vienna in 1529 and the submission of all of Hungary during the 1540s. Thus, Luther refers to 'the Turk' throughout his writings, in particular when discussing the threat that Islam posed to Christianity. In one of his publications addressing the Turkish threat, for instance, he writes, 'Since we now have the Turk and his religion at our very doorstep our people must be warned lest ... they deny their Christ and follow Muhammad' (cited in Levin 2011: 98). Despite his proximity to the Ottomans, however, and his unfulfilled wish to read the Koran himself, Luther's knowledge of the Turks and of Islam was primarily limited to texts of medieval origin or influence; it is therefore unsurprising that he tends to repeat medieval stereotypes in his own writing (Levin 2011: 100–104), in particular those of the Turk as God's wrath and as the Antichrist. The image of the Turk as the 'wrath' or 'rod' of God was also used by Catholics; Spanish clergyman Pero Mexia, for instance, described the Ottoman Turks as 'God's whip' (Kumrular 2008: 97).

This is a primarily defensive image and one that does not tend to promote military aggression as it laid the blame on Christians themselves; therefore it was hoped that, if Christians prayed, mended their ways and repented of their sins, God would ultimately save them. Thus, Luther argued that 'to make war against the Turk is nothing else than to strive against God, Who is punishing our sins by means of the Turks' (cited in Levin 2011: 103). By 1529, the year of the siege of Vienna, Luther had somewhat modified his position, arguing that 'I will fight against the Turks and their gods until I die' (cited in Kumrular 2008: 95). For Luther, however, any war against the Ottomans should be a secular one, fought under the banner of the Emperor, not that of Christ. In Luther's view, though, victory on the battlefield would only be possible if, with the guidance of the clergy, 'Sir Christian' first became aware of and repented of his sins and ingratitude to God (Levin 2011: 104–5).

Luther also saw the expansion of the Ottoman Empire as a sign that the Apocalypse was at hand. In this context, he cast both 'the Turk' and the Pope at various times as the Antichrist (Kumrular 2008: 95). The Ottoman Turks, thus, generally play the part of the harbinger of the Apocalypse in Luther's discourse, where they are also described as 'Gog and Magog', the two nations/giants/beasts unleashed by the devil after his thousand-year imprisonment (Levin 2011: 108–9).

Another discursive strategy used both by Protestants against Catholics and vice versa was to accuse the other of being 'Turks' (Kumrular 2008: 98). Luther calls the Pope's decretals his 'Alcoran', arguing that the Pope claimed for himself the 'power, rule and authority over the Christian church and over the Holy Scriptures, the Word of God' (cited in Levin 2011: 113). The same strategies were employed by Luther's Catholic opponents; for instance, an English translation of a French anti-Huguenot pamphlet entitled 'Luther's Alcoran' argued that Lutheranism agreed with 'Mahometism' on forty points of faith and religion (Levin 2011: 120–21). Being compared to Turks was also a strategy that Catholics used to complain about their own church; Machiavelli, for example, caused a scandal when he compared the Sultan's empire to the Vatican (Kumrular 2008: 98).

The Treaty of Westphalia of 1648 put an end to decades of clashes between Protestants and Catholics (Soykut 2003: 85). Under the new system, the sovereignty of states was advanced through a reaffirmation of the principle of *cujus regio, ejus religio,* or 'whose region, his religion', a concept which had first been advanced at Augsberg in 1555, according to which it was up to the king to decide which religion should be followed throughout his realm. On this basis, a legal system of autonomous states was set up, which formally succeeded the medieval notion of Christendom as one political unity (Neumann 1999: 49–50). Moreover, this new state system was coupled with the consolidation of the power of the old nation states, such as France and England (Soykut 2003: 85).

As Soykut notes, it is during this period that Orientalism in the modern sense was born and became part of the European perception of the Orient (2003: 85). Notably, the Ottoman Empire was seen in European discourse as profoundly unsuited to the new state system as Muslim political theory, according to which God is the source of all authority, was viewed as incompatible with a system of territorially defined states organised in accordance with man-made rules. Thus, when William Penn put forward his ideas for a European society of states in 1693 he recommended that the Ottoman Empire be allowed to join only on condition that it renounced Islam (Neumann 1999: 51).

The halting of the Ottoman army outside the gates of Vienna in 1683 by a league of Christian forces led by the Polish Prince Sigismund was a turning point in the relationship between the Europeans and 'the Turk' in that it marked the end of the concept of the 'undefeatable Turk' in Europe (Kuran-Burçoğlu 2007: 159) (İnalcık 2010: 217). In 1699, the Treaty of Karlowitz was signed between the Ottoman Empire and the Holy Union of Austria, Poland, Venice and Russia, signalling both the Europeans' military superiority and the beginning of the Ottomans' retreat from Central Europe. This treaty represents the Ottoman Empire's acknowledgement of the existence of European states for the first time (Neumann 1999: 51). As Neumann notes, during this period, there is a marked increase of the term 'barbarians' to describe 'the Turk', as opposed to those with strictly religious overtones such as 'infidel' or 'unbeliever'. Thus, for Europeans, it was now primarily civilization based on principles such as 'humanity', 'law' and 'social mores' rather than religion which served to distinguish Europeans from the Ottomans (Neumann 1999: 52).

A consequence of the Treaty, however, was the beginning of closer diplomatic, cultural and trade relations between the Ottomans and European states. The Ottoman Empire, notably, began to send ambassadors in a systematic fashion to Europe (Ortaylı 2008: 157). This exchange, in particular the founding of Mehmed Efendi's embassy to France in 1720–21, brought with it an increased European interest in all things Ottoman (Wheatcroft 1993: 210). This culminated in the *Turchomania* or *Turchophilie* movement, according to which all things Turkish, including Ottoman styles of dress or Turkish-themed parties, became fashionable (Kuran-Burçoğlu 2007: 159–160).

The Ottoman craze also influenced art, music and literature, where it was known as *Turquerie*. In music, for instance, a new genre known as *alla Turca* developed, works such as Mozart's *The Abduction from the Seraglio* were inspired, and new, Eastern-influenced musical instruments were introduced. In literature, a new genre of tales appeared which reflected the mystery and glamour of the Orient, while art began to take on Orientalist themes, depicting, for instance, everyday life in Oriental cities or Westerners dressed in Eastern costume (Kuran-Burçoğlu 2003: 29–30) (Kuran-Burçoğlu 2007: 159–60). However, as a result of this peaceful contact, and building upon earlier stereotypes of the 'Lusty Moor' and the 'Ensanguined Turk', it was deduced that the exotic Ottomans, who spurned alcohol and contact with women in public, led a private life of drunken debauchery, intrigue,and sexual excess (Wheatcroft 1993: 209–210).

The Enlightenment: The 'Despotic' Turk

The view of 'the Turk' as barbarian became even further entrenched in European discourse throughout the following century, with the development of greater European self-confidence and the development of the Enlightenment. In the latter part of the eighteenth century, it became usual to associate Europe and civilization with each other, indicating a growing feeling of European superiority based on factors including but certainly not limited to Christianity, in contrast to the late medieval equation of Europe with Christendom (den Boer 1993: 64). However, despite the self-consciously secular and progressive discourse of the Enlightenment *philosophes* and their vision of an inclusive European self-understanding based on a set of universal values rather than on a shared religion, their discourse on Islam carried a heavier debt to earlier Christian discourse than is commonly believed (Levin 2011: 123–4); they continued to discuss the Ottoman Empire in terms of the struggle between Christianity and Islam (İnalcık 2010: 222). However, eighteenth century images of the Ottomans, in contrast to the variety of images prevalent during the Renaissance, originated in the widely accepted idea of Oriental despotism derived from a comparison of political structures and belief systems based on theoretical deductive analysis (Çırakman 2003: 227). It is during this century, then, that a coherent and constant image of the Ottoman Turks first emerged (Çırakman 2001: 50).

Montesquieu is perhaps the first of the *philosophes* to portray an unbridgeable gap between Eastern and Western societies, their manners, customs and political life, and his work made a strong impact on eighteenth century writing about the Ottoman Empire (Çırakman 2003: 237). According to Montesquieu's *De l'esprit des lois* (The Spirit of Laws), despotism is fabricated by continuous corruption; thus, a despotic government does not have the ability to correct itself because it is naturally corrupt (Çırakman 2003: 237–8). Therefore, for Montesquieu and his contemporaries, despotism and slavishness are oscillating qualities of 'the Turk'; they were described as passive, timid and servile towards their superiors, but ferocious and despotic towards their subordinates (Çırakman 2001: 62). It will be noted that these are also the 'qualities' that, millennia before, had been ascribed by the ancient Greeks to the Persians. Moreover, Montesquieu derives despotism from climatic conditions and, again in a manner strikingly reminiscent of the ancient Greeks, argues that climate is the major explanation for the strength and freedom of Europe as contrasted with the weakness and enslavement of Asia.

His *Lettres Persanes* (Persian Letters), a political satire written in the form of letters by fictional Persian visitors to Paris, also reflects his belief in the disparity between European and Asian mentalities, the former being characterised by their work ethic and dynamism and the latter by inertia, placidity and indolence (den Boer 1993: 58–9). Montesquieu, then, sketches what he perceives as the contrasting 'essences' of East and West; science versus religion, reason versus mysticism, restraint versus eroticism, masculine versus feminine, industrious versus indolent (Salter 2002: 22). It is in this context that he argues that the Ottoman Empire, where the Sultan united the legislative, executive and judicial powers in himself, suffered under the most appalling despotism (den Boer 1993: 58–9). For Montesquieu, then, the endurance and stability of the Empire acquired a negative connotation, being reformulated as stagnation and backwardness (Çırakman 2003: 238).

A similar association of the East with despotism can be seen in the works of another important Enlightenment *philosophe,* Voltaire. Despite his rejection of 'fanatical' religion, for Voltaire the Christian heritage of Europe, along with its shared principles of civil law and politics, is considered an important factor in Europe's high level of civilization and Enlightenment (den Boer 1993: 60). In his view, then, although civilization had its roots in the East due to a favourable climate, it reached its greatest heights in modern Europe, which was gradually overcoming its benighted past, while Eastern empires such as the Ottomans had stagnated (Levin 2011: 134) (den Boer 1993: 60–61). Thus, for Voltaire, by the early seventeenth century the Ottoman Turks were 'no longer what they had been under the Selims, the Mahomets and the Soleymans; effeminacy corrupted the seraglio, but did not banish cruelty' (cited in Levin 2011: 134).

Although Voltaire considered Europe to be the most civilized continent, he frequently used the examples of non-European countries as a means of exposing European abuses and evils (den Boer 1993: 61). In this context, then, his play

Mahomet ou le Fanatisme can be read as a veiled attack on the Christian establishment and on religious fanaticism in general. However, it is also true that Voltaire relied heavily on medieval Christian images of Islam and of Mohammed in his creation of the character Mahomet. Thus, in the play, Mahomet represents a despotic Oriental Other, lustful, ruthless and cruel, who was defined by his lack of Enlightenment and who belonged to the past. Moreover, there is no suggestion on Voltaire's part that these differences would eventually be overcome (Levin 2011: 139–51).

Thus, an examination of the discourse of the Enlightenment *philosophes* regarding the Ottoman Empire, or the Muslim East more generally, reveals a fundamental contradiction in eighteenth century discourse. On the one hand, civilization is seen as potentially available to all. On the other hand, Eastern societies such as the Ottomans are viewed, for climatic, religious or cultural reasons, as *inherently* more despotic and, therefore, uncivilized. As will be argued in the next section, this dichotomy in European discourse persisted throughout the nineteenth century and the declining years of the Ottoman Empire.

Moreover, by the end of the eighteenth century, military defeat and belittlement in the political sphere had shaken the Ottomans' faith in their invincible and unchanging superiority. Thus, the Ottoman Turks began to examine the factors behind their relative political and military decline, as well as those which had allowed the West to rise to a predominant position. This eventually provoked a series of Westernising reforms within the Ottoman Empire (Akça and Hülür, 2004: 262–3), as is discussed further below.

The Sick Man of Europe

Although the epithet the 'Sick Man of Europe' with reference to the Ottoman Empire was originally attributed to Tsar Nicholas 1 in 1853,[10] similar imagery can be traced back as far as the late sixteenth and seventeenth centuries. As early as 1595, for instance, Lorenzo Bernardo, the Venetian envoy to Constantinople, argued that the Ottoman Empire 'rose to great strength very rapidly, in the same way that plants which quickly mature and produce fruit are also quick to wither' (Wheatcroft 1993: 205). However, such imagery is more typical of the declining years of the Ottoman Empire, namely the nineteenth and early twentieth centuries. Notably, the 'Sick Man of Europe' stereotype appears to have been constitutive of an increasingly self-confident and potentially expansive European self-image (Levin 2011: 162).

By the late eighteenth century it was believed that the destruction of the Ottoman Empire would take a matter of decades, particularly after the Russians

---

10   In fact, Tsar Nicholas described the Ottoman Empire as a 'sick man' that Europe had 'on its hands'. Thus, the 'of Europe' was added later, ambiguously suggesting to the Ottomans that, if they could only be cured, there would be a place waiting for them among the healthy European nations (Neumann 1999: 55).

seized Crimea. This decline was attributed to the perceived corrupt and despotic nature of the Empire, originating from the character of the Turkish people, a situation that was thought to result in, and be perpetuated by, weak, dissolute rulers and corruption among officials and in the army (Çırakman 2002: 164–5). Thus, as Levin notes, the Ottoman government was viewed as 'brutal, stagnant, oppressive, and barbaric', while Turkish society was considered to be 'effeminate, exotic and ripe for conquest and/or in need of protection' (Levin 2011: 162). Such imagery is typical of Orientalist discourse, whereby the Orient is portrayed as irredeemably backward, its only hope of development being the good leadership of the prosperous, rational West (Said 1995).

The culmination of the Ottoman Empire's increasing reliance on Europe came in 1799 with the Tri-Partite alliance with Britain and Russia against Napoleonic France, motivated by the need both to check Napoleon's hegemonic aims and to prevent, or at least postpone, the crumbling of the Ottoman Empire. Although the alliance collapsed with the end of the Napoleonic threat, the need to preserve the Ottoman Empire in order to prevent a dangerous power vacuum in Europe became a recurring theme in European discourse, an issue that would become known as 'the Eastern question'. This was reflected, for instance, in the policy led by Lord Palmerston, who organised, following the second Mohammed Ali crisis which began in 1838,a collective effort on the part of the European great powers to prevent Ottoman collapse (Neumann 1999: 54–5) considered particularly important as the Ottoman Empire was seen as a *cordon sanitaire* against Russia. Thus, until the end of the nineteenth century, the 'Eastern question was a question not of destroying the Ottoman Empire but of allowing it to survive, albeit as a semi-colony' (Baysoy 2011:63–4).

In this context, while the Ottoman Empire was never actually colonised by the European powers, it did increasingly come under their financial and political control. In the eyes of many progressive Europeans, the 'Sick Man of Europe' had to be cured of himself and the different Christian communities under Turkish rule had to be liberated from his oppressive yoke (Levin 2011: 162). As Zarakol argues, intervention on behalf of the Ottoman Christian minorities by the Western powers was often justified by arguments that the Ottoman Empire was an absolutist regime and that there was no constitutional protection of individual rights within its borders. However, she notes that, given the record of the Ottoman *millet* system up to the nineteenth century, there appeared to be no particular reason why Christian groups needed special protection (Zarakol 2011: 117). This can be better understood, perhaps, in the context of the development by nineteenth century lawyers of the European 'standard of civilization' based on (supposedly) long-standing European practices such as;

> the protection of individual rights (life, dignity and freedom of travel, commerce and religion); an organised and efficient state bureaucracy; a fairly nondiscriminatory domestic system of courts, codes and public laws; adherence to international law and the maintenance of avenues for diplomatic interchange;

and conformity with accepted norms and practices of civilised international society. (Neumann 1999: 57)

This was also linked to the nineteenth century French notion of *la mission civilisatrice*, or civilizing mission. The nineteenth century European concept of civilization, inherited from the Enlightenment and the French Revolution, was contradictory; on the one hand, civilization was potentially a path which could be taken by anyone, and it was the job of the European powers (the 'white man's burden') to lead less enlightened peoples along this path. The concept of the *mission civilisatrice,* then, was based on the idea of the inherent superiority of some cultures and their 'natural' entitlement to dominate others (Adib-Moghaddam 2011: 52). On the other hand, again reminiscent of the Enlightenment concept of the incurably 'despotic East', such discourse tended to devolve into 'more exclusive, chauvinistic and essentialist identities' (Levin 2011: 163); the 'barbarian was often represented as so beyond redemption that all efforts to improve his condition would be met with frustration' (Salter 2002: 25). In other words, while the Ottomans were generally viewed as a sick man, there was no consensus on whether the patient's disease was curable with a strong dose of European medicine or if it was suffering from an innate and eventually mortal illness.

Under pressure from the Europeans, then, the Ottomans issued the *Tanzimat* declaration in 1839, intended as a binding agreement between the Sultan and his subjects. As Akça and Hülür note, the Tanzimat reformers themselves had internalised the equation of civilization with *Western* civilization and argued that it was necessary for the Ottoman Empire to join this Western civilization if it was not to be left behind (2004: 263). According to the Tanzimat declaration, then, the Sultan accepted limitations on his authority, recognised the sanctity of life, property and individual honour, and declared that his government would be formed according to 'fundamental principles' embodied in written laws rather than by his own will. As Zarakol points out, however, as it was not clear what these 'fundamental principles' actually were, the Ottoman High Council ruled that they would have to be derived from *Shar'ia* law, thus ironically putting the rights of non-Muslims into question (Zarakol 2011: 118). Following the *Tanzimat* reforms, in response to Western pressure a further declaration, the *Islahat fermanı,* was issued in 1856. This declaration recognised all Ottoman subjects as citizens, allowed equal treatment, jurisdiction and representation of Muslims and Christians and recognised freedom of speech (Zarakol 2011: 118).

However, this declaration satisfied no-one, either at home or abroad; local Christian leaders were unhappy as their authority was reduced, while European ambassadors were dissatisfied as they did not think that the declaration went far enough in various ways (Zarakol 2011: 118). Thus, in Zarakol's view, the Ottoman leaders were under the (mistaken) impression that they would be left alone in their domestic affairs and their sovereign rights recognised if they met European 'standards of civilization'. However, this European civilization would never treat a Muslim power as an equal, and the Ottoman attempts to adhere to it would eventually undermine its sovereign rule over its territories still further (Zarakol 2011: 118–19). However, one month after the *Islahat fermanı* the Treaty of Paris was signed, formally including the Ottoman Empire into the Concert of Europe, and thus into the European state system (Neumann 1999: 56–8).

Therefore, in order to play in the Concert of Europe the Ottomans had had to 'learn new tunes' (Neumann 1999: 58). Despite these developments, the Ottomans were sometimes considered culturally and/or racially 'beyond the pale' of European civilization even after 1856. This is illustrated, for instance, by the discourse of James Lorimer, the nineteenth century theorist of international law, who argued that the inclusion of the Ottomans into the Concert of Europe had been premature (Neumann 1999: 57);

> In the case of the Turks, we have had bitter experience of the consequences of extending the rights of civilization to barbarians who have proved to be incapable of performing its duties, and who possibly do not even belong to the progressive races of mankind (cited in Neumann 1999: 57).

As Zarakol notes, the 1856 declaration had two major destabilising consequences within the Ottoman Empire. Firstly, it increased the speed of nationalisation processes among Christian groups, who were also those who benefitted most from increased commerce with Europe. Secondly, it created a backlash among the Empire's Muslim subjects, now disgruntled because they felt excluded from any benefits that this new, European-style administration was supposed to provide (Zarakol 2011: 123).

By the last quarter of the nineteenth century, the image of the Ottoman Empire as the 'Sick Man of Europe', became further entrenched with the considerable reduction of its territory by a series of wars, leading to their independence from the Ottoman Empire. It was, by then, becoming clear to the European powers that the sick man was on his deathbed. It was only with this understanding, as Baysoy notes, that the European powers began to contemplate the division of the Empire, although, even until the end of the first World War, the question of how the post-Ottoman power vacuum should be filled was approached with great caution due to the sensitivity of the issue (Baysoy 2011: 65–6).

However, in the context of these wars, including those in Bulgaria and Bosnia in 1875–77, older stereotypes of the cruel 'Infidel' or 'Terrible Turk' persisted; despite the weakness of the Ottomans the West was 'roused in horror' against the Turks for their 'atrocious violence' towards Christians (Wheatcroft 1993: 232–4). For William Gladstone, writing in 1876, these atrocities were a consequence of an innate Turkish barbarism which went deeper than Islam;

> What the Turkish race was, and what it is. It is not a question of Mahometism simply, but of Mahometism compounded with the peculiar character of a race … They were, from the black day they entered Europe, the one great anti-human specimen of humanity. Wherever they went, a broad line of blood marked the

track behind them, and as far as their dominion reached, civilization vanished from view (cited in Wheatcroft 1993: 234).

The further decline of the Ottoman Empire went hand in hand with continued attempts at modernisation. In 1876, the Ottoman Empire adopted a constitutional monarchy regime, and assembled its first Parliament, which was disbanded two years later following the Turco-Russian war of 1877–78; the constitution was restored following the 1908 Young Turk revolution (Zarakol 2011: 123). Thus, the interim period was characterised by autocratic rule on the part of Sultan Abdulhamid reminiscent of the 'classical' Ottoman period where 'the 'king' with an absolute sovereignty given to him by God reigns over his subjects, with 'justice' (Tezel 2005: 69). The Sultan chose to emphasise pan-Islamism, and stressed his position as Caliph in an attempt to maintain Muslim peoples such as the Kurds or Albanians in the Empire (Zarakol 2011: 123). However, he also saw the necessity for Westernisation, and, French speaking and fond of Western music, was himself a product of the *Tanzimat alla franca* environment. The reformist nature of his rule was reflected in his statement that the Empire 'should benefit fully from the development of contemporary civilization', and resulted in wide-ranging Western-oriented reforms in, among other sectors the economy and trade, education, the state bureaucracy and the army. As Tezel notes, some of these reforms had the effect of turning the Ottoman empire into a semi-colony of the European powers (Tezel 2005: 69–78).

As the breakup of the Empire progressed, however, the Ottoman intelligentsia itself became increasingly radicalised. The main opposition to Abdulhamid's autocratic rule, known as the Young Turks, was originally formed in 1895 by exiles in Paris. The main aim of the Young Turks was, in spite of their opposition to Abdulhamid's autocratic rule, to *preserve* the Ottoman Empire by synthesising 'Western' and 'Eastern' cultures (Tezel 2005: 78). However, the leaders of the CUP, originally a secret society within the ranks of the Young Turk movement, increasingly turned to pan-Turkism, an ideology with xenophobic overtones that sought to create a new Empire based on Turkish ethnicity and Islam (Zarakol 2011: 124); in effect, they envisaged that the Turkish-speaking, Muslim majority would dominate the Ottoman Empire and that the non-Turks should adopt a Turkish/Muslim linguistic, cultural and religious identity (Tezel 2005: 83). Thus, as Morozov and Rumelili argue (2012: 39), this can be seen as a form of reverse Eurocentricism, 'which accepted the hierarchy of civilization/barbarity, but questioned the superior positioning of Europe *vis à vis* the Turks in that hierarchy'.

However, Westernism also remained a strong force among Ottoman intellectuals. The Westernists described the relationship between the West and the Ottoman Empire as that between a strong, rich party and a weak, poor one; their aim was to Westernise the 'Asian mind' as, without this, they believed that no progress could ever be achieved. In 1912, for instance, the Westernists published an article called *Pek Uyanik bir Uyku* (A Very Awake Sleep), which contained a detailed programme of modernisation, in many ways anticipating Atatürk's reforms (Kučera 2010: 19–20).

In 1913, the CUP took *de facto* control of the Empire and, between 1913–1918, it followed an aggressively revisionist agenda intended to capture the Ottoman Empire's glory days (Zarakol 2011: 35). The CUP argued that its government was legitimate as it was based on the delegation of the Sultan's legitimate power. Ziya Gökalp, who had become the main 'ideologue' of the Unionists, combined elements of pan-Turkism and pro-Westernism in his philosophy, proposing simplification of the Turkish language, secularisation of the civil law and diversion of the Ottoman government's attention to the wider Turkic world. More generally, he argued that it was possible to combine Western scientific and technological skills and institutions without also borrowing 'cultural' institutions and value orientations from the West (Kučera 2010: 22–3).

However, the Ottoman Empire, defeated along with its allies Germany and Austria-Hungary in World War I, found most of its territories under occupation at the end of the war, ostensibly to provide for the security of Ottoman non-Muslim subjects (Zarakol 2011: 125–6). As Zarakol notes, 'the Ottoman Empire had failed miserably in her quest to regain equal footing with Europe' (2011: 156). In this context, older stereotypes of the Ottomans persisted in European discourse. As Marriot, for instance, wrote in 1919;

> The primary and most essential factor in the situation is the presence, embedded in the living flesh of Europe, of an alien substance. That substance is the Ottoman Turk. Akin to the European family neither in creed, in race, in language, in social customs, nor in political aptitudes and traditions, the Ottomans have for more than five hundred years presented to the European powers a problem, now tragic, now comic, now bordering almost on burlesque, but always baffling and paradoxical. (1919: 3)

Conclusion

This chapter has discussed how the image of the Ottoman Turks in Europe underwent considerable variation from the Renaissance to the early twentieth century. What is particularly notable, however, is the way that earlier images were revised and adapted over the centuries. In particular, the ancient Greek image of the Persians as barbarians continued to be influential in Renaissance and, especially Enlightenment images of the Ottoman Empire as barbaric and despotic.

What is also notable, particularly from the nineteenth century on, is the Ottomans' reaction to European Othering, particularly in the context of the Concert of Europe and the European 'Standard of Civilization'. To a large extent, these were internalised by the Ottoman elite, resulting in a period of considerable Westernising reform; in other words, Europe at this time was both frequently mistrusted and depicted as a 'superior' Other to be emulated, although this view was later significantly challenged by the Young Turks. As will be discussed further in this book, these have also been important themes in more contemporary Turkish debate, particularly in Kemalist and nationalist discourse.

Within Europe too, there was a division in discourse on the Ottoman Empire regarding the European 'Standard of Civilization'. It can be argued that there was a general consensus in Europe at this time that the Ottomans, compared to the (supposedly) civilized, enlightened Europeans were despotic barbarians, a state that had caused the stagnation and eventual decline of their empire. However, more controversial was whether the Ottomans, with European help, could ever hope to reach European standards of civilization, or whether, for religious, cultural, geographic and/or racial reasons, they were inherently condemned to a state of despotism. This last point is particularly important in the context of contemporary debates on Turkey's EU accession process; as will be discussed further in Chapter 4.

Chapter 3

Constitutional Patriots or Inhabitants of 'Fortress Europe'? Public Attitudes to Europe, the EU and Turkish Accession

As has been argued in Chapter 1, the discourse of political elites plays a determining part in the construction of collective identities. However, it was also noted that elite discourse has more impact on collective identity formation when it does not fundamentally clash with public opinion. Thus, it is worth attempting to examine the EU public's attitudes towards Turkish accession and trying to comprehend the factors behind these attitudes as a comparison with the discourse of the political elites, which will be studied in later chapters.

Although the main focus of this book, then, is how Turkey's accession is framed in elite discourse in the context of visions of the EU's *finalité*, this chapter aims to study public perceptions of and identification with Europe and the EU, and, within this broad framework, to analyse public opinion towards Turkish accession. While the evidence in this chapter is primarily based on opinion polls, it also uses commentaries by 'ordinary Europeans', principally from Internet discussion groups, in an attempt to illustrate the variety of opinions more fully. In addition, this chapter discusses, in a comparative perspective, Turkish public attitudes towards and perceptions of the EU and of Turkey's accession.

Creating Europeans? Attempts to Construct a European Identity from Above

European integration has been an elite-driven process, driven mostly by political elites together with experts and officials rather than by popular movements (Citrin and Sides 2004: 163). While the EU public feels that it has little influence over EU decision-making, the increasing use of referenda means that, on occasion, it can have the power to take part in history-making decisions (Taggart and Szczerbiak 2004: 82). This was the case, for instance, when the French and Dutch public rejected the Constitutional Treaty in 2005; several countries have also indicated that they will hold referenda over Turkey's accession.

The question of a European identity in the context of the EU began to gain prominence in the 1970s. The Declaration on European Identity, which was signed in 1973 in Copenhagen by nine member states, argues that European identity combines a 'diversity of cultures' and a 'common heritage', and is based upon the rule of law, social justice, and respect for human rights. As Grillo argues, this declaration was made in anticipation of membership applications from Greece, Spain and Portugal, which were still under fascist rule at the time (2007: 69). The Copenhagen Declaration was followed by the 1975 Tindemans report, which recommended the creation of a specific policy to help transform the 'technocrats' Europe' into a 'People's Europe', eventually resulting in the development of a EU cultural policy by the Commission in order to promote an awareness of a European cultural identity (Öner 2007: 6).

In spite of this, up to the 1980s public support for integration was not a high priority for EU elites (Shore 2000: 18). The momentum of the development of a European cultural policy increased, however, with the appointment of the Addonino Committee for a People's Europe in 1984, which produced the Addonino Report in 1985. The Report's proposals included proposals for a Europe-wide audio-visual area including a multilingual European TV channel, a Euro-lottery, a European academy of science, the formation of European sports teams, and a stronger European dimension in education. Moreover, it proposed the adoption of a European flag, and common European documents including passports, driving licences and emergency health cards. As Öner points out, most of these initiatives have since been carried out (2007: 6–7). As Grillo notes;

> National icons (Beethoven, Comenius, Erasmus, Shakespeare, Socrates, etc) have been recuperated and incorporated into EU iconography as representatives of European culture, and a 'community history' has been invented. Schemes such as educational exchanges and Women of Europe awards, along with the euro, are all thought to contribute to Europeanisation. (2007: 72)

Such attempts to create a European cultural identity from above are not without their critics. Grillo, for instance, describes it as an 'essentialist, elitist and ethnocentric' vision of European culture (2007: 72), while for Shore it represents a 'stereotyped Occidentalism' (1993: 792). As Kaelble notes, of these only the European flag, the Erasmus exchange programme and, eventually, the Euro have fully succeeded as cultural symbols, the others having remained weak or ambiguous in comparison, for instance, with national cultural symbols (Kaelble 2009: 206).

Despite these efforts to create a European cultural identity from above, then, it has been argued that, while a broad 'permissive consensus' on European integration existed prior to the early 1990s, this has since been challenged resulting in historically low levels of support for European integration (Diez Medrano 2009: 81). The overall level of support for European integration was at around 70 per cent until the early 1990s; it dropped to an all-time low of 45 per cent in 1997 and has since fluctuated between 48 per cent and 58 per cent (Risse 2010: 4). This can be explained as a consequence of the increased deepening and widening of the EU as a result of the Maastricht and subsequent treaties, and enlargement to 27 member states. In other words, as Citrin and Sides point out, the EU has 'slouched towards statehood' (2004: 161) increasingly encroaching on the lives of European citizens without a corresponding increase in their democratic participation. As Duchesne argues;

> The European Union has an increasing influence over European lives: People travel easily throughout the union; students are encouraged to spend part of their time abroad; working in other European countries has become much easier and more commonplace. Within the Euro zone, citizens experience the Union all the time. More generally, an increasing number of national laws and norms are now nothing more than the application of European decisions. (2008: 397)

In consequence of these factors, as well as of other, broader factors including globalisation and the resulting waves of immigration European integration has become increasingly politicised (Kaelble 2009: 194–7). Thus, given the increasing salience of the EU in citizens' everyday lives, the need to construct a European identity at mass level in order to maintain the legitimacy of the EU has been stressed with increasing urgency. As Risse, for instance, notes;

> In general, political scientists and practitioners alike see a clear link between identity and a functioning political order. Accordingly, a democratic polity requires the diffuse support of the citizens in order to be legitimate. Identification with a political order is seen as a source of diffuse support and, thus, of legitimacy. The higher the sense of loyalty toward a political community among the citizens, the more they are prepared to accept inconvenient decisions and policies of their governments, that is, to pay a price for their identity. Europe as a polity should be no exception. (2004: 270)

Indeed, many scholars have argued that the lack of such an identity could impede the process of European integration (Demossier 2007: 62). Starting from the mid to late 1980s, anthropologists, psychologists, political scientists, sociologists and cultural theorists have all contributed to the academic debate on European identity (Demossier 2007: 51). In addition, prominent intellectuals including Habermas, Derrida, Eco and many others have touched upon this subject (Kaelble 2009: 194). As Vaclav Havel,for instance, proclaimed in a 1994 speech to the European Parliament;

> Reading the Maastricht Treaty, for all its historical importance, will hardly win enthusiastic supporters for the European Union. Nor will it win over patriots, people who will genuinely experience this complex organism as their native land or their home, or one aspect of their home. If this great administrative work, which should obviously simplify life for all Europeans, is to hold together and stand the tests of time, then it must be visibly bonded by more than a set of rules and regulations. (Havel 1994)

It is, however, put forward here that a European identity, or identities, of some sort already exists for most European citizens, although this is usually secondary to national identity. Cram argues that 'the production and reproduction of EU identity is much more extensive than these grand efforts and their critiques suggest' and that, instead, the increasing encroachment of the EU into its citizens' daily lives encourages them to perceive it as 'normality', and leads to a 'collective forgetting that life was ever otherwise'. Thus, for Cram, 'Implicit identification with the EU is manifested in an, often unconscious, normalization of the EU as a legitimate political authority such that to challenge this norm is to challenge the status quo' (2012: 84).

As is discussed below, however, it is important to distinguish between an identification with Europe and with the EU, between identification with Europe and *support* for the EU (Cram 2012: 72), and between civic and cultural conceptions of Europe. Finally, it is also suggested that attitudes to enlargement may help to shed light on *how* the public identifies with the EU; on whether it is conceived primarily as an entity underscored by universal rights, as a cultural union or as a pragmatic organisation with the purpose of maximising security and economic advantages.

The main evidence is taken from opinion polls, particularly the EU's regular *Eurobarometer* polls. However, the examination of opinion polls also has its shortcomings. According to Habermas, 'opinion polls merely reflect 'latent' opinions in their raw and dormant state'; instead an examination of public debate in the public sphere may prove more fruitful (Habermas 2009: 135). Bogdani (2011: 89) agrees that letters to newspapers can be useful in gauging public opinion in that, in contrast to opinion polls, they are not determined by the formulation of questions. Bearing this in mind, then, the data from opinion polls presented here will be supplemented and illustrated by examples of opinions given in public debate, particularly Internet discussions.

Multiple Europes: Evidence for the (Partial) Existence of a Mass European Identity

According to social identity theories it is possible to hold more than one social identity at a time. In addition, these identities may be of different strengths; as Tajfel stated, social identities vary in their value and significance, with implications for how the individual treats insiders and outsiders (1982). In the context of European identity, it is therefore put forward that it is possible to hold several identities at a time (Strath 2002) including the local, regional, national and European levels, although there are different ideas about how this may occur.

In the first instance, these identities may be nested within each other in the manner of a 'Russian doll'; a person may identify themselves simultaneously, for instance, as Parisian, French and European. In the second case, the multiple identities may bear more resemblance to a marble cake, in that it is difficult to separate the different identities neatly as they mesh and blend into each other.

French identity, for instance, in the marble cake model, would inherently include aspects of European identity and vice versa (Risse 2004: 166–7).

Moreover, the marble cake concept would be compatible with the 'Europeanization' of national identities (Risse 2010: 45). As Kaelble points out, it is sometimes argued that each nation 'develops its own characteristic identification with Europe, based on its specific national experiences including perceptions of national security, national past and future, and basic national values' (2009: 202).

Empirical research appears to confirm the view that European identity is often held alongside other territorial identities. Firstly, it is important to point out that European identities are weaker than national identities (Ruiz-Jimenez et al. 2004: 16) and that identification with the nation state remains quite high (Citrin and Sides 2004: 168). Only 3.9 per cent of European citizens view themselves as Europeans exclusively (Fligstein 2009: 138). Notably, however, European and national identities often go together; as Mummendey and Waldzus argue, 'Europe provides a kind of dual identity for its citizens' (2004: 60). Eurobarometer polls suggest that national and European identities, as well as other territorial identities, co-exist for many people. While an overwhelming 86 per cent of respondents are proud to be citizens of their country, 68 per cent are proud to be European (European Commission 2006: 94–105), while 74 per cent feel European to some extent (European Commission 2009a).

Moreover, when asked whether they felt attached to their city, their region, their nation or Europe the majority of respondents claimed to be attached to all of them. Respondents felt mainly attached to their country (92 per cent), then their region and city (88 per cent and 87 per cent respectively) and finally 68 per cent felt attached to Europe (European Commission 2006: 94–105).

This research, then, illustrates two important points. Firstly, Europeans do appear to be able to hold several territorial identities at a time. Secondly, for most people some kind of European identity already appears to exist, although it is held alongside, rather than instead of, national identity and other territorial identities. Moreover, as Citrin and Sides argue (2004), a significant and increasing number of people identify equally with their nation state and Europe. As Habermas points out, then, '… a latent, rather Europe-friendly, mood predominates among the citizens in all of the member states, with the exception of Great Britain and the Scandinavian countries' (2009: 102). In Kaelble's view;

> An implicit identification with common European lifestyles and values does not necessarily signify a decline in the identification with national ones. To the contrary, the two might go together. Furthermore, identification with European values does not necessarily mean a rejection of non-European values. (Kaelble 2009: 204)

However, as Risse argues, attitudes towards Europe are more consistent with the marble cake model than the Russian doll model. He argues that the main split is not between those who identify primarily with Europe and the EU on the one hand and those who identify primarily with their nation state on the other, as the majority of respondents identify primarily with their nation state. The main dividing line, instead, is between 'inclusive nationalists', who identify both with Europe and their nation state on the one hand and those who only identify with their nation state on the other. Risse thus puts forward that the former have already integrated support for Europe and the EU into their national identity, indicating cosmopolitan values and support for European integration, while the latter are far more likely to show xenophobic and Eurosceptic attitudes (Risse 2010: 46).

Moreover, the marble-cake model depends on how European identity intertwines with national identity. This may explain differences in degrees of identification with Europe between member states. In other words, it is worth examining how Europe and the EU have been constructed in national discourses. According to Hooghe and Marks, the relationship between national identity and European integration is double-edged (2005: 423). In some cases, European identity may be an integral part of national discourse while in other cases national identity may have been constructed with Europe as its Other. Indeed, there may be significant variation not only between but even within member states: in the case of Britain, for instance, while English identity has been constructed with Europe as a friendly Other, positive associations have been found between both Welsh and Scottish identity and European identity (Haesly 2001). Citrin and Sides emphasise the variety of ways in which discourse on Europe may be intertwined with national identity constructions;

> The British consider continental political and legal systems alien; Europe is the Other – them, not us. By contrast, the French readily may claim a European identity because they imagine its culture and institutions as a replica of their own. And, for Germans, the primary meaning of a European identity is a denial of their country's recent history. (2004: 183)

As Hooghe and Marks argue (2005: 424), 'citizens who conceive of their national identity as exclusive of other territorial identities are predisposed to be considerably more Euro-skeptical than are those who conceive their national identity in inclusive terms'. Castano points out that, with the notable exception of the UK, national and European identities go hand in hand, with a positive correlation between the two (2004). Diez Medrano and Gutierrez, meanwhile, argue that Spanish national and regional identities are not only unthreatened by European identity but empowered by it (2001). This research thus contradicts the idea that there is a 'zero-sum game' between national and European identity. In cases where there is a positive correlation between national and European identity perceived positive national characteristics may be reflected onto the concept of Europe as a whole; thus the individual's nation state is perceived as being more European than the other member states. As Mummendey and Waldzus point out;

> The struggle for the best Europe is likely to be biased by an ethnocentric view, with citizens generalising some characteristics of their own nation as *pars pro*

toto to the whole of Europe – not because it makes the most sense but simply
because of a basic psychological principle. Examples of such tendencies have
been observed already. For instance, when the so-called Maastricht-Criterions
were introduced, people in Germany became upset about the supposedly wrong
handling of these criteria in other European countries. (2004: 68)

In addition, as Ruiz-Jimenez et al. argue (2004: 17) the co-existence of civic
elements of attachment both to the nation and Europe, as in the case, for instance
of Spain and Italy, tends to favour the compatibility of national and European
identities, whereas national identities which include strong feelings of pride, such
as British and Greek identity, tend to be comparatively incompatible, perhaps
because of a sense of 'humiliation' in having to co-operate with other countries
(Ruiz-Jimenez et al. 2004: 18). In general, as Risse points out (2010: 46), the
populations of continental Western and Southern Europe, with the exception
of Greece, are more likely to be attached to Europe than the British, Northern
Europeans or Central/Eastern Europeans.[1]

Moreover, attachment to Europe also correlates significantly with other
attitudes and demographic factors. In particular, younger, wealthier and better
educated individuals and men rather than women are more likely to identify with
Europe (Taggart and Szczerbiak 2004: 78), while holding cosmopolitan values,
having positive attitudes towards immigrants and having left-wing political views
also have a positive correlation to European identity (MacLaren 2002: 562).
According to Fligstein's research, which is based on Karl W. Deutsch's theory of
nationalism and social communication, this may be because younger, well educated
people from high-status socio-economic classes are more likely to speak another
European language and to travel to other European countries for work or pleasure
(Fligstein 2009: 142). Thus, in his view, those people who interact with other
Europeans on a regular basis are more likely to think of themselves as Europeans.
As he argues, survey data indicate that knowledge of a second language and travel
to other European countries are both correlated with identification with Europe,[2] a

---

1   As Risse argues, 'Membership matters' in that older EU members, particularly the
original six, tend to be more supportive of the EU. Thus, in his view, 'the EU has had
significant constitutive effects on European statehood' (2010: 11). However it is argued
here that positive attitudes to the EU may not only be a consequence of but also a *cause*
of early EU membership. Thus, those countries which, traditionally, have identified more
with Europe also tend to be those which joined the EC at the first opportunity. The case of
Britain, particularly England, whose national identity has been constructed with Europe as
an Other, and did not originally wish to join the EC, is illustrative here. The same may be
argued for the Scandinavian countries.

2   Interestingly, Fligstein points out that citizens of small countries are more likely
to identify with Europe than those of larger Member States, and that the former are more
likely both to speak another language and to travel frequently to other European countries
(2009:143).

finding which is also supported by Bruter (2004: 206–7). In this way, the following commentator is, perhaps, typical;

> I've grown up, lived and worked in three, no, that's four bits of Europe and hence had to pick up four languages to different degrees. And been to a fair few other bits and nations of Europe. What that tells me is that different bits of Europe are very very different indeed. And those bits are all better off in the EU. (BBC 2010)

In addition, left-wing supporters are more likely to identify with Europe as they are less likely to perceive European integration as a threat to national identity than right-wing supporters (Fligstein 2009: 141). Moreover, those who identify exclusively with their nation state are less likely to travel to other European countries, thus reinforcing their lack of a European identity.

In line with the above, perhaps the group who hold the most clearly defined European identity are the so-called 'Eurostars' (Favell 2009), who, taking advantage of EU free movement legislation, are defined as European 'free movers'. In contrast to traditional working class, South to North migration, the 'Eurostars' are from upper-middle class backgrounds (Fligstein 2009: 171); they are the professionals, the skilled and the educated who tend to move to urban hubs, or 'Eurocities', such as London or Amsterdam (Favell 2009: 178–80). Living in a different European country tends to have a profound effect on identity, an idea which has been supported by the PIONEUR (Pioneers of European Integration 'from below' study), an EU-sponsored survey of intra-EU migrants. As has already been argued, the sense of a European identity is more developed among this group, with 68.9 per cent of respondents claiming to have a European identity. Interestingly, however, 67.4 per cent of respondents identified with both their host country and country of origin; in other words they saw themselves as holding 'hyphenated identities'. Thus, almost half (49.7 per cent) of respondents identified with their country of origin, their host country and Europe. Perhaps unsurprisingly, such people are also particularly supportive of European integration (Recchi 2006).

Regarding the non, or even anti-Europeans, called 'exclusive nationalists' by Risse, they form a 'mirror-image' of 'the Europeans' in that they are predominantly older and less educated blue collar workers, while women also tend to be more Eurosceptical than men (Taggart and Szczerbiak 2004: 78) (Risse 2010: 49). They are also more likely to hold negative attitudes to immigration. As MacLaren argues, 'antipathy towards the EU is not just about cost/benefit calculations or about cognitive mobilisation … but about fear of, or hostility towards, other cultures' (McLaren 2002: 553). Notably, across wide samples of the European population, support for European integration decreases the more xenophobic attitudes increase (Lahav 2004: 172–3). A British Conservative MEP, interviewed by Lahav, illustrates this point by referring to his/her constituents, who live in a predominantly white agricultural area:

> … If I stood up and made a speech saying 'really it's better for humanity if we all start mixing up and having our share in here,', they would be very unhappy with me indeed. It's the fear of the unknown. It is not just black men they resent. If I actually stood up and said I think we ought to import half a million Frenchmen they would be equally angry. And Germans. We are British. We don't want the other people. It's the fear of the unknown, that they are slightly different to us. The French eat frog legs! (Lahav 2004: 171)

However, Risse (2010: 230) has noted that, while the exclusivist nationalist vision used to be simply Eurosceptic and anti-integrationist, it now supports a 'Europe of the nations' and rejects supranationalism rather than EU integration *per se*. Thus, this represents an alternative vision for the EU, a form of 'nationalism beyond the nation state', in that values traditionally identified with nationalism, including Christianity and exclusionary policies, are transferred to the European level (Risse 2010: 230–31). As is discussed later in this chapter, the rise of this 'European nationalism' is both partly a consequence of Turkey's EU accession bid and, potentially, has important consequences for its final outcome.

As Taggart and Szczerbiak point out, nationality is also an important variable in rates of Euroscepticism. Levels of Euroscepticism vary across the member states, with Britain, Sweden, Estonia, Austria, Latvia, Malta and the Czech Republic the most Eurosceptic, Luxembourg, the Netherlands, Ireland, Belgium and Italy the most supportive of the EU, and France, Germany, Poland and Spain in between.[3] However, 'hard'[4] Euroscepticism is relatively rare. From the early 1990s to the mid 2000s, according to Eurobarometer surveys support for EU membership was relatively consistent, with an average of 52 per cent of people thinking that their country's membership of the EU was 'a good thing'. In contrast, only an average of 13 per cent of respondents saw EU membership as 'a bad thing' (Taggart and Szczerbiak 2004: 75).

In 2010, notably, support for EU membership fell slightly, possibly due to the effects of the economic crisis; however, while 49 per cent of citizens from the EU-27 continue to think that their country's membership of the EU is a good thing, only 18 per cent think it is a bad thing (European Commission 2010a). Even in Britain, which is the most Eurosceptic member state, the Eurosceptics are slightly outweighed by Europhiles (Taggart and Szczerbiak 2004: 75–7), while only a small minority of respondents, 13 per cent in 2010, appear to think that the EU represents a threat to their cultural identity (European Commission 2010a).

---

3   It is notable that the post-communist CEECs do not cluster together in terms of their attitudes to European integration; rather they are scattered among the existing member states (Taggart and Szczerbiak 2004: 80).

4   'Hard' Eurosceptics advocate withdrawal from or non-membership of the EU, whereas 'soft' Eurosceptics are not against membership of the EU *per se* but are suspicious of the granting of the further extension of the competences granted to the EU (Taggart and Szczerbiak 2004: 83).

Interestingly, while trust in the EU appears fairly low across the member states, with 42 per cent of respondents saying they trust the EU while 49 per cent do not, when compared to trust in both national governments and parliaments the EU figure looks much better; only 29 per cent trust their national governments and 31 per cent their national parliaments, while they are distrusted by 60 per cent and 62 per cent respectively. In the UK, however, a 68 per cent majority claim not to trust the EU, while those who mistrust the EU are also in the majority in Greece, Germany, Austria, France, Latvia and Sweden (European Commission 2010a).

It is, however, also important to question how far identifying with Europe in general and the EU in particular are synonymous and it may not be advisable to conflate the two (Breakwell 2004: 38). As Diez argues, at a geographical level EU membership hardly comprises what most people would describe as Europe, with Switzerland, Norway, most parts of the former Yugoslavia and some Eastern European states remaining outside[5] (Diez 2004: 320). It is theoretically possible for a person to feel a strong attachment to Europe while feeling none to the EU, or vice-versa (Risse 2004: 169). Research suggests that the European public does distinguish between the two; while only 49 per cent of people feel attachment to the European Union,[6] 68 per cent feel proud to be European (European Commission 2008).

However, attachment to Europe is strongly correlated with support for European integration (Citrin and Sides 2004) (Hooghe and Marks 2005) (Risse 2004: 170) (Van der Veen 2002: 17). As Citrin and Sides note, the percentage of those saying that EU membership is a good thing ranges from 70–76 per cent among those who identify exclusively, primarily or secondarily with Europe, while it drops to 38 per cent among those who identify with the nation only. Similar results were obtained when the effects of attachment to and pride in Europe on support for the EU were examined. Thus, 'creating support for a stronger European state does not require a European identity that dominates national identity. It is sufficient if a European identity is established alongside one's national identity' (Citrin and Sides 2004: 175). There may however be exceptions to the correlation between identification with Europe and support for the EU. Cram compares the cases of Ireland and the UK where, in both cases, identification with Europe is lower than the EU average. While this is translated into low support of the EU in the UK, however, Irish respondents are, in general, amongst the most supportive of the EU (Cram 2012: 72).

Moreover, trust in specific EU policies has been stronger than overall identification with the EU, although there are variations between the member states, with a majority of citizens supporting a common currency, a common foreign policy, a common defence and security policy and a policy of teaching children

---

5   As Diez notes, however, the concept of Europe is a contested one, on geographical as well as cultural terms.

6   This figure, however, shows considerable variation among the member states. While 65 per cent of Belgians and 63 per cent of Poles claim to identify with the EU, this figure is only 25 per cent in Cyprus and 27 per cent in both the UK and Finland (European Commission 2008).

about the EU (Citrin and Sides 2004: 175). Support for a common environmental policy and a common policy on organised crime and terrorism is also high, while support for education, health, housing and pensions policies at EU level is much weaker (Kaelble 2009: 209).

Bruter argues that it makes a difference whether Europe is identified with in civic or cultural terms (Bruter 2004). Here, a cultural identity may be defined as an individual citizen's sense of belonging to a particular social group, while a civic identity implies identification with a particular political structure, such as the EU. Thus, at the nation-state level, attachment to the nation would be an example of cultural identity, while that to the state is a civic identity. However, the two may, of course, be parallel (Bruter 2004: 190).

As Bruter points out, in the case of Europe civic identity will probably refer to the EU while cultural identity is more likely to refer to Europe as a whole; it is unlikely that a definition of a European cultural identity would embrace France and Germany but not Switzerland and Monaco (Bruter 2004: 188). Thus, in Bruter's view;

> Indeed, while conceiving of Europe as a cultural identity would imply a reference to Europe as a civilisation that stretches from the Atlantic to the Urals, conceiving of Europe as a civic identity would imply a reference to the European Union, which covers less than half the continent. (Bruter 2004: 190)

Thus, while Europe in general tends to be associated with history, ethnicity, heritage and civilization, the EU is primarily associated with 'universal' or Enlightenment values such as human rights and democracy (Risse 2010: 50).[7] Eurobarometer surveys tend to support the predominantly civic vision of the EU. According to a 2006 Eurobarometer report in which respondents were asked what best described the idea they had of the European Union, for instance, 70 per cent chose 'democracy' and 'modern' (European Commission 2006). Pragmatic or instrumental factors also seem to be an important component of EU identity (Ruiz-Jimenez et al. 2004: 16). The EU is also strongly associated with the freedom to travel, work and study anywhere in the EU (European Commission 2010). It is also interesting, as pointed out above, that most people support their country's membership of the EU, even in so-called Eurosceptic countries. Thus, as Diez Medrano argues, although their sense of who they are may remain anchored at the national and local levels, most European citizens tend to approach the EU as

---

7   As Bruter points out, such a situation is not unique to the case of European identity. The United Kingdom, India and Belgium could also provide examples where 'cultural' identities may be smaller in scale than 'civic' identities (2004: 188). To expand on the example of the UK, a British citizen may simultaneously identify with Wales or Scotland, for instance, on a cultural level and with the British state at a civic level. Thus, this explains a sometimes puzzling phenomenon where such an individual may happily admit to being, say, both Welsh and British but is likely to object to being defined as English.

Habermasian 'constitutional patriots'[8] in that they support the principles and goals that it embodies (2009: 86).

Finally, while the civic and instrumental perceptions of the EU appear to be dominant, there is also a certain amount of cultural identification with the EU. For instance, 27 per cent of respondents to a 2007 Eurobarometer survey included culture as one of the three most important elements of a European community sentiment, making it the most frequently chosen element together with the economy, also chosen by 27 per cent of respondents. In contrast, only 20 per cent chose values. Regarding more specific cultural attributes of European identity, in the same survey, 21 per cent of respondents chose history, while 13 per cent chose religion as important factors (European Commission 2007). Notably, there is a strong correlation between self-identification as being politically right-wing and cultural identification with Europe (Bruter 2004: 207). Thus, as Bruter argues, 'Common sense might naturally lead us to expect left-wingers to be on average more cosmopolitan and right-wingers more likely to oppose a consistent European, Judeo-Christian, Western civilization to the rest of the world' (2004: 208).The perception of a 'cultural Europe' then appears to be more widespread amongst the group which is traditionally more Eurosceptic – Risse's 'exclusive nationalists'.

EU Identity and Attitudes Towards Enlargement

As Risse points out, 'the 'widening' of the EU concerning both enlargement and immigration policies cannot be explained without taking identity issues into account' (Risse 2010: 224). Moreover, as Sjursen (2002) (2006) (2008) and Ruiz-Jimenez and Torreblanca (2007), among others, argue, arguments for and against enlargement can help to shed light on which kind(s) of EU citizens may identify with. These arguments can be broadly classified as civic, cultural and pragmatic. Firstly, *Moral,* or civic, arguments are related to 'universal values' such as democracy and human rights, and indicate that the EU is seen primarily as a *post-national rights based union* based not on common cultural values and traditions but on a set of legally entrenched fundamental rights and democratic procedures, and potentially open to any country which fulfills these criteria. Secondly, *ethical-political,* or cultural, arguments are those that relate to religion and culture and indicate that the EU is seen as a *value-based community* based on a sense of common identity, which serves to deliminate its borders. Finally *pragmatic* arguments, such as those related to the economic or security benefits of enlargement, indicate that the EU is seen as a *problem-solving entity* whose

---

8   Habermas has proposed 'constitutional patriotism' as the basis for political identity at European level. Although this is a kind of 'patriotism' it is based on a civic, even cosmopolitan, understanding of the principles underlying the European polity rather than on a thicker 'cultural' understanding. Thus, while it is rooted in a self-understanding of the European perspective it is therefore potentially open to the Other.

existence is justified not by norms but by the practical benefits it can provide for the member states.

Prior to the accession of the CEECs in 2004, enlargement was not met with overwhelming enthusiasm by EU citizens. Indeed, attitudes were more or less evenly split between supporters and opponents of enlargement; just before the 2004 Eastern enlargement only 42 per cent supported imminent enlargement, while 39 per cent opposed it (Risse 2010: 208). Since then, however attitudes to further enlargement seem to be somewhat more positive, with 49 per cent of respondents endorsing future enlargement and 39 per cent against although, as is discussed below, opposition to Turkish membership in particular is considerably higher (European Commission 2007). However, support for enlargement varies significantly across EU member states, with the post-Communist EU member states in particular tending to be more in favour of further enlargement. There is also a considerable difference in levels of support for enlargement among the older member states; in 2005, for instance, opposition to Romania's accession in Germany was 66 per cent, while it was only 23.3 per cent in Sweden (Dixon 2010: 130). In addition, support for enlargement varies considerably according to the (potential) applicant country. According to a 2006 Eurobarometer survey, 77 per cent of respondents declared that they would support enlargement to Switzerland and Norway, while only 31 per cent were in favour of Turkish accession (European Commission 2006: 37).

Interestingly, there is a positive connection between enlargement and 'universal norms' in the minds of most European citizens, confirming the idea that the EU is frequently perceived as an organisation based on 'universal' norms such as democracy and human rights. A survey led by Boğaziçi University and carried out in five large EU member states (France, Germany, Poland, Spain and the UK) indicates that the applicant's performance in democracy and human rights is considered the most important factor when considering new admissions to the EU (Boğaziçi University et al. 2009).

Other surveys suggest that the European public considers that enlargement has, so far, improved democracy and human rights and increased freedom in Europe. According to a 2006 Eurobarometer survey 67 per cent of respondents agreed that enlargement would improve democracy in the European continent while 65 per cent agreed that it would improve protection of human rights and minorities in Europe (European Commission 2006: 35). According to a 2009 Eurbarometer survey, 73 per cent of respondents from the EU-27 agreed that enlargement to the CEECs had facilitated the spread of democratic values and the protection of human rights. In addition, 92 per cent of respondents agreed that the 2004 and 2009 enlargements had increased people's possibilities to freely move and travel within the EU (European Commission 2009b: 4). Moreover, freedom and democratic values were considered to be the most important criteria to take into account when considering future enlargements (European Commission 2009b: 21).

From a pragmatic point of view, the applicant country's possible contribution to Europe's economic development and welfare was considered the second most important factor in assessing new admissions to the EU (59.1 per cent), following democracy and human rights. The applicant's contribution to Europe's defence and security was considered the third most important factor, although this was chosen by only 26.4 per cent of respondents. However, enlargement so far was judged to have had mixed benefits and disadvantages. While 76 per cent of EU citizens agreed that enlargement had led to growth and modernisation in the CEECs, over 56 per cent considered that it had contributed to job losses in their country. Moreover, opinions on the security effects of enlargement were mixed, and even contradictory; while 58 per cent of respondents agreed that enlargement to the CEECs had improved security and stability in Europe, in particular by improvements in the fight against organised crime and illegal immigration, 50 per cent agreed that enlargement had led to an increased feeling of insecurity in the EU as a whole (European Commission 2009b: 4–5).

Finally, cultural and religious issues, together with immigration, were evaluated as being the least important when considering future enlargement rounds, where it was seen as relatively important only in Italy (European Commission 2009b: 21). The Boğaziçi survey also confirms the relative unimportance of cultural issues; only 21.5 per cent of respondents chose cultural and religious differences between the applicant country and Europe as an important factor in considering its accession, making it the fourth most important factor out of five[9] (Boğaziçi University et al. 2009). As is discussed below, Turkey appears to be the exception to the rule in this respect.

However it is interesting to note that respondents judged the cultural/religious criteria to be most important to them personally, rather than to their member state or the EU. Thus, the culture and religion of candidates appears to be particularly emotive in comparison with other criteria (European Commission 2009b). In addition, qualitative data indicate that, for many citizens of the older EU-15 member states, particularly in the Southern and Central member states, there is a sense of empathy and moral duty to admit countries which are considered part of Greater Europe, in spite of perceived difficulties. This feeling of being part of a 'common European family' is, however, less evident in the UK and the Scandinavian countries, perhaps because of a generally weaker identification with Europe and higher rates of Euroscepticism in these countries.

In conclusion, then, European citizens appear to justify enlargement to the CEECs primarily in terms of universal norms rather than in pragmatic terms. In contrast cultural issues appear to be relatively unimportant. This seems to confirm the idea that the majority of European citizens view the EU as primarily a kind of rights-based postnational union. However, as discussed below, an examination of attitudes to Turkey's accession appears to paint a rather different picture. As Dixon notes, for instance, Turkey's entry elicits more opposition than that of other

---

9   Perhaps surprisingly, the number of immigrants that may come from the applicant country to Europe was considered the least important of the five factors, chosen by only 20.5 per cent of respondents.

candidates – and this is the case in every member state (2010: 130). Eurobarometer surveys, among others, appear to support the view that enlargement to Turkey is particularly unpopular, and that support fell between 2001–2005. According to Eurobarometer 64 (2005), for instance, opposition to Turkey's membership was 55 per cent in the EU-25, reaching as high as 70 per cent in France, 74 per cent in Germany and 80 per cent in Austria (Ruiz-Jimenez and Torreblanca 2007: 7). A 2008 Eurobarometer survey suggests that opposition to Turkey's accession remains at 55 per cent, higher than that to the accession of 11 other potential candidates. In addition, 45 per cent of respondents declared themselves against Turkey's accession even if it fulfills all the criteria for membership (European Commission 2008: 28–9). Moreover, 52 per cent of the respondents stated that they would vote against Turkey's accession in a referendum (Boğaziçi University et al. 2009: 25, 42). Other polls tend to confirm EU citizens' negative attitude towards Turkish accession. A June 2007 Financial Times Harris poll, with the title *Is Europe Big Enough for Turkey* argued that it was not, with only 16 per cent of French respondents and 21 per cent of Germans in favour of Turkish accession[10] (cited in Bogdani 2011: 86–7).

However, public support for Turkish accession varies considerably between the member states, with, generally speaking and allowing for some exceptions, higher support in CEE countries, Southern Europe, the Nordic countries and the UK and more opposition in the 'core' EU states of continental Western Europe. More specifically, member states which are rather in favour of Turkish accession include the Czech Republic, Denmark, Estonia, Finland, Poland, Romania, Slovenia, Spain, Sweden and the United Kingdom, while those with a mixed opinion include Bulgaria, Greece, Hungary, Italy, Malta and Portugal. Finally, Austria, Belgium, Cyprus, France, Germany, Ireland, Latvia, Lithuania, Luxembourg, the Netherlands and Slovakia are rather against Turkish full membership (Oğurlu 2010).

Interestingly, however, on an individual level, Gerhards and Silke show that people who see themselves as a citizen of the EU as well as belonging to a nation or region are *more* likely to support Turkish accession to the EU (2011: 20). As has been argued above, younger and more socially and economically advantaged people, as well as those to the left of the political spectrum, are more likely to identify with Europe; they have therefore been dubbed 'the Europeans'. Thus, it is 'the Europeans' who are more likely to support Turkish accession. This may

---

10　Interestingly it would be too simplistic to explain this merely on the basis of negative attitudes towards Turkey. Overall, according to the Boğaziçi University survey, an average of 68 per cent of respondents claimed to have a positive opinion of Turkey, with only 25 per cent owning up to a negative opinion. Even in France and Germany, two of the member states most opposed to Turkish full membership, 65.5 per cent and 60.0 per cent respectively said that they had a positive attitude to Turkey. Even among respondents who were opposed to Turkish accession, a slightly larger proportion had a positive opinion of Turkey (48.2 per cent) than a negative one (44.3 per cent).

seem surprising at first glance as enlargement has often been seen as hindering deepening, but is less surprising if we consider that a fear of other cultures, linked to support for the right, has been correlated with a non-European identity, as well as with Euroscepticism.[11]

Given the large minority against Turkish accession even in the event of it fulfilling all the accession criteria, it is clear that opposition to Turkey's membership is also, to a large extent, based on factors other than the perception that Turkey has not fulfilled the Copenhagen criteria. Thus it should be reiterated that doubts about Turkey's democratic or human rights credentials alone do not seem sufficient to explain the large degree of opposition to Turkish accession. In this case, then, pragmatic and cultural objections to Turkish accession should be explored. In contrast, citizens who think that Turkey must respect human rights before entering the Union have a 70 per cent probability of supporting that country's accession (Ruiz-Jimenez and Torreblanca 2007: 13).

Thus, those who hold a post-national view of the EU are most likely to support Turkish accession (Ruiz-Jimemez and Torreblanca 2007: 23). In this view, then, if Turkey fulfills the official criteria for membership it should be allowed to join. As a Scottish commentator, for instance, argues; 'If the EU denies Turkey the right to accession, it would be nothing short of scandalous. If any country wants to join, and they meet the criteria, then there should be nothing to stop them' (BBC 2004a: 2). Similarly, a British commentator succinctly notes that 'I would like to see a completely secular EU, and Turkey should be admitted' (BBC 2004a: 8). This is also linked to arguments on the basis of *pacta sunt servanda.*[12] In a French commentator's view; 'Yes, Turkey should join the EU or we should have told them from the start (as we did to Morocco), that it was not possible. They have worked hard to reach EU standards in all sorts of domains, so it would be incorrect to tell them we don't want them now' (BBC 2004a: 2). However, there is also a concern that the entry criteria should not be relaxed in order to allow Turkish accession. As a commentator from Germany argues;

> Before Turkey can join the EU, it must stop being necessary to be Turkish and a Muslim to live there. Turkey continues to persecute religious and cultural minorities, which is rather strange for a secular state. The current government is a huge step forward, and it shows that it is possible to have a moderate Muslim government, but it still has a long way to go. Turkey knows what it needs to do, so if it really wants to join it should be allowed to do so, but not by changing the rules, as that will devalue EU membership for everyone. (BBC 2004a: 3)

---

11   De Vreese et al. have also noted a negative correlation between right wing ideology and support for Turkish accession (2007: 523).

12   The legal term *pacta sunt servanda* refers to the principle that 'agreements must be kept'.

Public opinion is mixed on the pragmatic benefits of Turkish accession to the EU. Fifty-two per cent of respondents see Turkish accession as primarily benefiting Turkey itself (European Commission 2006). According to Ruiz-Jimenez and Torreblanca, however, evaluations of the Turkish economy 'are not relevant' when evaluating the likelihood of support for Turkish accession. In contrast, the security dimension appears to be highly relevant. The likelihood that citizens who consider that Turkish membership will improve security in the area will also support Turkish accession is a massive 97 per cent, a 44 per cent higher probability than for those who do not think it will improve security (2007: 12). Moreover, Gerhards and Silke (2011; 19), as well as De Vreese et al. (2008: 519), argue that, while perception of a respondent's personal economic situation does not affect attitudes to Turkish accession, perceptions of their country's economic situation do have a significant effect; in particular those who assess their country's economic situation positively, as well as those who come from recipient countries, are more likely to support Turkish accession (Gerhards and Silke 2011: 759).

However, various studies have also confirmed the importance of culture and identity in the formation of attitudes to Turkish accession (De Vreeseet al. 2008) (Ruiz-Jimenez and Torreblanca 2007) (MacLaren 2007) (Gerhards and Silke 2011). Opinion polls also indicate that cultural differences are perceived as an obstacle to Turkish accession, with 61 per cent of EU citizens feeling that the cultural gulf between Turkey and the EU is too great to allow it to join the EU (European Commission 2006). A survey led by Boğaziçi University also confirms this, with an average of 40 per cent of respondents agreeing that cultural factors were the most influential for determining attitudes to Turkey's EU accession (Boğaziçi University et al.2009)[13,14]. Moreover, according to this same survey, 38.9 per cent of respondents agreed that Turkey was a Muslim country and therefore not compatible with the EU's common Christian roots.

Thus, in their analysis of Eurobarometer surveys on Turkey's accession, Ruiz-Jimenez and Torreblanca argue that, although there are national variations, the EU public tends to make judgements about Turkey's EU accession bid on the basis of culture, history and geography rather than on the basis of universal values or cost/benefit analysis.[15] Moreover, this identity dimension correlates most weakly with support of Turkey's full membership in the EU (European Commission 2005) (Ruiz-Jimenez and Torreblanca 2007: 17).

---

13   This is compared to 27 per cent for mostly political factors and 26 per cent for mostly economic factors.

14   The proportion of respondents against Turkish membership who chose cultural factors as primarily determining attitudes to Turkish accession was even higher at 45.7 per cent. Cultural factors were also particularly important for the French population in general, at 47.7 per cent.

15   The Bogaziçi survey suggests, however, that geographical and historical arguments against Turkish accession are much less widespread than cultural arguments.

In contrast, citizens who think Turkey belongs to Europe owing to its history or geography have an 85 per cent probability of supporting Turkish accession (Ruiz-Jimenez and Torreblanca 2007: 12), while those who perceive Turkey as fundamentally non-European tend to have a more negative attitude to its full membership. As one commentator from the Netherlands, for instance, argues when asked if Turkey should join the EU, 'No, no and no. Why should Turkey be in the EU? Turkey is simply not in Europe. It will endanger the foundations of the EU. Only a privileged partnership must be envisaged for Turkey' (BBC 2004a: 2).

Lauren MacLaren (2007: 272–3) also argues that opposition to Turkish membership cannot be explained by economic self-interest as those at varying income levels appear to be equally opposed to Turkish accession. Instead she argues that this opposition results from a perception of threat to both group-resources and culture, and that negative attitudes to Turkish accession are more pronounced in countries which have experienced high levels of Turkish immigration[16,17].

According to Manco (2007) the negative image of the Turkish community in Europe stems from a variety of factors, including, among others, its largely rural origins, lack of mastery of the language of the host country, ethnic family traditions and a lack of educational and vocational qualifications which force Turkish workers into low-paid, unskilled jobs. Similarly, according to a regression analysis by Saz (2011: 487), disapproval of Turkish accession is correlated with the size of the Turkish population in the country in question. However, he notes that 44.4 per cent of the total variation could not be explained by the size of the Turkish population and must, therefore be due to other factors.

Ruiz-Jimenez and Torreblanca's study confirms the connection between attitudes towards immigration and Turkish accession; the probability of citizens who fear immigration endorsing Turkish accession is only 36 per cent, 16 per cent lower than that of those who do not fear immigration (2007: 12). Religion appears to be an important factor; while Christians (Catholics, Protestants and Orthodox Christians) on the one hand and atheists and agnostics on the other tend

---

16   It is interesting to note, however, that in Caldwell's view, for instance, these are not the countries which are likely to experience the most difficulties resulting from immigration from Muslim countries. He argues that Britain is 'by far, the European country with the most serious dangers of violence and political extremism', while Spain 'is the country most at risk of being swamped by the sheer volume of immigration' (Caldwell 2010: 246–7). Moreover, surveys indicate that the British are far more concerned about immigration than the French, with 62 per cent of British respondents and only 35 per cent of French respondents agreeing that immigration was 'more of a problem' rather than 'more of an opportunity' (Transatlantic Trends 2008).

17   Interestingly, however, according to Eurobarometer, the countries whose citizens were more likely to evaluate immigration as being important when considering future rounds of enlargement, namely Italy, Malta and the UK (European Commission 2009b: 21) are neither the countries with the highest proportion of Turkish immigrants nor strong opponents of Turkish accession.

to reject Turkish accession, Muslim respondents are more likely to be supportive[18] (Gerhards and Silke 2011: 760).

How, then, to reconcile the fact that democracy is cited as the most important factor for enlargement with the large proportion which would reject Turkey on a cultural basis? As suggested above, mistrust of Islam is linked to its perceived implications for secular democracy, and for 'European culture' in general. This, then, appears to play an important part in popular misgivings about Turkish accession, as do related fears of immigration; thus those who hold a 'cultural' view of European identity tend to be those most likely to oppose Turkish accession.[19] In particular, there is a sentiment that Muslims cannot easily fit in with pluralist, multicultural or 'European' ideas (Lahav 2004: 161).As Roy, for example, argues;

> Turkey will be rejected from the EU not because the Turkish state fails to satisfy the EU demands to democratise, which would be a good reason, but because Turkish society is not 'European' … The reluctance shown by European public opinion to envisage the entry of Turkey into the EU is largely linked to it being a Muslim country. (Roy 2004: 16)

It is important to reiterate that cultural rejection of Turkish membership often appears to go hand-in-hand with mistrust of the EU in general. This perhaps underlines the connection described above between xenophobia and immigration with Euroscepticism, as both often imply a mistrust of other cultures. In particular, the question of Turkish accession often appears to be linked to the fear of domination by a faceless Brussels bureaucracy. As one commentator from Amsterdam, for instance, argues;

> One thing is for sure, if Turkey joins the EU then it can no longer be called the EU or European Union. What next? WU or World Union? World power and world domination? Exactly what is the plot of these unelected officials who are running the EU? (BBC 2004a: 1)

In conclusion, then, an examination of attitudes to Turkish accession indicates that many Europeans do view the EU in cultural terms; in other words they

---

18   According to Gerhards and Silke (2011: 760), however, Christians and those with no religious affiliation are likely to oppose Turkish accession for different reasons. While the first group may feel a threat to their own Christian belief, the latter may feel that the accession of a Muslim-majority country such as Turkey threatens the secular nature of the EU.

19   Bogdani makes an important point when she asks why the same level of opposition has not been directed against other potential Muslim-majority candidate countries, namely Bosnia-Herzegovina, Albania and Macedonia. She concludes that it is due to their small size, as each have a population of 3–4 million, in contrast to Turkey's population of 68.7 million. Thus, in her view, it is the *combination* of large size and religious/cultural differences that accounts for the opposition to Turkish accession (Bogdani 2011: 167–8).

perceive the EU as a value-based community. Here Islam appears to be the defining factor; as discussed above many EU citizens feel that Islam is not compatible with other 'European' values such as democracy and human rights. Thus, broadly speaking, an examination of attitudes to enlargement reveals two competing visions of the EU among the European population; on the one hand there is a kind of constitutional patriotism based on universal norms, albeit in their specific European interpretation. On the other, however, there is a more culturally defined 'Christian' Europe, which tends to exclude Turkey on cultural grounds as it sees these norms as being specifically 'European', rather than potentially universal, in nature. As will be discussed in the following chapters, this split between 'civic' and 'cultural' Europe can also be noted in elite discourse across Europe.

Which Kind of Europe? The View from Turkey

As Cautrès and Monceau (2011: 133–4) note, identification with Europe in Turkey appears to be much weaker than in Europe as a whole. According to a 2007 Eurobarometer survey, for instance, 96 per cent of Turkish respondents said that they felt attached to their country, 94 per cent to their town or village and only 25 per cent to the EU. This represents the lowest level of attachment to the EU in all 30 territories included in the survey (European Commission 2007). Similarly, according to a 2004 Eurobarometer survey, 64 per cent of Turkish respondents asked whether they identified with their nationality and/or Europe declared that they felt only Turkish while 26 per cent said that they felt first Turkish and then European, and 7 per cent claimed to feel equally Turkish and European, while only 1 per cent felt European then Turkish and 1 per cent only European. The amount of people claiming to identify only with their nationality was higher than in any of the member states, and was followed by Hungary (54 per cent) and Greece (51 per cent) (European Commission 2005).

Moreover, in Turkey, in contrast to the relatively stable support in the member states, support for accession has declined precipitously over the last few years. While in spring 2004 71 per cent of Turkish respondents thought that Turkish membership was a good thing, this had fallen to 41 per cent in autumn 2010. Similarly, the proportion of Turkish respondents who thought that Turkish accession was a bad thing rose from 9 per cent to 32 per cent over the same period (European Commission 2005) (European Commission 2010b). As Yılmaz argues, Euroscepticism among the Turkish population is mainly determined by levels of nationalism. While support for the Turkish nationalist *Milli Hareket Partisi/* National Movement Party(MHP) and the Islamist Saadet (Felicity) party is highly correlated with Euroscepticist views, supporters of the Kurdish ethnonationalist party HADEP – DEHAP had higher levels of Eurosupportiveness than average. (Yılmaz 2011: 17–18). Like Eurosceptics from EU member states, Abusara argues that Turkish Eurosceptics are more likely to be poorly educated, right wing, belong to a low or middle-income group and be potential losers from accession (2010: 84)

Yılmaz argues that a majority of the Turkish population is most concerned about the effects of EU membership in the area of culture, in terms of the weakening of national or religious values, while issues such as the constriction of national independence, the breakup of national unity and the violation of the secular social and political order were considered much less important (2005: 175). Similarly, a 2004 Eurobarometer survey suggests that Turkish respondents are concerned with the identity effects of accession. According to this survey, more than one Turkish citizen in two fears a 'loss of the language' (59 per cent), the end of the national currency (52 per cent) and the loss of national culture and identity (52 per cent) (European Commission, 2005). In contrast, as Cautrès and Monceau note, the fears of the European population as a whole *vis à vis* European integration tend to be of an economic or security nature rather than identity concerns (2011: 135).

In addition, growing public Euroscepticism in Turkey is fuelled by overall mistrust of the EU and uncertainty about Turkey's accession prospects, provoked especially by right-wing reluctance in the EU to accept Turkey as a full member (Taraktaş 2008: 253–4). A 2008 survey carried out among the Turkish public confirms this; when asked for the best explanation of the decline in Turkish public support for EU accession, 36 per cent agreed that it could be explained by the EU's sometimes negative attitude towards Turkey, while 25 per cent thought it was due to the increasing disbelief that Turkey would ever be accepted as a full member (A&G Araştirma 2008). The comments of one Turkish reader of *The Economist* perhaps illustrates this sense of unfair treatment on the part of the EU; 'On joining the European Union, the EU set their conditions, which the AKP fulfilled to 100 per cent. After which the EU started making new conditions and it is clear that Turkey will not be admitted no matter what the AKP does' (*Economist* 2011).

This is sometimes considered as the EU's, rather than Turkey's, loss. The *Economist* reader cited above argues that, 'The West is ruining their relationship with the only real ally they had in the Islamic world'. As another Turkish reader comments,

> In the seventies, the leaders of France and Germany chose Greece over Turkey for participation in their European project. Now the chickens are coming home to roost. Turkey's leaders should brush aside the riff-raff in Europe, consign the EU to the rubbish bin and pursue a policy based on Turkey's own historic experience as a great power. (Economist 2011)

Turks appear, on average, to have a more 'cultural' understanding of the EU. In contrast to most EU citizens, in a 2007 Eurobarometer survey the majority of Turkish citizens view religion (41 per cent) and history (26 per cent) as the most important dimensions of a European identity (European Commission 2007). This is consistent with the perception that the EU is increasingly viewed as a 'Christian Club' in Turkey, and may be linked with the growing importance of the religious element in the self-definition of Turkish identity according to several surveys

(Cautrès and Monceau 2011: 132–3). Indeed, this view is dominant particularly among those individuals who are right-wing and/or religious (Yılmaz 2005: 172).

Thus, as Cautrès and Monceau point out (2011: 145), many Turkish citizens view this as a reason why Turkey will not be accepted into the EU. As one Turkish commentator noted, 'Turkey has been waiting for over 40 years to enter the European Union, and it appears we will wait another 10 to 15 years. The main handicap is being a Muslim country and the cultural differences with other members' (BBC 2004a: 5). As Yılmaz argues, this view of the EU as a Christian club partly echoes European exclusionary narratives against Turkish EU accession based on Christianity, but is also partly rooted in Turkey's own history and culture, notably the *Tanzimat* and *Sèvres* syndromes (2005: 172) as well as the fear that Turkish religious and cultural values will be eroded by EU membership.

Conclusion

Research indicates that some form of European identity already exists among the majority of the European population, although normally this is complementary and secondary to other forms of territorial identity, including national and regional identity. Broadly speaking, the European public can be divided into two groups. The first of these is 'the Europeans', a relatively prosperous and well-educated group who tend to support European integration and perceive the EU as resembling a Habermasian rights-based, post-national union based largely on 'universal values' rather than a 'thicker' cultural identity. The second group, who tend to be 'blue-collar' workers and relatively right-wing, are comparatively Eurosceptic in terms of EU integration, although they may identify with Europe in a cultural sense. This group, then, which is relatively xenophobic and anti-immigration, tends to support an EU which is based on European *cultural* values.

The prospect of Turkish accession accentuates these differences. 'The Europeans' tend to support Turkish accession at least in principle, on condition that Turkey completely fulfills the economic and political conditions for accession; there is, then, little cultural objection to Turkish accession among this group, which can be explained by their predominantly rights-based vision of the EU. In contrast, the second group tends to oppose Turkey's full membership of the EU on the grounds that it is not European in cultural or religious terms; this group, then, tends to view the EU as a 'Christian club'. Interestingly, many Turks also view the EU as a 'Christian club' and consider that they will be excluded as a result no matter how much their country carries out economic and political reforms. This perception thus leads to increased disillusionment with the EU and to a rise in Euroscepticism among the Turkish population. Thus exclusionary narratives of the EU, and their support by the 'exclusive nationalists' in turn fuel Euroscepticism among the Turkish population and undermine electoral support for tough EU-related reforms in Turkey.

Chapter 4

A Deliberative Approach to EU Enlargement: The Case of Turkish Accession

The Application of Habermasian Theories to the Case of the EU: A Short Overview.

The discourse analysis used in this section is based on an approach developed primarily by researchers linked with the ARENA centre in Osloon the basis of Habermas' theories of communicative action, as well as his related work on discourse ethics and deliberative democracy. As Diez and Steans argue, for instance, the work of Habermas provides 'a tremendous resource that IR is only now beginning to explore (2005), by 2009, as Parker points out, his discourse ethics has become 'highly influential in international relations and European Studies' (2009b).

For Habermas communicative action can be distinguished from rhetorical action in that, while actors engaging in rhetoric are not prepared to change their own beliefs, communicative action presupposes that actors not only try to persuade others but they are themselves prepared to be persuaded by the 'better argument' (Risse 2000: 8–9). Thus, the goal of communicative action is to achieve argumentative consensus, not to push through one's own values or views of the world. It is more likely to occur when actors are 'uncertain about their own identities, interests and views of the world and/or if rhetorical arguments are subject to scrutiny and counterchallenges leading to a process of 'argumentative entrapment'' (Risse 2000: 23). As Habermas argues,

> I speak of communicative actions when the action orientations of the participating actors are not coordinated via egocentric calculations of success, but through acts of understanding. Participants are not primarily oriented toward their own success in communicative action; they pursue their individual goals under the condition that they can co-ordinate their action plans on the basis of shared definitions of the situation. (1981: 385)

Moreover, the attempt to reach an argumentative consensus as a result of communicative action can also have a *constitutive* effect on actors, as the questioning of identities and interests is at stake; thus 'agents are not simply the the puppets of social structure, since they can actively challenge the validity claims inherent in any communicative action (Risse 2000: 10). In this sense, then, 'the more we debate issues, the more we create political communities' (Risse 2010: 110).

However, Habermas emphasises that several preconditions are necessary for communicative action to take place. Firstly it requires empathy; the ability to see things through the eyes of one's interaction partner. Secondly, it requires that actors share a 'common lifeworld', consisting of a shared culture, a common system of norms and rules perceived as legitimate. In turn, communicative action reproduces and nourishes the common lifeworld. Finally, actors must recognise each other as equal and have equal access to the discourse, which must be public in nature. On this basis, Risse offers some indications to recognise an arguing situation in international politics;

- The absence of references to rank and power by actors.
- Arguments should be consistent, as actors who change their arguments depending on the audience with which they are dealing probably engage in rhetorical behaviour.
- Weaker actors, such as small states, should be disproportionately empowered as stronger actors do not necessarily have the better arguments.
- Actors who change their mind in spite of the fact that their instrumental interests would suggest otherwise.
- Actors' reactions to accusations of violating certain norms of appropriate behaviour to which they have previously agreed; they should try to justify their behaviour, or even apologise rather than simply dismiss the accusation (Risse 2000: 19).

As authors including Eriksen (2003) and Risse (2000) argue, the EU provides a likely arena for communicative action to develop. In Eriksen's view supranationalisation cannot be explained by the fixed preferences of the member states. Moreover, it cannot be explained by coercion as the EU lacks many of the traditional features of state power by which they can impose their will, such as a monopoly on violence, taxation and majority voting (Eriksen 2003: 172). The absence of power structures in the EU thus tends to predispose it to deliberative outcomes; as authoritative ways of resolving conflicts are absent in the EU, reason-giving becomes the only way to reach a consensus (Eriksen 2003: 183). However, it is important to point out that, while deliberation may end in agreement, it may also end in conflict, and may be succeeded by voting or bargaining (Eriksen 2003: 174).

Müller, for instance, notes that the EU's constitutionalisation has been 'an essentially open process of deliberation and political struggle' (2006: 21). However, one potential limiting factor for deliberative democracy in the EU is the relatively small size of the public sphere, and the lack of 'equal access' to the public discourse as it is dominated by elites (Risse 2010: 170). In Habermas' view there can be no European identity without a European public sphere;

> The development of a Europe-wide political public sphere – that is, of a communicative network extending across national boundaries and specializing in the relevant questions – is of central importance for the emergence of such a

> European identity, however weak it may be, relatively speaking ... A European
> public sphere can arise only if the national public spheres become responsive
> *to one another,* which would also remove the problem of multilingualism.
> (Habermas 2009: 87)

In a 2003 article co-signed by Jacques Derrida, however, Habermas sees the protests against the Gulf War as a sign of an emerging European public sphere[1] (Parker 2009b: 398). In addition, an extensive study by Risse (2010) concludes that, although it is uneven and dominated by elite discourse, a Europeanisation of public spheres with regard to visibility and meaning structures can indeed be observed, at least in Western Europe, and that this Europeanisation tends to increase over time. However, while there is convergence in broader frames, such as 'widening or deepening', national differences become more evident in detailed subframes. As Risse argues, then, 'The general frames might be available everywhere, but they often appear in national colours' (2010: 155).

The importance of discourse in Habermasian thinking can be explained by the fact that, for Habermas, language itself contains certain rules which facilitate agreement. In this sense, discourse itself embodies the foundation of a universal ethic for Habermas (Parker 2009b: 392) in that discourse is understood as 'a process whereby reflexive agents turn back upon their habits and assumptions and subject them to a communicatively rational interrogation and evaluation' (Diez and Steans 2005: 134). This, in turn, implies that rational reflection on actions and beliefs is an inherent possibility for all, perhaps leading to a consensus if all parties are able both to rationally express themselves and remain open to others' perspectives (Parker 2009b: 392). Thus, for Habermas, 'all speech is oriented to the idea of a genuine consensus – discursively achieved consensus – which is rarely realized' (Held 1980: 256).

In his later work, Habermas develops the distinction between moral, ethical and pragmatic discourse, each of which designates a different use of practical reason (Habermas 1993: 1). *Pragmatic* discourses concern the rational choice of the means to a given end; according to Habermas practical problems 'have to be' mastered if we are to avoid suffering negative consequences (1993: 2). Importantly, Habermas also distinguishes between *moral* and *ethical* discourse. *Moral* norms or rights are universal in that they belong to humanity as a whole, irrespective of cultural identities and belongings. In this way, they are behavioural rules anchored in the lifeworld which are based on universally shared interests; thus they may refer to questions which may be settled with reference to justice, and include principles such as human rights, democracy and the rule of law (1993: 15).

Ethical norms or values, on the other hand, are connected both with the characteristics of a specific community and to the identity of the members of that community, and are thus only binding upon members of the community in question.

---

1 For a detailed critique of this article, and of Habermas' writings on the EU in general, see Parker (2009b).

Therefore, they are collective representations of the 'good life' which are bound to a particular cultural and social context. In other words, ethical discourse assesses what is 'good for me' or 'for us'; it thus refers to *particular,* rather than universal goods. According to Habermas, then, values are the basic symbolic constituents of culture or ethical life, and also form an integral part of an individual's self-identity as they are internalised as a result of that individual's socialisation into the institutions and practices of their community (Habermas 1993: 1–17).

According to Habermas, traditional societies are held together by a shared ethos; in modern, multicultural societies, however, values are more likely to create conflict than cohesion. In his view, then, the moral has priority over the ethical; however important a particular cultural value may be it can always be overridden by a valid moral norm as, in Habermas' view, modern citizens have abstract self-identities that are not rooted in any particular tradition. In this way, then, moral discourse is appropriate for modern, culturally diverse societies as it allows individuals to determine the rules of their co-existence for themselves. While values still have a certain importance, morality sets limits for ethics as ethical discourse functions within the bounds of moral permissibility (Habermas 1993: 14–16).

On this basis, Habermas' own view on the development of the EU is that it should be underscored by a form of *constitutional patriotism* which is anchored in the universal principle of the constitutional state; in this way, then, there is 'a peculiar switch in emotional fixation from the state to the constitution' (Habermas 2006: 78). In other words, for Habermas, if there is a 'European people' it should be a demos rather than an ethnos; a common political culture cannot, in his view, be based on a shared religion. However, for Habermas, for a truly democratic constitution to take root, it must not only be consistent with post-conventional morality but must also resonate with the ethical understanding not only of the majority culture but of *all* cultural groups in the political community (Habermas 1998: 159).

Thus, constitutional patriotism also implies 'a distinctive interpretation of those constitutional principles that are equally embodied in other republican constitutions' with references to the particular historical circumstances that rooted them in practice. In turn, this imbues them with values and affection (Habermas 1998: 118). In this way, then, constitutional patriotism comprises both universalistic and particularist features (Castiglione 2009: 39).[2] As Habermas argues;

> Any political community that wants to understand itself as a democracy must at least distinguish between members and non-members ... Even if such a community is grounded in the universalist principles of a democratic constitutional state, it still forms a collective identity, in the sense that it interprets

---

2   Indeed, as Parker, for instance, argues Habermas' view of the EU is not entirely cosmopolitan; in the article co-signed with Derrida appears to 'Otherise' the USA, as well as the CEE member states (2009b).

and realizes these principles in light of its own history and in the context of its own political form of life. (Habermas 2001: 107)

As is discussed further below, Sjursen, for instance, in her analysis of arguments used by EU and national elites regarding the accession of the CEECs concluded that EU identity did, in fact, appear to be developing into something resembling a Habermasian constitutional patriotism. However, it is argued later in this chapter that an examination of the discourse pertaining to Turkish accession reveals that the 'constitutional patriotism' vision of the EU is being challenged by an alternative view.

Deliberative Approaches to Enlargement

It has frequently been argued that instrumental or pragmatic arguments cannot sufficiently account for the EU's decision to enlarge. Schimmelfenning (2001) argued that enlargement to the CEECs was beneficial to certain member states which then used normative arguments to 'shame' the others into compliance; in other words they acted as 'norm entrepreneurs'. However, according to Sjursen this is an insufficient explanation as those countries, such as Germany and Denmark, which had most to gain from enlargement did not primarily use arguments based on the economic or security benefits of enlargement. Instead, they rather appear to have viewed enlargement as a moral duty and an act of solidarity with the CEECs. Moreover, she points out that there is no evidence that those countries which would receive less benefit from enlargement, such as France and Spain, were 'shamed' into supporting it (Sjursen 2008: 6). Thus, in her view, there is no reason to believe that the norms referred to were not honestly believed in;

> even if enlargement had come about as a form of 'hypocrisy', where some states would have used normative arguments regarding the 'duty to enlarge' in order to ensure an outcome in line with their own interest, they would not have succeeded unless the norms that they appealed to were considered valid, true or right in the first place. (Sjursen 2008: 6)

In Sjursen's opinion, then, a Habermasian approach can help to explain support for enlargement to the CEECs. She argues that:

> support for a policy such as enlargement can be obtained as a result of deliberation where arguments and reasons are provided in favour of this policy, on condition that the arguments are deemed legitimate by the parties involved. Or, to put it differently, the arguments and reasons provided in favour of enlargement have to be of a type that others can support; they have to be considered legitimate. (Sjursen 2002: 493)

This approach has several advantages. Firstly, it can be seen as a way of solving collective action problems in a manner which is consistent not only with the interests of the individual member states but also with those of the EU as a whole, as it examines action co-ordination as a process of establishing mutual understanding between diverse actors (Torreblanca 2002: 22) (Eriksen 2003: 3). Secondly, deliberation does not force us to choose between interests and norms; indeed, enlargement involves both (Torreblanca 2005: 23–4).

Torreblanca also supports the view that governments have traditionally exchanged arguments about how to make sure that successive enlargements were compatible with EU values and identities and the integration process. In turn, these have resulted in decisions which have gradually constituted the enlargement *acquis,* consisting of a set of criteria and principles culminating in the Copenhagen criteria and the accession principles. The latter include points such as the indivisibility of the *acquis,* 'non-discrimination' in the decision to open negotiations and 'relative merit' for determining the conclusion of negotiations (Torreblanca 2005: 21). As Piedrafita and Torreblanca argue, then;

> It is undeniable that significant enlargement decisions have been reached through a deliberative process in which member states have exchanged 'reasoned reasons' for their respective claims and preferences (i.e. arguments rather than threats). Thus, proposals and stances not necessarily supported by the most powerful states have prospered as the result of reflecting on the 'better argument' on the table. (Piedrafita and Torreblanca 2005: 14)

Following Habermas' distinction between pragmatic, moral and ethical discourse, which has been discussed above, Sjursen posits that arguments used in this context could be based on material gain (pragmatic arguments), but they could also be based on actors' conceptions of what is just or fair (moral arguments), or on identity concerns (ethical political arguments) (Sjursen 2002: 492–3) (2006: 8).

Moreover, each kind of argument speaks to one of the ideal types of the EU. While pragmatic arguments are linked to the conception of the EU as a problem solving entity, moral arguments are linked to the idea of the EU as a post-national, rights-based union and ethical-political arguments to that of the EU as a value-based community. As Sjursen argues, pragmatic arguments have much in common with March and Olsen's (1989, 1998) concept of the 'logic of consequence' and moral and ethical-political arguments with the 'logic of appropriateness', although the 'logic of appropriateness' could be applied to both moral and ethical-political arguments as it could imply rule-following as a result of habit or a particular identity on the one hand, and rule-following based on a rational assessment of morally valid arguments on the other. Thus, in Sjursen's view, clarity can be increased if three types of logic and discourse are put forward rather than two: she adds the concept of the 'logic of justification' pertaining to the latter case, i.e. to a rational assessment of morally valid arguments (Sjursen 2006: 9).

Thus, these logics and discourses can be identified by different criteria; those of utility, values and rights. *Utility* refers to an effort to find efficient solutions to concrete dilemmas or problems; policy is therefore legitimised by achieving an outcome which would maximize given interests and preferences. *Values* refers to a particular idea of the good life, which is grounded in the identity of a specific community. In this case, policy would be legitimised by its appropriateness to the group's identity and sense of what it represents. Finally, *rights* refers to principles that can be recognised as just by all parties regardless of their interests or cultural identities and perceptions of 'the good life'. Here, then, policy would be legitimised by reference to mutuallyrecognised principles (Sjursen 2006: 9).

The EU as a Problem Solving Entity

According to this view, actors' decisions are considered to be defined basically by a logic of consequentiality (Piedrafita and Torreblanca 2005: 32). This outlook thus conceives of the EU in pragmatic terms: EU membership is motivated by the benefits it can provide, while policies are supported or opposed according to a means-end calculation. In this view, the EU is seen as *derivative* of the nation states and is thus characterised by an intergovernmental rather than a supranational logic; sovereignty and democracy are associated with the nation state. Thus, the EU is conceived of simply as an international organisation, and the member states' right to veto further integration is taken for granted (Sjursen 2008: 3). The EU's legitimacy, in this vision, is based on its performance, and support may be withdrawn if expectations are not met. Eriksen and Fossum, therefore, note that interests alone provide only an unstable basis for co-operation as actors will opt-out as soon as they find a better option; instead, some kind of common identity is necessary to motivate collective action (Eriksen and Fossum 2004: 439–40).

In the case of EU enlargement, pragmatists tend to support enlargement if it is considered to maintain or enhance the economic prosperity and physical security of national and EU citizens. In this vision the EU is optimally without borders as enlargement is seen as a question of efficiency and utility, and often linked to arguments about extending the free market or reinforcing security (Schmidt 2009: 215). Similarly, from this point of view, if an enlargement round is considered to endanger prosperity or security it is likely to be opposed. Thus, it follows that a candidate country is not merely accepted on cultural terms, and may be rejected for full membership even if it fulfills the formal membership criteria if this is seen as going against the interests of the EU or of some of the member states in question (Sjursen 2008: 3–4).

While pragmatic arguments regarding the accession of the CEECs were certainly not absent, a pragmatic approach alone is not enough to explain the unanimous consensus in favour of enlargement, particularly as some of the member states that would be expected to be 'losers' from CEE enlargement, such as Spain, eventually supported it,due in the Spanish case to its own experiences of EC/EU membership as a way to consolidate democracy and economic growth in the transition from dictatorship (Sjursen 2008: 5). Moreover, Verney (2006) and Torreblanca (2005: 34) argue that earlier rounds of enlargement to Greece and Spain could also not be entirely explained instrumentally. As Verney argues in the context of Greek accession, for instance;

> The economic arguments in favour of Greek accession were peripheral, weak and nebulous. They certainly did not add up to a strong case in favour of admitting Greece. The discourse around the second enlargement clearly did not speak to an image of the European Community as primarily a Common Market. (Verney 2006: 207)

Thus, with the gradual development of the enlargement *acquis,* it eventually became impossible for a member state to validate its opposition to enlargement on the basis of pragmatism alone; instead, it had to refer to the candidate country's inability to fulfill the political criteria for membership (Torreblanca 2005: 35).

The EU as a Post-National, Rights Based Union

Unlike the view of the EU as a problem-solving entity, the conception of the EU as a post-national, rights-based union is based on a rights-based procedural notion of legitimation (Eriksen and Fossum 2004: 445). This conception, like that of the EU as a value-based community, is normative in that both are based on norms and values rather than merely on pragmatic or utility based arguments. In this case, however, the norms, or rights, in question are not cultural but 'universal'; the legitimacy of a community is based not on common cultural values and traditions but on a set of legally entrenched fundamental rights and democratic procedures which serve the purpose both of protecting the freedom and integrity of the individual and of permitting public participation in opinion-formation and decision-making processes through a public sphere characterised by freedom, equality and an open agenda. In short, this normative vision is founded on respect for the dignity and integrity of the individual, and is rooted in a political culture based on tolerance of difference (Eriksen and Fossum 2004: 445–6). However, Eriksen and Fossum note that a potential difficulty lies in the challenges, exacerbated by enlargement, posed to the political discourse necessary for rights-based integration by different histories, traditions, languages and experiences (Eriksen and Fossum 2004: 448).

In the rights-based view of the EU, particular solutions or policies are preferred if they are considered to fulfill universal criteria of being just or right. In the context of enlargement, the argument is that a candidate country should be allowed to accede to the EU if it is considered to fulfill conditions based on 'universal' liberal democratic norms such as respect for human and minority rights, democracy and the rule of law (Sjursen 2008: 3). Thus, the EU's boundaries are determined by the limits of the functionality of representative democracy in Europe; they are drawn with regard to what is necessary for the Union to be a self-sustainable and well-functioning democratic entity (Eriksen and Fossum 2004: 447).

The conception of the EU put forward in the Treaties is close to a rights-based union, as will be discussed further later in this chapter. The Copenhagen criteria, set out by the European Council in 1993, are also broadly in line with this vision. They demand that the candidate countries meet the four broad political conditions cited below, in addition to the economic criteria:

> The stability of institutions guaranteeing democracy, the rule of law, human rights and respect for and protection of minorities, the existence of a functioning market economy and the capacity to cope with competitive pressure and market forces within the Union … [and] the ability to take on the obligations of membership, including adherence to the aims of political, economic andmonetary union. (European Council 1993)

As Ruiz-Jimenez and Torreblanca point out, then, 'whether the candidate country is Turkey, Norway or Switzerland it should not make much difference' (2007: 6). Thus, from this point of view, there is no cultural criteria for EU accession; instead any country that is accepted as geographically European and which fulfills the Copenhagen criteria should be allowed to join regardless of broader identity questions such as religion or history. Here, as Hülsse notes, the enlargement process may be metaphorically compared to a path, the 'one metaphor that the enlargement discourse apparently cannot do without', or the related metaphors of a railway or highway. In this case, there is no natural or cultural conception of EU identity as there is nothing uniting the current members apart from their position at the end of the path; the EU is conceived of as the 'final destination' of political integration towards which the candidates are heading (Hülsse 2006: 411).

The EU as a 'Value-Based Community'

In this view, which is also normative, the borders or cultural values of a community are emphasised; a political community should be based on a sense of common identity, or 'we-feeling', rather than simply on common benefits or 'universal' norms. This 'we-feeling' may be based on a common history or religious tradition (Sjursen 2008: 3). In the case of the EU, as Eriksen and Fossum note, it is difficult to identify values which are uniquely European as opposed to universal or local (2004: 444). Revitalising Christian and humanist values as a source for a deeper sense of community and unity is one option in this respect, and the question of whether a reference to Christianity should be included in the Charter of Fundamental Rights and, later, the Constitutional Treaty proved to be a matter of intense debate (Eriksen and Fossum 2004: 441).

It is important to recall here that the construction of an identity also involves the construction of its Other (or Others). In the value-based view, people can be regarded as genuine members of a community only if they are born or assimilated into it culturally. If not, they are doomed to remain outsiders. In this context, then, the border has an important symbolic meaning as it is used as a 'demarcating identifier between the in-group and the out-group' (Cassarino 2006: 6). Thus, the sense of common identity is upheld by a system of border control, which excludes those defined as Others, and a system of military defence that protects against external aggression, influence and control (Eriksen and Fossum 2004: 442). One potential difficulty with a 'value-based' EU, therefore, is that it implies the tendency to develop into a 'fortress Europe', thus potentially endangering the rights of minorities (Eriksen and Fossum 2004: 443–4).

From this perspective, enlargement is encouraged only into spaces which are considered to have a similar cultural heritage: its aim is to bring together the 'European family' (Schmidt 2009: 15) and is justified by referring to duties and responsibilities resulting from belonging to a particular community (Sjursen 2002: 494). As a result, it is possible to establish a clear set of territorial boundaries for the further extension of the EU (Eriksen and Fossum 2004: 443).

As Torreblanca argues, while ethical-political arguments have been used against Turkey's accession, as will be discussed further in this chapter, they were also used by De Gaulle against British membership in the 1960s (2002: 21). In fact, the following speech of De Gaulle's taken out of context could easily be mistaken for contemporary French right-wing discourse on Turkish accession;

> Here is a country which is not European, its history, its geography, its economy, its agriculture and the character of its people – admirable people though they are – all point in a different direction. This is a country which cannot, despite what it claims and perhaps even what it believes, be a full member (cited in Cameron 2010).

In contrast, as Sjursen (2002, 2006, 2008) and Lundgren (2006) argue, ethical-political arguments were used together with moral ones in support of enlargement to the CEECs. In particular, the argument of 'reuniting Europe' or bringing the candidate countries 'back to Europe' was frequently used. Thus, the closeness between the two 'halves' of Europe was described as consisting of a common history, common values and a common culture (Lundgren 2006: 135). As the European Parliament (EP) argued in 1995, for instance; 'Europe as a whole has a common cultural heritage which has its roots as much in the East as in the West' (European Parliament 1995: 22). In turn, this sense of a common culture and history resulted in a sense of duty or responsibility on the part of the EU.

Hülsse also notes that many of the metaphors used in the 1990s in German discussions of enlargement to the CEECs imply a primordial conception of EU identity according to which Europe is constructed as a *Kulturnation* like Germany on a wider scale. In particular, the CEECs were described as part of the 'European family' and enlargement as a family reunion or homecoming (Hülsse 2006: 406–10). As former Chancellor Kohl argued in 1994, for example; 'The Poles, the Czechs the Slovaks, the Romanians, the Bulgarians and the Hungarians are our European brothers [...] and need to attain their European rights' (cited in Hülsse 2006: 407).

Moreover, Verney argues that the concept of bringing the candidate 'back to Europe' had also been used in arguments to support enlargement to Greece (2006: 34);

> Analysis of the accession debate indicates that the perception of Greece as indubitably European was based on a civilisational frame of reference. Echoing the value-based 'Declaration on European Identity', Greece was essentially seen as European due to its supposed adherence to European ideals, which in turn had been born in the shadow of the Acropolis. Moreover, EC accession was represented as a way of reinforcing and guaranteeing Greece's 'European' nature. (Verney 2006: 34)

Conclusion: Implications of Previous Enlargement Rounds for EU Identity

The prospect of enlargement inevitably provokes a certain amount of reflection within the EU on its 'ideal' nature and identity. As Sjursen notes, 'Enlargement may be seen not only as a process that reinforces the applicants' European nature but also the Union's own 'Europeanness' (Sjursen 2008: 11).

Enlargement to the CEECs, or even to Greece and Spain in the 1980s cannot be explained by instrumental factors alone (Sjursen 2006: 204) (Torreblanca 2005: 34) (Verney 2006). Moral arguments, such as respect for human rights and democracy, have played an important part in considering enlargement from the beginning. In addition to moral arguments, however, ethical-political arguments played an important part in the enlargement to the CEECs, in particular in the sense that, as members of the European family, the EU reiterated its 'sense of responsibility' to the CEECs (Piedrafita and Torreblanca 2005: 40). Neumann (1999: 143–60) also notes that such value-based arguments were used by the CEECs themselves during their candidacy for EU accession by representing themselves as European historically, geographically and culturally, in stark contrast to their neighbours to the East which were portrayed as less European. In contrast, as will be explored in more detail below, value-based arguments used by the EU in support of Turkish accession are far less evident. Therefore, the argument that Turkey is a natural part of the European family and that the EU consequently has a sense of responsibility towards it has generally been absent in EU discourse (Piedrafita and Torreblanca 2005: 41).

Despite this, as Sjursen argues in the context of the CEE enlargements, evidence of a sense of 'thick' collective identity reflecting, for example, religious, ethnic or linguistic commonalities is scarce. According to Sjursen, then, the view of the EU which emerged from the debate on CEE enlargement is close to Habermas' conception of constitutional patriotism, implying an entity based on moral norms such as democracy and respect for human rights but also linked by a 'thin' ethical sense of belonging. In this context, then, the consensus reached on CEE enlargement also seems to corroborate the idea of 'Europe's past as its Other' (2006: 210–15). However, as is discussed below, this vision has been challenged in the wake of Turkey's candidacy for accession.

The following section aims to give an overview of attitudes towards Turkish accession across the EP and European Commission, and across the member states and party lines. Following this, a broader analysis of pragmatic, rights-based and value-based arguments used by the European elites (including that of Turkey itself) both in favour and against Turkey's EU membership is carried out.

Elite Attitudes to Turkey's EU Accession: Variations by Country and Political Affiliation

The European Commission

As Suvarierol and Aydın-Düzgit point out, the power of the Commission in enlargement policy is twofold. Firstly, the Commission employs a significant amount of discursive power through shaping the terms of the enlargement debate via the regular reports it provides on the candidates' progress towards accession. Secondly, it also wields power through 'governing' through its official/legal role as negotiator and initiator of policy, and through its recommendations to the Council (2011: 157).

The European Commission's attitude to Turkish accession has been broadly supportive although certainly not overwhelmingly so. According to the European Elites survey carried out in 2008, only 45 per cent of Commission officials agreed that 'Turkey's membership of the European Union would be a good thing' (European Elites Survey 2008). The Commission has generally argued that Turkish accession is dependent upon Turkey's fulfillment of the Copenhagen criteria, and it has also stressed the pragmatic benefits of Turkish accession. However, as Lundgren notes (2002: 6–10) there is a considerably different tone in Commission discourse on Turkish accession to that used regarding the CEECs.

While enlargement to the CEECs was often phrased in terms of 'reuniting' Europe, or 'returning' to the 'European family', discourse regarding Turkey's membership bid has tended to be described as a relationship of neighbours rather than brothers.[3] Turkey is thus frequently described as a 'partner' of the EU rather than a country which, for cultural reasons, forms a 'natural' part of the EU. Thus, in EU discourse about CEE accession a greater sense of its responsibility, or even duty, for supporting democratic and economic reform is expressed, as might be expected towards 'family members', than towards Turkey. The question of Turkish reforms has, instead, tended to be expressed as being in the EU's interest, or as a matter of concern for the EU (Lundgren 2002).

---

3   There are exceptions to this. Following the earthquake in Van (South-East Turkey), Kristalina Georgieva, the Commissioner for International Co-operation, Humanitarian Aid and Crisis Response, said that the EU saw Turkey 'as part of the European family'(Cümhüriyet 2012).

Contemporary Commission discourse therefore tends to focus on the strategic benefits that Turkey would bring to Europe. As Commissioner Verheugen, for instance, argued in 2000;

> The European Union and Turkey are linked in a strategic partnership. The Union wants to further integrate Turkey into the European structures. We need Turkey as a reliable partner in foreign and security policy. We want Turkey to be a stable democracy, respecting the rule of law and human rights. Our interest is that Turkey plays a constructive role in our common efforts to contribute to peace and stability in the region. (Verheugen 2000)

However, as Casanova points out, the meeting of the European Commission on June 29 2005 to determine the rules for membership negotiations with Turkey reveals a schism within the Commission regarding Turkey's accession; Commissioners from Austria, Poland, Greece and Luxembourg called for a halt in the negotiations with Turkey, which ultimately resulted in a considerably tougher negotiation framework for Turkey when compared to that demanded of the CEECs (Casanova 2006: 234–5).

Moreover, studies among Commission staff also indicate that, while many are in favour of Turkish accession for strategic reasons, Turkey is still viewed as fundamentally 'different'. As Suvarierol and Aydın-Düzgit note, in spite of their encounters with Turkish officials, and their often positive opinions of the latter, Commission officials frequently appear to stick to stereotypical depictions of the country as predominantly backward and traditional. Thus, Suvarierol and Aydın-Düzgit conclude that, for Commission officials, 'the borders of cosmopolitan Europe still appear to stop at the borders of Turkey' (2011: 165).

The European Parliament

The EP, consisting of a broad representation of nationalities and party positions, provides a 'semi representative' sample of the diversity of views in the European public sphere. Unsurprisingly given the broad spectrum of political views and member states which it represents, the EP does not have a common position on Turkey's accession, although members of the European Parliament (MEPs) generally view Turkish accession more positively than the broader European public (Levin 2011: 182–3). According to the 2008 European Elites survey, 48 per cent of MEPs agreed that Turkish accession would be a good thing (European Elites Survey 2008).

While almost all MEPs converge on a position of sharp criticism of the Turkish reform process, the main division appears to be between those who support eventual Turkish membership on condition that it continues to take steps towards democratisation and those who consider that it is simply too culturally different to ever be considered as a full member of the EU at all. In fact, the question of Turkish accession has caused divisions within as well as among parties (Bogdani 2011: 93).

Overall, however, it can be argued that the EP has been 'more a handicap than a facilitator' of Turkey's integration into the EU (Dodd 2002) in the sense that it has been a vocal critic of what it sees as Turkey's 'lack of commitment' in fulfilling the political criteria, particularly in areas such as the status of minorities, human rights and democracy (Levin 2011: 184) and has been particularly outspoken on the Kurdish and Armenian issues. The Armenian question, notably, has not been present in the Council's or Commission's demands (Soler i Lecha 2005: 2). Levin notes that, in EP debates, while Turkey is sometimes depicted as a valuable and important neighbour, it is frequently portrayed as a 'dangerous place to live' and the 'troublemaker of the international community', which he ascribes to the persistence and reworking of much older stereotypes such as the 'Terrible Turk' or 'the Sick Man of Europe'[4] (Levin 2011).

Moreover, since the acceptance of the Turkish candidacy in 1999, ethical-political arguments have also increasingly been used against Turkish accession. Levin, based on the analysis of a series of EP debates on Turkish accession between 1996 and 2010, notes a marked and continuous rise in essentialist arguments against Turkish full membership during this period. While at the beginning of this period it was only the nationalist fringe that rejected Turkish accession on value-based grounds, such arguments have become increasingly widespread on the mainstream right as well (2011: 187–8).

Broadly speaking, the more right-wing the party the more likely it is to be opposed to Turkish accession on essentialist grounds. Both the European People's Party (EPP), which includes centre-right and Christian Democrat parties, and far-right MEPS generally oppose Turkish accession on cultural grounds. The EPP, however, is more divided, with the dominant German Christian Democratic Union (CDU) and Christian Socialist Union (CSU) and the French *Union pour un Mouvement Populaire* (UMP) against Turkish membership while parties from Southern Europe,[5] Sweden and Finland and the CEECs are generally more supportive. In addition, the British Conservative Party, which, in June 2009, split from the EPP together with the Polish Law and Democracy Party and the Czech Civic Democratic Party to form the 'European Conservatives and Reformists' group, are also in favour of Turkish accession (Bogdani 2011: 93–6).

The opposition of the EPP, however, is particularly important as it forms the largest group in the EP (Casanova 2006: 235). Indeed, the need to strengthen the EU before carrying out any further enlargement is often stressed in EPP discourse as it is seen as potentially weakening the European integration project. In the view of EPP MEP Markus Ferber, for instance, 'First steps first: Europe has to concentrate on addressing its own future before embarking on further enlargement' (European Voice 2008). However, Turkish accession is often seen as particularly problematic due to cultural and religious differences. As EPP

---

4   For a similar argument, see MacMillan (2010b).

5   Including Greece's Neo Democracia, Italy's Forza Italia and Spain's Partido Popular (Bogdani 2011: 94).

MEP Bernd Posselt argues, for instance, 'Turkey is not a European state. I am a supporter of a strong, federalist Europe. With Turkey as a full member this will not be the case' (European Parliament 2012b). The official view of the EPP, then, is that Turkey should be granted a more limited 'privileged partnership' with the EU rather than full membership. As former EPP chairman Hans-Gert Poettering put forward in 2004;

> Contentious though the issue of Turkey is for us, it is important that the criteria should be complied with, that there should be no political opportunism and, should negotiations take place, that consideration be given to alternatives, such as, for example, a privileged partnership with Turkey. (Poettering 2004)

The far right, unsurprisingly, also argues against Turkish accession. The view of MEP Philip Claeyes, for instance, is fairly representative; 'Turkey is not a European country and does not belong in Europe, and a privileged partnership would be preferable to fully-fledged membership' (Bogdani 2011: 96).

In contrast, liberal and socialist parties, as well as the Greens, tend to be in favour of Turkish accession providing the relevant criteria are met. The Party of European Socialists (PES), the second largest group in the EP after the EPP, is broadly in favour with the exception of some German and Austrian MEPs, as are the Greens. As European Socialist Véronique de Keyser, for instance, argued in a 2006 EP debate on Turkish accession; 'Our long term aim is to have Turkey join because we believe – and this is a genuine political project – in a Europe that is multicultural, secular, multi-faith and open to the rest of the world' (European Parliament 2006). Similarly, while the European Liberal Democrats are generally supportive of Turkish accession, MEPs from the Union for French Democracy (UDF) and the German Free Democratic Party tend to have more reservations (Bogdani 2011: 94–5). Generally speaking, although the Socialists and Greens have traditionally been the strongest opponents of Turkish accession on the grounds of violations of human and minority rights, they now increasingly argue that the country has sufficiently fulfilled the political criteria (Soler i Lecha 2005: 2).

Overall, a study of the 2012 EP Resolution on the 2011 Progress Report on Turkey/EU relations, which was later adopted by the EP, indicates a primarily pragmatic and rights-based view of Turkey's accession to the EU. While praising Turkish efforts to prepare a new Constitution, the Resolution emphasises the need for Turkey to accelerate its political reforms, and is often heavily critical of the situation in Turkey, expressing concern, for instance, over freedom of expression and media pluralism and minority and women's rights. However, the Resolution also argues that Turkish accession would bring geopolitical and economic benefits to both parties. It is notable that the resolution makes no allusion to value based arguments for Turkey's inclusion in or exclusion from the EU, and there is no mention of a 'privileged partnership' (European Parliament 2012a).

The Member States

There is also a considerable split in the attitudes of the member states towards Turkish accession. This division can be observed both between and within member states, and sometimes even within political parties. However, an overall pattern of elite support and opposition can be noted in the member states which is broadly consistent with their attitudes to EU integration. Moreover, this split along member state lines is reflected in the EP and even in the Commission, as has been pointed out above. The division appears to be,broadly speaking, between states which have traditionally preferred a 'federalist' or 'supranationalist' EU and those which have supported integration along 'intergovernmental' lines.

Opponents of Turkey's EU accession include France, Germany, Austria, Belgium and Luxembourg, which have generally tended to be those which are most supportive of 'deeper' integration. According to the dominant opinion in France, Germany and Belgium in particular, Turkish accession would threaten European integration; these states have thus tended to propose a 'privileged partnership' for Turkey rather than full membership. Opposition to Turkish membership has also been tied up with concerns about increasing immigration and the transition to a multicultural society, most strikingly in the case of Austria (Oğurlu 2010). Notably, France and Austria have declared that they will hold referenda on Turkish accession, which, given the high level of public opposition in these countries, would almost certainly produce negative results (Redmond 2007: 309). In general, however, there are divisions of opinion within these countries, with right wing parties tending to oppose Turkish accession more strongly than those further left. Germany in particular underwent a significant change in its policy towards Turkey following the change in government, and there continues to be a heated debate over Turkish accession there (Şenyuva and Akşit 2009: 220–21).

Another group of member states are more supportive, with the UK being one of the staunchest advocates of eventual full membership for Turkey (Redmond 2007: 309). Spain has also been strongly in favour, although a certain amount of reluctance has begun to appear on the right. Greece, which used to oppose Turkish accession, has undergone a significant change in its attitude in recent years, having become much more supportive of it. This change in Greek policy from a confrontational to a co-operative approach can be dated to the 1999 Helsinki summit (Şenyuva and Akşit 2009: 223). Italian support rests on the idea of a shared Mediterranean spirit and identity, as well as on strategic factors such as Turkey's geopolitical situation and economic dynamism (Alessandri and Sali 2009: 60–61).

In addition, Poland and Romania have publicly declared their support for Turkish membership. Romanian elites tend to argue in favour of Turkish accession from a pragmatic point of view, focusing on the potential gains for Romania, while the Polish standpoint can best be seen in the context of Polish support for enlargement in general, including that to its neighbour Ukraine, as well as on the *pacta sunt servanda* argument (Şenyuva and Akşit 2009: 224–5). Smaller CEECs such as the Czech Republic, Slovakia, Bulgaria, Hungary and the Baltic countries are either divided or cautiously in favour of Turkish accession (Redmond, 2007: 309) (Şenyuva and Akşit 2009: 224–5).

Thus, it can be noted that the pattern of elite support across the member states is broadly consistent with patterns of public opinion on Turkish accession, although overall public support for enlargement to Turkey is weaker than that at elite level. This disparity between elite and public opinion on Turkish accession is particularly notable in certain countries, especially in Greece and Italy. While there is an elite consensus in both of these countries in favour of Turkish accession, this is coupled with considerable public scepticism (Şenyuva and Akşit 2009: 227).

It should, of course, be reiterated here that, mirroring the case of the EP, national views on Turkish accession tend, logically, to be split according to political affiliation. Notably, Christian parties in general are significantly less positive about Turkish EU membership and use fewer positive arguments relating to Turkey's accession than other parties, although the effect is less for Protestant than for Catholic parties (Boomgarden and Wüst 2012: 185). Despite differences in the attitudes of centre-right and centre-left parties across Europe, far right and far left parties in most EU member states generally appear to be against Turkish membership. In the case of the far-right, who are also backed in this case by some segments of strongly Catholic parties across the EU, the rejection is usually on value-based, essentialist grounds. Far left parties, in contrast, tend to oppose Turkish accession using moral arguments based on perceived deficiencies in Turkey's willingness and ability to reform, such as insufficient protection of human rights, the Kurdish issue and/or its refusal to recognise the 'Armenian genocide', although they would be ready to accept Turkey if it were to reform. Notably, in contrast to the extreme right, the left tends to be 'enthusiastic about the assets Turkey would bring to a multicultural Europe' (Tocci 2011: 93).

Arguments Used in Relation to Turkey's EU Accession

Pragmatic Arguments: The EU as a Problem Solving Entity

It has been noted that pragmatic arguments are rarely used alone in national discourses on EU enlargement; instead they are often found in combination with rights-based arguments. Thus, not even a relatively Eurosceptic member state such as the UK sees the EU in purely pragmatic terms; it is also perceived as based upon 'universal' rights and values. To recap, pragmatic arguments speak to a vision of the EU as a problem solving entity, based primarily on the benefits, particularly in the areas of economics or security, that EU membership can provide. This implies that the EU is optimally without borders as enlargement is seen as a question of efficiency and utility, and often linked to arguments about extending the free market or reinforcing security (Schmidt 2009: 215). Enlargement is, then, supported or opposed on the basis of the advantages or disadvantages the candidate country is perceived to bring to the EU, particularly in the areas of economics and security.

As mentioned above, it has been argued that pragmatic arguments have been prominent in the discourse of supporters of Turkey's EU membership, both among national and European level elites. As Nugent points out (2007: 483–4), the perceived benefits of Turkey's EU accession are based around the following five key Turkish characteristics, including;

- The size of Turkey's market, which is projected to reach 100 million by around 2020,[6] as well as its fast rate of economic growth.
- The nature of its labour-force, which is young and fast-growing, and could thus provide personnel and help maintain welfare systems in demographically ageing European countries.
- Its key geo-political position between the Balkans, the Middle East, the Caucasus and Central Asia, which would help the EU to gain leverage in these areas. In turn, this would contribute to greater security in these areas. Moreover, due to its borders with energy-rich regions Turkey is fast becoming a major gas and oil transit country; thus Turkey could link Europe to the energy markets off its North-Eastern borders thereby reducing the EU's dependence on Russia (Barysch 2007).
- The fact that it is a Muslim-majority country; it could potentially contribute to extending the EU's 'soft' influence in Islamic countries, while encouraging moderate Islamism.
- Its considerable military capacity, which could contribute significantly to the development of the European Security and Defence Identity (ESDI).

The Commission, for instance, has often cited the strategic and economic benefits that the EU would reap from Turkey's accession. As Commission President Durão-Barroso, for instance, argued in a 2008 speech;

> The EU and Turkey cooperate to make the world more safe and secure Turkey is a key partner for Europe on foreign and security policy. Its responsibilities can only increase in the future, to address the challenges of our common neighbourhood … Turkey is a major partner for energy supplies to Europe from Central Asia and the Middle East. The Baku-Tbilisi-Ceyhan pipeline is a major step towards increasing security. In the light of the challenges that the European Union faces, regarding diversification and security of energy supplies, Turkey-EU co-operation is certainly set to grow further in the coming years. (Durão-Barroso 2008)

Such arguments are also frequently used in EP discourse. As EP deputy Ria Oomen Ruijen argued in a recent EP debate, for example; 'Turkey is a key country for the

---

6   With a population of around 70 million people, Turkey's population is almost twice as large as Poland's, the largest of the CEE Member States. Turkey is predicted to become the most populous country in the EU within a generation (Kubicek 2004: 46). Moreover, Turkey has an exceptionally high rate of economic growth by European standards.

security and the prosperity of the EU. Turkey has enormous potential for economic growth and it has a strategic role as a corridor for the EU's energy' (European Parliament 2012b).

Pragmatic arguments have also been widely used by supporters of Turkish accession in the member states. There has been an important pragmatic element, for instance, in British discourse in favour of Turkish accession, according to which Turkey's entry into the EU would be beneficial for both Britain's and the EU's strategic, political and economic interests. This has been clearly emphasised by former Prime Minister Tony Blair, who argued that the EU's decision to open accession negotiations with Turkey was important for the world's future 'peace and prosperity' (BBC 2004b).

These arguments are echoed among other supporters of Turkish accession who, as has been noted, are mostly concentrated in Southern Europe, Central and Eastern Europe and Scandinavia. According to Soler i Lecha and Garcia, pragmatic arguments including those referring to Turkey's geostrategic value have also frequently been used in support of Turkish accession in Spanish political discourse particularly on the left (2009: 74). As former Prime Minister José Luis Rodríguez Zapatero succinctly argued in 2009, for instance, 'Turkey's entrance is good both for Turkey and for the EU' (Rodríguez Zapatero 2009). Similarly, former Italian Foreign Minister Franco Frattini declared that 'the EU and Turkey need each other' (Frattini 2010). Swedish Foreign Minister Carl Bildt also argued, in an interview with French newspaper *Le Figaro* that 'the EU has a strategic interest in Turkey's full membership' (Vucheva 2009), while Romanian MEP Cristian Dan Preda recently noted that 'Turkey plays an increasingly important role at regional level, and not only' (European Parliament 2012b).[7]

Another argument that has frequently been used in favour of Turkish accession by the Commission (Aydın-Düzgit 2009) and other supporters of enlargement to Turkey is that, with its predominantly Muslim population, a Turkey anchored in the EU could contribute to avoiding a 'clash of civilizations' within and beyond Europe. This view was reinforced following the events of September 11, the Al-Qaida attacks on Madrid and London, and on two synagogues and two British targets in Istanbul in November 2003. Such views are also echoed by the Independent Commission on Turkey, which states that;

> In the great cultural debate of the twenty-first century, all too often fuelled by ignorance and prejudice and misused by criminal phenomena such as international terrorism, a multiethnic, multicultural and multifaith Europe could

---

7   For those with more essentialist, 'value-based' conceptions of the EU, however, such arguments are irrelevant. As MEP William the Earl of Dartmouth recently argued, for instance, 'Mrs Bozkurt, you used the phrase in your speech that Turkey is a growing economy and a regional power. Well the same could be said of South Korea. Why do these two facts, if they are facts, justify political union with Turkey? (EP 2012b).

> send a powerful message to the rest of the world that the 'Clash of Civilizations'
> is not the ineductable destiny of mankind. (2004: 6)

Javier Solana has also recently emphasised the geopolitical advantages that Turkey could bestow on the EU, this time in the context of the Arab Spring;

> For Europe, the 'Arab Spring' should refocus attention on an issue largely
> ignored in recent months: the benefits of Turkey's full membership of the
> European Union. Given the tremendous opportunities present in the current
> circumstances, the advantages for Europe of Turkish accession should be
> obvious. (Solana 2011)

Such arguments have also been used at member state level in favour of Turkish accession. British Labour politician Jack Straw, for instance, put forward the view that EU entry would prevent Turkey from falling into the hands of Muslim extremists: if the terrorist attacks were attacks against civilization, EU accession would place Turkey firmly on the side of the civilized world (Happold 2002). Similar arguments have been used on the German left, for example. As Joshka Fisher, for instance, argued in 2004;

> After 11-S the situation requires that we support the transformation in the Arab-
> Islamic world or that we accept being a target for an explosion that may arrive
> at any moment […] In this situation, I think that saying no without necessity is
> so short-sighted and against the interests of Europe, of the whole Western world
> and Germany, that I would like to urge you again to deeply revise your position
> in the light of the facts. (Deutscher Bundestag, 2004: 13792, cited in Herranz-
> Surralles, 2012: 398)

Turkey itself has used pragmatic arguments in favour of its accession bid. Turkish Minister for Europe Egemen Bağış, for instance, stressed in 2009 that 'Turkey will be an honourable member of the EU and not the sick man of Europe' (Taylor 2009). On the contrary, as is discussed further in the following chapter, Turkey is portrayed as being of significant benefit to the EU in economic and security terms, particularly in the context of the current economic crisis. Thus, this can be seen as an inversion of the traditional European metaphor of Turkey as the 'sick man of Europe';[8] in the AKP's discourse, it is Europe itself which is the 'sick man', particularly in the context of the current economic crisis.

On the other hand, pragmatic arguments have also been used against Turkey's accession although, again, they are rarely used in isolation. Indeed, ironically,

---

8   As noted in the previous chapter, the metaphor of the Ottoman Empire as 'the sick man of Europe', attributed to Tsar Nicholas 1 in 1853, became widely used in Europe during the late nineteenth and early twentieth centuries, the period during which the Empire was in decline.

these arguments often focus on the same factors as pragmatic arguments in favour of Turkish accession. In this view, Turkey's large and youthful workforce, coupled with its relative economic underdevelopment, is likely to provoke considerable immigration into current EU countries. In addition, it is argued that Turkey's large agricultural sector and relatively low GDP per capita will prove a drain on the EU's resources, while its large population means that Turkey would dominate decision-making in the EU.[9] As French PS deputy Laurent Fabius, for instance, has argued in the context of Turkish accession, 'Our regions would no longer have any financial support … [Turkey] would have 20 per cent more votes in the EU than France would' (cited in Agence France Presse 2004).

In addition, Turkey's geopolitical position has been viewed as a disadvantage in that, it is argued, the EU is more likely to become entangled in conflicts in Turkey's often troubled neighbourhood. As well as this, due to its close relationship with the USA, Turkey is sometimes viewed as a 'Trojan horse' for American interests by those who support a more independent foreign policy, particularly France. Moreover, it is also argued that Turkey's nationalist traditions will hamper EU decision making (Kubicek 2004: 53).

It is important to reiterate, however, that pragmatic arguments either in favour of or against Turkish accession are rarely if ever found alone. Instead, pragmatic arguments supporting Turkey's EU membership are often found together with moral ones, while pragmatic arguments against Turkish accession often go hand-in-hand with ethical-political ones which reject Turkey on cultural or religious grounds.

Moral Arguments: The EU as a Post-National, Rights Based Community

As has been explained in more detail earlier in this chapter, moral arguments, like ethical-political ones, are normative in that they are based on norms and values rather than pragmatic or utility based arguments. In this case, however, the legitimacy of a community is based not on common cultural values and traditions but on a set of legally entrenched fundamental rights and democratic procedures. In this view, the EU is conceived of as a post-national, rights-based union, and particular solutions or policies are preferred if they are considered to fulfill universal criteria of being just or right. This discourse tends to be the dominant one among European 'liberal' or 'cosmopolitan' elites as well as by EU level officials (Schmidt 2009: 16).

---

9   In fact, on accession Turkey would be entitled to 100 MEPs, compared to Germany's 99, thus entitling it to more MEPs than any other member state. Moreover, and perhaps more importantly, Turkey would have a strong impact on voting within the European Council, which is to be carried out under the double majority system. According to this system, a proposal would be adopted in the Council if at least 55 per cent of the member states representing at least 65 per cent of the population approve (Müftüler-Baç 2008: 213).

Indeed, the 'official' identity of the EU, i.e. that stated in the Treaties and the *acquis communautaire* in general, tends to emphasise an identity based on 'universal norms' such as democracy and human rights rather than a 'deeper' cultural identity. As can be seen in the Preamble to the Treaty on European Union (TEU), this is based on a concept of civilization that is close to the 'French Enlightenment' view. In this view,while Western Europe is seen as the source of civilization, the resulting values, such as democracy, human rights or the rule of law, are potentially universal in nature. Here, then, civilization is not a given; instead it can only be achieved as the result of progress and development (Kuzmanovic 2008: 57). It also implies a *mission civilisatrice* for Europe to spread these values as much as possible. These features can be clearly discerned in the Preamble to the TEU;

> Drawing inspiration from the cultural, religious and humanist inheritance of Europe, from which have developed the universal values of the inviolable and inalienable rights of the human person, freedom, democracy, equality and the rule of law [...] Believing that Europe, reunited after bitter experiences, intends to continue along the path of civilisation, progress and prosperity for the good of all its inhabitants [...] and that it wishes to deepen the democratic and transparent nature of its public life, and to strive for peace, justice and solidarity throughout the world. (European Union 2007: 12)

As discussed earlier, further analysis of the TEU[10] supports the idea that the identity referents are generally of a universalist nature rather than based on a common past, and are limited to universal principles. Article 2(1a) of the TEU affirms that 'the Union is founded on the values of respect for human dignity, freedom, democracy, equality, the rule of law and respect for human rights, including the rights of persons belonging to minorities'. In addition, article 3(2) of the TEU stresses 'unity in diversity', as it emphasises the EU's commitment to respect the 'rich cultural and linguistic diversity' of the member states, and 'shall ensure that Europe's cultural heritage is safeguarded and enhanced' (European Union 2007: 13–14).

Moreover, the focus on the preservation of national identities, cultures and traditions means that there is room for a certain degree of divergence of interpretations and implementation of these norms between the member states. This implies the appreciation and tolerance of differences between countries, regions, political orientations and individuals, in other words respect for and interest in the internal Other, at least in so far as the 'universal values' underpinning the EU are respected. Thus, the appreciation of difference is seen as one of Europe's greatest achievements, and a stimulant for democratic institutions as well as for cultural and economic innovation (Kaelble 2009: 201).

---

10   The numbering of the TEU is that used following its amendment to the Lisbon treaty.

Importantly, the Preamble to the TEU does not mention 'a community of Christian values' although, as discussed below, during the European Convention some member states, as well as the Catholic Church and some intellectuals wanted Judeo-Christian values to be more openly mentioned in the Constitutional Treaty. Instead, the Preamble makes a more general allusion to European religious values as the foundation of universal values on which the EU is based: 'Drawing inspiration from the cultural, religious and humanist inheritance of Europe, from which have developed the universal values of the inviolable and inalienable rights of the human person, freedom, democracy, equality and the rule of law'[11] (European Union 2007: 12).

Thus, while the Treaty mentions 'Europeanness' and 'European values', these values are actually understood as being potentially universal in nature. More specific references to 'Europeanness' and 'European values' were avoided in order to prevent dissent and to bolster the EU's legitimacy among European citizens. The emphasis, then, is again more on the creation of a future common identity through universal values and integration than on a shared past. In addition, the Charter of Fundamental Rights also emphasises universal values coupled with respect for diversity in areas such as religion, language and custom (Zürcher and Van der Linden 2007: 449). Moreover, as has been noted above, the Copenhagen Criteria do not include cultural or religious criteria for accession.

Thus, from this point of view, any country that is accepted as geographically European and which is considered to fulfill these criteria should be allowed to join regardless of broader identity questions such as religion or history. According to Commission President Durão-Barroso, '[Accession] negotiations are based on shared values and a common understanding of the rule of law, democracy and human rights' (Durão-Barroso 2008); as former EU enlargement commissioner Olli Rehn has argued, it is these values, rather than religious or cultural issues which underscore the EU's enlargement policy;

> Any European country that respects values like democracy, human rights and rule of law can apply to be a member of the EU. That does not mean that we have to accept every country. But it would also be wrong to close the door forever by drawing a line in a map that forever sets the borders of Europe. (AB Haber 2006)

Similarly, in MEP Emma Bonino's view,

> I believe that the identity of the European Project consists in its being a political project and not a geographical project or a religious one …I believe instead that our identity is represented by the last fifty years, in

---

11 As Kylstad, among others, has noted (2010: 6), these are certainly not features which have always characterised Europe; Europe's history of feudalism, Communism, Fascism and the lack of universal suffrage until the twentieth century is enough to prove this. Instead, these ideas represent an idea of Europe as it ought to be rather than a shared history.

which we have tried and to some extent succeeded in bringing about the rule of law, the separation of powers and the secularisation of our institutions, as well as the protection of human and political rights as an essential part of human development. (European Parliament 2004)

This view of the EU's identity and the consequent attitude towards enlargement can also be seen in the discourse of many individual member states. As Schmidt points out:

> Many supporters of enlargement, including those in the UK, legitimate the argument not so much on grounds of its pragmatic utility and efficiency as of the rights-based post-national union. They fear that setting borders will in fact destroy what the EU has achieved in enlargement after enlargement, which has been to ensure the democratization of its expanding borders through its extremely strong 'power of attraction'. (Schmidt 2009: 12)

In this view, Turkey, regardless of its religion and culture or even of its potential benefit to the EU and its member states, should be offered membership on condition that it fulfills the political criteria. According to former UK prime minister Tony Blair, for instance, Turkish accession would prove that the EU is 'committed not just in word but in deed to a Europe of diverse races, cultures and religions all bound together by common rules and a sense of human solidarity and mutual respect' (BBC 2004b). Similar arguments are used by other actors who (conditionally) support Turkish accession. Former Spanish prime minister Zapatero, for instance, argues that 'Spain firmly supports Turkey's candidature to enter the EU, provided it meets the necessary requisites' (Rodriguez Zapatero 2009) while, for Javier Solana, 'The developing culture in Europe encompasses all civilizations. We have in the EU millions of citizens or residents who recognise both the values of Europe and those of Islam' (Solana 2002).

Moreover, moral arguments, along with pragmatic ones, are also used by Turkey itself. As Avcı argues, particularly in the period 2002–2005, the EU issue in Turkey was increasingly discussed in rights-based terns. Thus, accession-oriented reforms were justified by political elites in Turkey on the basis of 'the right thing to do' rather than 'who we are' or 'what we get'. Prime Minister Erdoğan, for instance, argued that the EU 'is a union of values' and that he wants to make 'European values Ankara's values' (Avcı 2006: 64–5). This rights-based conception has continued since 2005, despite the decline in Turkish public support for EU accession and of the increasing 'reform-fatigue' in the government. Erdoğan, for instance, argued in 2007 that 'Turkey's membership of the EU will demonstrate that different cultures with varying traditions can accommodate globally recognised values and principles' (Marbeyed 2007). Similarly, in his view, there is no contradiction between Islam and democracy; rather Turkey is a country where 'the cultures of Islam and democracy have merged together' (Castle 2004). In this discourse, then, the EU is portrayed as a rights based union open to any country (including Turkey) which adheres to the 'universal values'which, in this view, underpin the EU integration project.

A strong argument in favour of Turkish accession has been that EU membership will lead to greater democracy and human rights protection and strengthen the rule of law in Turkey (Diez 2011: 163). Moreover, rights-based discourse in favour of Turkey's accession argues that a Turkey firmly anchored within the EU and which fully respects the 'universal values' on which it is constructed will be an example to other Muslim societies and will prove that civilization is indeed available to all, regardless of religious and cultural background. This argument also overlaps with pragmatic arguments in that they often also allude to Turkey's importance in contributing to European security by avoiding a 'clash of civilizations'. In this case, as Kalypso Nicolaidis points out (2003), Turkish membership of the EU would be the most powerful signal yet that the EU is a normative global power which is able to include a Muslim country as its largest member state. As Commissioner Olli Rehn argues, for instance;

> In my view, we are not doomed to an eternal conflict between the West and the Muslim world. As we used both containment and co-operation to win the Cold War, we should today show resolve against Islamic fundamentalism and firmly contain all kinds of terrorism, while continuing to build bridges with Islam and respect universal democratic values. Turkey plays a key role in this. (Rehn 2008)

In this argument, then, there is no fundamental contradiction between Islam and Western or European values. According to former Enlargement Commissioner Günther Verheugen, Turkey's accession to the EU would provide 'living proof that it is perfectly possible for such a country to share our values. One of the great questions of the twenty-first century will be how we shape the relationship between the West and the Islamic world. Turkey has a key role to play here' (European Parliament 2003).

In 1999 Gerhard Schroeder argued that Turkish membership of the EU would 'initiate a process of accommodation between Western Enlightenment and non-radical Islam (cited in Öner 2011: 138), while according to a text by a group of French intellectuals pleading in favour of Turkish accession Turkey embodies 'a compromise between secularism and Islam' (Morin et al. 2004). The Independent Commission on Turkey states that 'Turkish membership would further give evidence of the compatibility of Islam and democracy' (2004: 7). Similarly, in the view of Spanish Socialist party politician José Ramon Villanueva Herrero, for instance;

> The values of democracy, human rights, fundamental freedoms, the rule of law, pluralism, justice, non-discrimination and tolerance can also be applied in a modern and secular country with a Muslim population, as is the case of Turkey. In this way the grim vision of the clash of civilizations preached by the prophets of doom will disappear like a bad dream as, with the EU offering freedoms and a better standard of living to Turkey, it will become an example of freedom

and progress for the rest of the Middle East which can be followed by other countries. (Villanueva Herrero 2009)

However, as Tocci notes, while such arguments about Turkish accession preventing a 'clash of civilizations', or Turkey's acting as a 'bridge between civilizations' or participating in an 'alliance' or 'dialogue' between civilizations appear to be inclusionary, they are, in fact 'based on precisely the same mental categories, the same form of othering as negative arguments shunning Turkey in term of its identity' (Tocci 2011: 100). The following quote from Bruno Gollnicht, an extreme right-wing MEP, gives an idea of just how easily the 'bridge' metaphor can become exclusionary;

> We consider Turkey as a bridge between Europe and Asia, but not as a European country. We want the EU to remain purely European. But this has nothing to do with being enemies of Turkey, just as we do not have anything against Morocco, Argentina or Canada, which are not EU members (cited in Bogdani 2011: 96).

These views are not confined to the extreme right, as the following quote from Angela Merkel demonstrates; 'a bridge ... should never belong totally to one side. Turkey can fulfill its function as a bridge between Asia and Europe much better if it does not become a member of the EU' (cited in Tocci 2011: 86).

The issue of fairness has also been an important one in rights-based discourse on Turkish accession. It is often argued by proponents of eventual full membership for Turkey that it would be unfair to offer Turkey anything less than full membership at this stage. In other words, the EU should act according to the principle of *pacta sunt servanda*. While, in international law, the principle of *pacta sunt servanda* only applies to treaties as such, Diez stresses that an institution such as the EU, which considers itself exemplary in its conduct in international politics, is certainly obliged to keep its promises (Diez 2011: 161).

Turkish discourse in particular has emphasised the unfairness and arbitrariness of the 'privileged partnership' proposed by the EPP as a substitute for Turkish full membership; in this case it is the EU that is accused of not playing by the rules. Erdoğan, for instance, who is an ex-footballer, commented that '[privileged partnership] is just as strange as someone changing the penalty rules in a football match' (*Spiegel* 2010). In a similar vein, Turkey's EU envoy Egemen Bağış has argued that it is wrong to single out Turkey for 'privileged partnership' when the other member states would never accept such an agreement for themselves. As Bağış points out, 'It is an insult because it does not exist. If some of the member states give up full membership and become privileged partners then maybe we can start to discuss it, but it is immoral to offer Turkey privileged partnership' (Karabat 2010).

In this view, then, an EU which rejected full membership for Turkey in spite of its fulfilling the accession criteria would, according to Turkish discourse, be 'a Christian club'. Here, then, Turkey is rejecting the value-based vision of an EU based on 'Judeo-Christian values' or on 'European civilization' in Huntingtonian terms proposed by the right in many EU member states. Erdoğan pointed out in 2004, for instance, that a rejection of Turkey would imply that 'the West is not ready to integrate with the people who do not share the same faith with them' (Erdoğan 2004). Here, then, it is Turkey's Western opponents who are accused of not living up to common standards of civilization.

The privileged partnership idea has also been rejected by supporters of Turkey's eventual accession within the EU. Olli Rehn, for instance, observes that Turkey may already be considered a privileged partner of the EU; 'There is a customs union for trade and economy. The political dialogue is deepening. Turkey is part of the EU's crisis management operations in the Balkans. In other words, some would say this already represents a privileged partnership' (Euractiv 2005).

However, the need to comply with these conditions also, of course, represents a constraint even for Turkey's most fervent supporters, just as it does for other candidate countries.[12] Having said this, a norms-based approach essentially represents an inclusive rather than an exclusive identity construction so, in this view, it is perfectly possible for Turkey to become included in the EU once it has fulfilled these conditions, but not before. In an interview of British Conservative MEPs and/candidates regarding Turkey's accession, for instance, while most of the respondents stated pragmatic reasons in favour of Turkey's accession, 'rights-based' arguments were used most often when arguing that Turkey's accession should not be rushed into (Conservative Party 2008).

Thus, in spite of the rapid pace of reform in Turkey, particularly from 2002–2005, criticism of Turkey's record in democracy, human rights and minority rights has continued by those who favour Turkey's eventual accession as well as by supporters of a 'privileged partnership' for Turkey. In the context of the EP, Levin notes that, in the Turkish case in particular, there is a profound significance attached to the political criteria and to the perceived need to carefully control whether Turkey actually abides by these in practice (Levin 2011: 193–4).

The main criticisms in this respect relate to fundamental freedoms and human rights (Bogdani 2011: 27–8), specifically the protection of the rights of women, ethnic and religious minorities (Minkenberg et al. 2012: 139). As Commission President Durão-Barroso argued in 2008;

> We all know that a lot remains to be done for Turkey to comply fully with European standards. Freedom of expression remains an area in which reforms are overdue. This concerns, amongst other legal provisions, article 301 of the Criminal Code. On the basis of this article, hundreds of cases have been brought

---

12   However, as Diez notes, in the case of the accession of Greece, Portugal and Spain as well as that the CEECs, the lack of their fulfillment of human rights and other political criteria for accession was used as an argument *in favour* of their accession to the EU. In this way, it was argued, the domestic human rights regime would be strengthened by placing it in the framework of EU law (Diez 2007: 2).

against Turkish citizens expressing non-violent opinions. I could come up with
a long list of issues on which further progress is needed for Turkey. They range
from the creation of an Ombudsman, the reform of the Court of Auditors, to civil-
military relations, judicial reform, the fight against corruption. It also includes
cultural and minority rights, social rights including trade unions, women's and
children's rights. (Durão-Barroso 2008)

The Cyprus issue has also been a motive for criticism of Turkey in this respect.
Greek President Karolos Papoulias, for instance, stated in November 2009 that
he would not support Turkey's accession 'as long as Ankara behaves as an
occupying force in Cyprus' (Müezzinler 2009). However, it has also been argued
that accession negotiations with Turkey should be persevered with, as this would
encourage improvements in these areas. In the context of the imprisonment of
journalists in Turkey, Hélène Flautre, Green MEP and head of the EP's delegation
to Turkey argued that; 'Clearly the most effective way to exert pressure on Turkey
to implement human rights reforms would be to open the negotiating chapter on
fundamental rights (chapter 22) as part of the accession talks … It is short sighted
in the extreme [not to open the chapter]' (Willis 2011).

As will be explored in the next section, however, most elites who are against
Turkish accession, most notably those on the French and German right, use
arguments related to democracy, human and minority rights and the rule of
law in a rather different way in order to reject Turkish full membership. Here,
in a framework reminiscent of Huntington's 'Clash of Civilizations' argument,
norms such as democracy, tolerance, the rule of law and so on are seen as being
culturally determined rather than potentially universal. As Turkey is perceived as
not belonging to 'Western' or 'European' civilization, seen as the origin of these
values, it is argued that it is not fundamentally European, and is thus incapable of
fully accepting and adopting such values.

Ethical-Political Arguments: The EU as a 'Value-Based Community'

Ethical-political arguments imply that a political community should be grounded
on a sense of common identity, or 'we-feeling'. This 'we-feeling' may be based
on a common history or religious tradition (Schmidt 2009: 15). Those who hold
an ethical-political view of the EU, then, view it as a value-based community
underscored by cultural and historical characteristics which serve to draw its
geographical boundaries. From this perspective, enlargement is encouraged only
into spaces which are considered to have a similar cultural heritage: its aim is to
bring together the 'European family'.

As has been discussed above, although the official EU discourse, for instance
that of the Commission, has generally tended to be supportive of Turkey's
accession bid, there is a considerably different tone to that used regarding the
accession of the CEECs. While CEE enlargement was often phrased in terms of

'reuniting' Europe, or 'returning' to the 'European family',[13] discourse regarding Turkey's membership bid has tended to be expressed in terms of a relationship of neighbours rather than brothers. Turkey is frequently described as a 'partner' of the EU rather than a country which, for cultural reasons, forms a 'natural' part of the EU. Thus, in EU discourse about the CEECs' accession a greater sense of its responsibility, or even duty, for supporting democratic and economic reform is expressed, as might be expected towards 'family members', than towards Turkey (Lundgren 2002: 6–10). On this basis, then, it can be argued that the EU holds a more rights-based and pragmatic, and less value-based, view of Turkish accession than that of the CEECs.[14]

However, centre-right politicians and intellectuals in many European countries, including France and Germany, tend to articulate their opposition to Turkey's full membership of the EU in value-based terms, emphasising cultural elements in addition to geography and universal values when defining European identity (Yılmaz 2007) (Szymanski 2007: 34). In this case, then, such discourse stresses Turkey's *inherent* Otherness rather than Otherness on the basis of acquired characteristics. Therefore, while, in the moral view Turkey may be constructed as less-Europe, in ethical-political arguments opposing Turkish accession it is constructed as *non*-Europe.

In addition, it is most notably on the Franco–German right, in addition to the right of many other smaller EU countries, that the specifics of what, in their view, a European identity beyond 'universal values' should consist of have been discussed. In short, while the linguistic and cultural diversity of the EU tends to rule out the development of a 'thick', national-type cultural identity for the EU, the Franco–German right has tended to promote a 'Huntingtonian' type of European identity based on a perceived common religious and historical experience. Thus, particularly for Christian Democrats, Christianity is thought to be an important element of European identity, a concept which appears to share considerable public support in spite of the decrease in the numbers of practicing Christians in Europe. The accession of Poland to the EU in particular has also raised the visibility of the question of Christianity's place in European identity; indeed, Casanova (2006: 67–8) refers to the 'great apostolic assignment' of Catholic Poland in the EU. Pope

---

13   Similar discourse continues to be used in the context of the Western Balkan countries. As European Commission President Durão Barroso argues, 'The reunification of Europe will not be completed without the Western Balkans as part of the European Union' (European Parliament 2011)

14   Even when discourse does refer to Turkey as being part of the 'European family, the use of this metaphor should be examined with caution, as Hülsse points out in his analysis of Klaus Kinkel's discourse on Turkey's EU accession;

> But –one may ask- why is there a need to signal that Turkey belongs to the family? … Someone who does not belong to the family by birth may become a member of the family only through marriage or adoption. Thus the signal given to Turkey makes sense only if Turkey is not considered to be an original family member. (2000: 12)

John Paul II, himself Polish, envisaged that the Polish Church could contribute to the formation of a European identity;

> The Church in Poland … can offer Europe as it grows in unity, her attachment to the faith, her tradition inspired by religious devotion … and certainly many other values on the basis of which Europe can become a reality endowed not only with higher economic standards but also with a profound spiritual life (cited in Risse 2010: 210–11).

Naturally, such discourse tends to exclude Turkey's EU accession on religious and cultural grounds. As Pope Benedict himself, then Cardinal Josef Ratzinger, argued in a 2004 interview;

> Europe is a cultural continent, not a geographical one. It is its culture that gives it a common identity. The roots that have formed it, that have permitted the formation of this continent, are those of Christianity. In this sense, throughout history, Turkey has always represented another continent, in permanent contrast with Europe. There were the wars against the Byzantine Empire, the fall of Constantinople, the Balkan wars, and the threat against Vienna and Austria. (de Ravinel 2004]

On another occasion, he argued that 'Christians and Muslims could be privileged partners', indicating that the Catholic Church would find it difficult to accept that Turkey could be a full member of the EU (cited in Rehn 2007: 146).

However, the importance of Christianity in the discourse of the right-wing elite, in spite of the decline of religious practice among the European population, can best be explained by the importance granted to Christianity in this discourse as a civilizational marker rather than for purely religious reasons. Here, an understanding of Huntington's approach to civilization can help to shed light on value-based arguments against Turkish accession. According to Huntington, there is no single civilization; instead, the world is divided into different civilizations,[15] each of which has a fundamentally different outlook, and different values resulting from the specificities of its religious foundation and historical development. In this way, then, a civilization is 'a culture writ large' (Huntington 1997: 41). Thus, in his view, the belief in the universality of the West's values and political systems is naive. Instead, each civilization has its own, unique values which may not be compatible with those of the West;[16]

---

15   According to Huntington, the major civilizations are Western, Latin American, Orthodox, Islamic, Sinic, Hindu, Japanese, and possibly African (Huntington, 1997: 26–7). Israel is considered a unique state with its own civilization, although this is extremely similar to the West (1997: 48). Ethiopia and Haiti are 'lone' countries in Huntington's view (1997: 136–7).

16   For İnalcık, for instance, Huntington's theory, which clearly rests on a division of the rational West from the religious East (including Turkey), and which sees Western

> The people of different civilizations have different views on the relations between God and man, the individual and the group, the citizen and state, parents and children, husband and wife, as well as differing views of the relative importance of rights and responsibilities, liberty and authority, equality and hierarchy. These differences are the products of centuries. They will not soon disappear. (Huntington 1993: 3)

Thus, so-called 'universal values' such as representative democracy, the rule of law or secularism are seen as resulting specifically from the European experience, notably the influence of classical culture (particularly Roman law) and 'Christian values', as well as the Renaissance, Reformation and Enlightenment (Huntington 1997: 69). Importantly, this implies that these values cannot easily be transferred to other 'civilizations' which have their own systems of values. Thus, according to Huntington, 'Western civilization' is informed by 'classical civilization', which, for him, includes Greek philosophy and rationalism, Roman law, Latin and Christianity (1997: 69). However, he also adds several features which are expressly linked to democracy and the rule of law;

- The separation of temporal and spiritual authority, also seen in Hindu civilization. Huntington argues that 'In Islam, God is Caesar; in China and Japan, Caesar is God, in Orthodoxy, God is Caesar's junior partner'.
- Representative bodies including parliaments, estates and other institutions which eventually evolved into the institutions of modern democracy.
- The rule of law, inherited from the Romans and developed by medieval thinkers, which eventually laid the basis for constitutionalism and the protection of human rights (1997: 69–72).

Importantly, in Huntington's view, Turkey is a 'torn country' whose leaders have tried to 'shift' its civilization from Islamic to Western civilization;[17] given his essentialist conception of civilizational identity, this is a difficult if not impossible task. Huntington argues that this could only be achieved if the national elite, national public opinion and dominant elements in the host society are staunchly supportive of the change in civilizational identity. However, in his view these conditions are not adequately fulfilled in the case of Turkey (1997: 141–9).

In this context, Yılmaz describes the role of Christianity in right wing discourse on European identity as an 'extinguished volcano'; thus Christianity is viewed not as a belief system but as a cultural marker (2007: 298). Similarly, Yeğenoğlu argues that 'the religious elements [in discourse] might not appear as religious *per se,* but displaced to and articulated with issues of culture and identity' (2006: 247).

---

superiority as natural and necessary, is no more than a development of a European discourse that has been developing since Montesquieu (2010: 227).

17 According to Huntington, Mexico and Australia are also examples of 'torn countries' (1997: 149–54).

Thus, in contemporary right-wing discourse, Christian heritage is viewed as the basis for some secular European values including the separation of religion and the state, the idea of the natural rights of man and even the culture of capitalism; in this way, 'this apparently new identity is in fact a displaced re-identification by reinvoking older values and ideals in secularised discourses' (Yeğenoğlu 2006: 254). In this view, conversion to Christianity is perceived as insufficient to acquire 'Judeo-Christian values', as the convert 'does not carry the Christian heritage in his or her "cultural genes"' (Yılmaz 2007: 298).[18] Shakman Hurd supports this analysis, particularly regarding secularism;

> Secularisation, in this view, is the realisation of a Western religious tradition. Religion is part of the moral basis of Western civilisation. A significant implication of this authoritative discourse is that the secularist separation of religion from politics, and the democratic settlement of which it is a part, is perceived as a unique Western achievement that is superior to its non-Western rivals ... The potential for secularisation is tied to a particular cultural identity, civilisational history and geographic location ... .(Shakman Hurd 2006: 409–10)

In particular, Islam is 'not treated as one religion among others' (Yeğenoğlu 2006: 251). Above all, Islam is seen as all-pervasive, encroaching on all aspects of Muslims' lives. As Bernard Lewis explains, for instance,

> Islam is not a location; it is a religion. But for the Muslims the word 'religion' does not have the same connotation that the word 'religion' has for Christians or even had for medieval Christians... For Muslims, Islam is not merely a system of belief and worship ... It is rather the whole of life, and its rules include civil, criminal,and even what we would call constitutional law. (Lewis 1993: 3–4)

Such discourse, then, reflects the 'difference within sameness' of history (Yeğenoğlu 2006: 247); old discourses such as the medieval 'clash' between Christendom and Islam, as well as older stereotypes of the 'civilized', free West and the 'barbarous' East, are rearticulated in twenty-first century terms. As Yeğenoğlu, for instance, notes, the Turkish bid for membership of the EU has 'exacerbated the deep-seated Orientalist anxieties about Islam among the liberal and extreme right in Europe'; in this way, then, Islam continues to be portrayed as the 'constitutive outside' of Europe (Yeğenoğlu 2006: 247).

While such discourse is more common among right wing politicians, it can also be found on the left in France, for instance. As former French Prime Minister Jean Marie Raffarin argued in 2004; 'We are not doubting the good faith of Mr. Erdoğan, but to what extent can today or tomorrow's government make Turkish

---

18   Diez notes that, given its exclusionary nature, the 'Christian club' argument is, ironically, fundamentally un-Christian as it undermines the Christian values of openness and responsibility to others (2011: 163).

society embrace Europe's human rights values? Do we want the river of Islam to enter the riverbed of secularism?' (Neumayer 2004).

From this point of view, then, the accession to the EU of a country like Turkey with a majority Muslim population is clearly seen as highly problematic. Speaking in 1997, Helmut Kohl succinctly pointed out that the EU was a 'civilizational project' in which 'Turkey has no place' (Nuttall and Traynor 1997). Similarly, in a 2002 interview, former French President and President of the European Constitutional Convention Valéry Giscard d'Estaing argued that Turkey should not be allowed full membership of the EU as it 'has a different culture, a different approach, a different way of life' (Leparmentier and Zecchini 2002). Giscard d'Estaing expanded on this idea of how Turkey did not fit into 'European civilization' as the European Convention attempted to define it;

> The European Convention sought a clearer definition of the foundations of this entity, which include the cultural contributions of ancient Greece and Rome, the religious heritage pervading European life, the creative enthusiasms of the Renaissance, the philosophy of the Age of the Enlightenment and the contributions of rational and scientific thought. Turkey shares none of these.
> (Giscard d'Estaing 2004)

As former Belgian prime minister and permanent President of the European Council Herman van Rompuy argues; 'The universal values which are in force in Europe, and which are also fundamental values of Christianity, will lose vigour with the entry of a large Islamic country such as Turkey' (Cronin 2010). Similarly, Angela Merkel argues that 'democracy is unthinkable without Christian values' (cited in Kösebalaban 2007: 102). Surveys among the European public tend to support a negative view of Islam, and indicate that many Europeans view Islam as being incompatible with so-called 'universal' values (Bardakoğlu 2008: 113) (Transatlantic Trends 2006).

Moreover, most notably but not exclusively in Franco–German right-wing discourse, Turkish full membership is construed as representing the 'death' of European integration as it would lead to the dissolution of European cultural/civilizational identity, thus undermining the EU's strength as a political actor. Giscard d'Estaing famously argued in 2002 that Turkish accession would mean 'the end of the European Union' (Leparmentier and Zecchini 2002), while Dutch politician and former Commissioner Frits Bolkestein argued that the EU would 'implode' if Turkey became a member (Evans-Pritchard 2004). In a somewhat milder tone, meanwhile, German chancellor Angela Merkel put forward that 'A Europe with Turkey as a fully-fledged member won't be a Europe that is fully integrated' (Williamson 2004).

This value-based construction of EU identity also contains an 'out group from within'; in this case Muslim immigrants from North Africa and Turkey (Risse 2010: 54) who are frequently invoked by the right in its discourse on the Turkish membership bid. Thus, in right-wing discourse, especially that of the extreme right, it is argued that Turkish accession would open the floodgates to let other 'undesirables' into the EU. Giscard d'Estaing accused those of supporting Turkish accession as being 'the adversaries of the European Union' as admitting Turkey would prompt demands for membership from North African and Middle Eastern countries, starting with Morocco (Leparmentier and Zecchini 2002). As François Bayrou, leader of the French centre-right party UDF, argued in 2002: 'No to a Europe which would include, in addition to Turkey 'the Mahgreb, the Federation of Russia, tomorrow Israel and why not Senegal' (Cited in and translated by Tekin 2008: 747).

Such views have also been put forward by former French President Nicolas Sarkozy, who points out that, although he does not consider the EU to be a future superstate, Europeans would close the doors to Turkey's full membership as they were 'a Europe of nations exercising their sovereignty and decided to stay themselves' (2007a). In this context, he argued that;

> Turkey is not a European country, and as such she does not have a place inside the European Union. A Europe without borders would be the death of the great idea of political Europe. A Europe without borders is to condemn her to become a sub-region of the United Nations. I simply do not accept it. (Sarkozy 2007a)

His reasons for viewing Turkey as a potential threat to European identity were put forward in more detail during his 2007 election campaign and in his book *Testimony*:

> Turkey's entry would kill the very idea of European integration. Turkey's entry would turn Europe into a free trade zone with a competition policy. It would permanently bury the goal of the EU as a global power, of common policies, and of European democracy. It would be a fatal blow to the very notion of European identity. (Sarkozy 2007b: 189)

Such views can also be seen on the German right. As EPP MEP Hans Gert Poettering argued in 2004, Turkey's accession 'might prove fatal and Europeans might lose their identity, that it might be detrimental to the sense of being 'us' on which solidarity in the European Union is founded' (cited in Soler i Lecha 2005: 14). These concerns are often linked to the fear of mass migration from Turkey and to the question of the EU's own large Muslim population, an issue that has also been securitised[19] (Huysmans 2000). As Sarkozy argues; 'We have a problem of integration of Muslims that raises the issue of Islam in Europe. To say it is not

---

19   In fact, the accession of Turkey would increase the Muslim element of the total EU population from 3 per cent to 20 per cent. However, of course, the vast majority of these would continue to be based in Turkey so there would be little effect on the visibility of Muslims in the current member states (Redmond 2007: 313).

a problem is to hide from reality. If you let one hundred million Turkish Muslims come in, what will come of it?' (cited in BBC 2006b).

Other right-wing discourse, particularly (but not exclusively) on the extreme right, tends to imply more directly that the EU (and therefore Europe) would be in danger of becoming a 'Eurabia' with Turkish accession. As Carr notes, the Eurabia discourse depicts Europe as a 'doomed continent, on the brink of cultural extinction in the face of a relentless and co-ordinated campaign of Islamicisation' (2006: 2).[20] Thus, the term Eurabia describes the emergence of a new 'Islamicized' European civilization in thrall to the Arab world (Carr 2006: 2). While it is often argued that Muslim immigration to Europe provides the greatest threat, Turkey's accession has also been depicted in these terms. Former EU Commissioner Frits Bolkestein, for instance, argued in 2004 that if Turkey entered the EU Europe risked becoming predominantly Islamic(Evans-Pritchard 2004).

Extreme nationalist discourse also tends to hark back more clearly to older stereotypes of 'the Turk' as barbaric or cruel and bloodthirsty. Levin notes how the comments of a Slovak MEP in a 2010 EP debate, who argued that [in Turkey] 'Fathers still sell their daughters or swap them for cattle' are strangely reminiscent of Martin Luther's comment that 'in Turkey women are held immeasurably cheap and are despised; they are bought and sold like cattle' (cited in Levin 2011: 190). Austrian discourse, particularly that of the media, has securitised Turkey's EU accession in even more striking terms, by alluding to the Ottoman siege of Vienna in 1683, and Kösebalaban argues that, over four centuries later, it is still the primary explanation for Austria's exceptionally strong opposition to Turkey's full membership of the EU (Kösebalaban 2007: 99). Examples of this discourse can even be found in the relatively liberal Austrian press, such as the weekly newsmagazine *Profile,* which, in a 2004 article headlined 'Turks at the Gates of Vienna', argued that Turkish demands for the opening of accession negotiations were 'not so much a risk as a danger' (Traynor 2004).

Such arguments are not confined to Austria, however; Dutch former Commissioner Frits Bolkestein argued that Turkey's accession to the EU would mean that the efforts of the German, Austrian and Polish troops that resisted the Ottoman Turks' siege of Vienna in 1683 would be in vain (Gow and MacAskill 2004). Dutch right wing populist leader Geert Wilders also argued in a 2009 visit to Italy that;

> The first Islamic invasion of Europe was stopped at Poitiers in 732. The second Islamic invasion was halted at the gates of Vienna in 1683. Now we have to stop the current – stealth- Islamic invasion. Ladies and gentlemen, once Islam conquered Constantinople, now it wants to conquer Rome. We have to stop

---

20   One of the main inspirations for the Eurabia discourse has been an Egyptian-born British citizen known by the pseudonym Bat Ye'or (daughter of the Nile). The discourse has since been popularised by, among others, the veteran Italian journalist Oriana Fallaci (Carr 2006: 5).

the Islamisation of Europe, because if we don't, Europe will become Eurabia.
(Underhill 2009)

At their most extreme, such arguments go beyond culture and religion to embrace
pseudoscientific theories of race and intelligence. In this view, expounded for
instance by Thilo Sarrazin, a former German senator and board member of the
Bundesbank, Muslim immigrants are genetically prone to lower intelligence and
productivity (Saz 2009: 480).

Thus, both on the extreme and centre right, proponents of these views tend
to be in favour of offering Turkey a 'privileged partnership' instead of eventual
full membership. This, as has been noted, is the official position of the EPP, the
largest group in the EP (Casanova 2006: 235). In addition to the Franco–German
right, prominent politicians such as Luxembourg's Prime Minister Jean-Claude
Juncker and Austrian Prime Minister Wolfgang Schüssel have been among the
proponents of a 'privileged partnership' rather than full membership for Turkey
(Kösebalaban 2007: 103).[21]

Moreover, EU documents regarding Turkey's accession demonstrate some
concessions to those who put forward such views. The Negotiation Framework
adopted by the European Council in October 2005 reflects these concerns,
emphasising the 'open-ended' nature of the negotiations. The Negotiation
Framework states that 'while having full regard to all Copenhagen criteria,
including the absorption capacity of the Union, if Turkey is not in a position to
assume in full all the obligations of membership it must be ensured that Turkey
is fully anchored in the European structures through the strongest possible bond'.
Therefore, the possibility of alternative outcomes, such as a 'privileged partnership'
is suggested in the document, and the EU's absorption capacity is emphasised
(Duyulmuş 2008: 28). This differs not only from the Negotiation Frameworks of
the countries which acceded to the EU in 2004 and 2007, but also from that of
Croatia, which was issued on the same date as Turkey's (Aydın 2006: 7–8).

In contrast, however, in relatively unusual cases ethical/political arguments
have been used in support of Turkish accession. These arguments focus on
the multicultural roots of European, and therefore Western, civilization, and
also on the importance of Anatolia and Constantinople in the development of
European culture. In this view, European civilization descends from a broader

---

21   Kösebalaban (2007: 105–6) notes that the concept of a privileged partnership is
not new; in fact it has its roots in eighteenth century political thinking. In order to tackle
the problem of Islam surrounding Europe, French social philosopher Charles-Irene Castel
de Saint Pierre suggested a defensive partnership with Europe's Mediterranean Muslim
neighbours, including the Ottomans. The Muslims, while being required to contribute
troops and finance to the union would not take part in decision-making processes. In de-
Saint-Pierre's view, the proposed partnership would also be advantageous for Europe in
that it would imply opening the borders of neighbouring Muslim states to unrestricted
commercial activity.

Mediterranean cultural area, and is formed by 'interaction, cross-fertilisation, cultural borrowing and diffusions' (Delanty and Rumford 2005: 38). Similarly, Amin (1989: 10–11) argues that prior to the Renaissance Europe 'belonged to a regional tributary system that included Europeans and Arabs, Christians and Muslims'. This view of European civilization is succinctly defined by Delanty and Rumford as follows (2005: 38);

> The historical roots of this Western civilisation – Athens, Rome and Jerusalem – were not European in the Western sense of the term European. Classical antiquity and origins of Christianity were Mediterranean … Western civilisation is based on a history that was never entirely European, but became Europe in a process of borrowing, translation and diffusion. The major examples of this are Hellinisation, Romanisation and the subsequent adoption of the Roman heritage by Christianity, the Renaissance and scientific revolution and age of discovery, and exploration and imperialism which led to the diffusion in Europe of non-Western inventions and marked 'the rise of the West'.

In this view, too, called *civilizational constellations*, while civilizations are considered formations of the *longue durée*, they are open to significant internal change and are more adaptable to new circumstances than Huntington's civilizations. Each civilization is a *constellation* of societies, in that it is a juxtaposed rather than fixed cluster of changing elements; in this context a civilization thus constitutes a unity in difference. Similarly, civilizations may also cluster together; a civilizational constellation is a configuration of civilizations (Delanty and Rumford 2005: 37).

On this basis, Delanty argues that Europe is not exclusively constituted by a familiar teleology of Latin Christendom, Renaissance, Reformation, Enlightenment and modernity (2003: 15), but is in fact made up of a tripartite set of civilizational constellations; the Occidental Christian constellation, the Byzantine/Slavic/Eurasian constellation and the Ottoman Islamic constellation (Delanty 2003: 16). In this way, then, Europe can be defined in civilizational terms without the associated Western-centric notions and assumptions. As Delanty and Rumford point out, 'the cultural diversity of Europe is more than the diversity of its nations' (Delanty and Rumford 2005: 36–40). Thus, the diversity of contemporary European experiences is a consequence of its multi-civilizational heritage, which has produced 'different traditions of modernity, experienced as Western capitalism/liberalism, Communism and statism, exemplified by Turkey' (Rumford and Turunç 2011: 139).

Such arguments, although apparently far less widespread than pragmatic and/or moral arguments in favour of Turkish inclusion in the EU, have been used by supporters of Turkey's eventual accession. As Aksoy points out, some members of the former British Labour Cabinet have stressed the long interaction and cultural links between the Judeo-Christian and Islamic traditions, and the values shared between them (2009: 489). Dennis MacShane, former Labour Minister for Europe, for instance, has stressed the medieval Islamic world's contribution to the humanities, sciences and arts, and its role as a shelter for the persecuted minorities of Europe. Thus, in his view, the EU's encouragement of Turkey's accession process would be a way both of recognising the Islamic influence on Europe's cultural heritage and of supporting the development of democracy in a predominantly Muslim nation (MacShane 2002). Such discourse has also been noted among political actors in the CEECs. Polish president Kaczinski, for instance, noted in 2007 that 'For ages, the history of European nations and Turkey were intertwined' (Çakır and Gergelova 2010: 123), while some members of the Czech Civic Democratic Party (ODS) have also argued that Islam played an important role in European history and culture (Çakır and Gergelova 2010: 122–3).

The Independent Commission on Turkey has also stressed cultural arguments for including Turkey in the EU. Instead of exploring the historical links between Islam and European civilization, these arguments focus more specifically on Turkey as heir to Byzantium, Christianity and classical civilization via the Ottoman Empire.According to this argument, then, Turkey is intimately intertwined with European cultural heritage,[22] in a way that other Muslim countries in North Africa and the Middle East are not (2004: 15). In this view, then, the Ottoman Turks:

> became heirs not only to the Byzantine and the Eastern Roman Empire, but also to a rich Greco-Latin and Judeo-Christian culture in Anatolia. Names such as the 'father of history', Herodotus of Halicarnassus; Aesop, who inspired La Fontaine's fables; Lucullus, the patron of gourmets; Saint Nicholas, bishop of Myra and ancestor of our Father Christmas; and Croesus, who became the richest man of his time, are connected with this region, as are places like Troy, Pergamon, Ephesus, and Mount Ararat where Noah's Ark came to rest. Saint Peter preached to the first Christian community in Antioch. Tarsus was the birthplace of Saint Paul, who made his first missionary journey to Anatolia, extending Christianity beyond the limits of Judaism and thereby laying the foundations of a worldwide religion. All this reminds us that the region which today is the heart of Turkey was one of the cradles of European civilization. (2004: 4)

Conclusion

In conclusion, an examination of elite discourse across Europe reveals that the apparent consensus that was reached on CEE enlargement no longer exists in the face of the question of Turkey's accession. Indeed, there is a split between those (potentially) in favour of Turkish accession provided that Turkey fulfills the political criteria for accession and those who favour a more limited 'privileged partnership'.

---

22   This argument is subtly different from the 'bridge between civilizations' one, which implies a connection between essentially foreign civilizations. By contrast, the above arguments stress the culturally European nature of Turkey.

This division is particularly important in that it is indicative of a fundamental difference in ideal visions of the EU. The first vision is close to that of a rights-based union, where legitimacy ultimately rests on the shared adherence to 'universal' values. According to this view of the EU, Turkey is welcome to join providing it is deemed to adequately adhere to those values. Indeed, Turkey is often held up as a positive example for other Muslim countries, and it is frequently argued that a Turkey firmly anchored within the EU could even prevent a 'clash of civilizations', thus disproving the Huntingtonian thesis that non-Western civilizations, in particular 'Islam', are incapable of wholeheartedly adopting Western values. Such rights-based arguments in favour of Turkish accession are often backed up with pragmatic arguments that Turkish accession would boost the crisis-ridden EU's economic and geopolitical weight, thus supporting a 'normative-power Europe'.

However, it is important to note that this discourse, inclusive as it may be, still often implies an Othering of Turkey. In this case, Turkey is considered an 'inferior', although not necessarily threatening, Other; it is 'less Europe' although it is not 'non-Europe'. In other words, Turkey is depicted as the barbarian struggling along the long path towards the enlightenment of Western civilization. Once it gets there, it is hoped, it will itself become a beacon of hope for even more Eastern (and thus supposedly benighted) peoples. As has been emphasised in Chapter 2, the dichotomy between the enlightened West and despotic East is an old one, associated with the Enlightenment, and with even more ancient roots in classical Greece.

The perceived opposition between an enlightened West and barbaric Muslim East is both more overtly stated and more exclusive in the main competing discourse, mostly associated with the countries of 'core Europe' and with the political right. In this discourse, the EU comes across more as a value-based union with a strong identity and fixed borders. Particularly in the context of Turkish accession, Christianity has been framed as an important marker of this European identity, along with other features including the influence of classical civilizations, the Renaissance and the Enlightenment. This conception of 'European civilization' bears a close resemblance to Huntington's 'Western Civilization', both in its defining features and in its rigidity. In both cases, these historical, religious and cultural features are seen as a prerequisite for the development of values such as democracy, respect for human and minority rights and the rule of law. Importantly, moreover, it is seen as close to impossible for a country historically belonging to another civilization ('Islamic' in the case of Turkey) to become truly European/Western.

In this view, Turkish full membership of the EU is rejected as it is seen as non-European, and thus unable to adhere to the values on which the EU is based because of its religious and cultural heritage. Therefore, in this value-based discourse, Turkish accession would mean the demise of the EU, at least in its current form; while, for those on the centre-right of the political spectrum, the EU would be diluted into just another international organisation, for the far-right it would become a 'Eurabia'.

Chapter 5

The Application of Foreign Policy Discourse Analysis to British, French and Turkish Discourse on Turkish Accession to the EU

An Overview of Foreign Policy Discourse Analysis

This chapter uses Foreign Policy Discourse Analysis (FPDA), developed by authors including Wæver (2002, 2005] and Larsen [1997, 1999] on the basis of Foucault's approach to discourse, in order to analyse the discourse of individual member states regarding Turkey's accession to the EU. While, optimally, an analysis of all the member states plus Turkey would be carried out, for reasons of space the analysis is limited to UK discourse which has a broadly supportive stance towards Turkish accession at elite level, to French discourse, which has generally been much more sceptical, and finally to Turkish discourse.

Foreign Policy Discourse Analysis

For Foucault, discourses organise knowledge systematically and delimit what can be said and what cannot; the aim of discourse analysis based on Foucault is, therefore, to look for these rules (Wæver 2002: 29).Thus, discourse analysis 'does not try to get to the thoughts and motives of the actors, their hidden motives or secret plans' (Wæver 2002: 26); instead 'our investigation into meaning has to take place at the level of the language' (Larsen 1997: 13). Analysis of political discourse can therefore be insightful in that, whatever their ulterior motives, policy makers must justify their policies in terms of how they resonate with the state's vision of itself (Wæver 2002: 29).

Thus, instead of being simply 'haphazard acts', political speeches are dependent on the basic conceptual logic available in a society. On this basis, certain basic codes exist in a particular political culture, and interests are constructed and transformed into policies formed on the basis of these codes. Moreover, discursive practice not only depends on but also reproduces (or reformulates) the discursive system (Wæver 2002: 29–31).

In Foucault's view, then, discourse is the precondition for statements in that it defines which speech acts are allowed and prohibited. As Foucault argues;

> I am supposing that in every society the production of discourse is at once
> controlled, selected, organised and redistributed according to a certain number
> of procedures, whose role is to avert its powers and its dangers, to cope with
> chance events, to evade its ponderous, awesome materiality. In a society such as
> our own we all know the rules of exclusion. The most obvious and familiar of
> these concerns what is prohibited. (1972: 216)

Following Foucault, therefore, discourse is seen as forming a system which is made up of a layered constellation of key concepts. They are related in a hierarchical way, 'like a tree with roots, trunks and branches'. The roots here represent the central concepts from which all the other concepts are derived. While discourses can change, then, they rarely do so radically; a change in discourse is rarely a complete change *of* discourse. While foreign policies may change, for instance, this does not necessarily imply that the underlying national discourse has changed (Larsen 1997: 17).

Discourses do not *a priori* have clear borders beyond which they do not apply (Larsen 1997: 24). However, according to FPDA, the concepts of nation and state, themselves constructed discursively, have an important effect on a country's foreign policy as they define national identity and have a constraining effect on which discourses are possible at the level of foreign policy, including those concerning European integration (Larsen 1999: 454). The primary focus of FPDA, then, is the nation state; it is therefore possible to talk about, for instance, a 'British', 'French' or 'German' discourse in this field. An advantage of FPDA is that it can help to shed light on the way that views may be shared across political parties (Larsen 1999: 455). As Larsen argues;

> When saying that a political discourse is present in the foreign political domestic
> environment of a given state, the implication is that we are dealing with a
> constraint that shapes the foreign policy of this state, a kind of framework within
> which the foreign policy of a particular country can take place. (Larsen 1997: 21)

This does not mean that there cannot be rival national discourses within a country. These rival discourses, however, do not necessarily contradict each other at every level; they may only differ in a single point, while agreeing at a deeper level (Larsen 1997: 25). Thus, even if a statement is apparently in 'opposition' or even 'marginalized' *vis à vis* the dominant discourse it is likely to share codes at a deeper level (Wæver 2002: 31). While the British Labour party appears to pursue a more 'Euro-friendly' policy towards the EU than the Conservative party, for instance, it does not automatically follow that attitudes towards the EU differ significantly at a more fundamental level.

Regarding EU issues, then, the discourse analysis takes place at three levels. Firstly, the dominant discourse regarding state and nation is examined, including the internal and external dimensions. Here, questions such as the basic conceptual constellation of state and nation, the perceived connection between the two and the attachment to state and nation, as well as the state's projection of itself onto the world are examined. France's first layer, for instance, consists of a fusion of state and nation, while the two remain distinct in the German case. The issue of how and if one can become a member of the nation in question is also dealt with at this level. While French nationality is traditionally open to anyone who is willing to assimilate culturally, for example, the concept of German nationality is closely linked to blood descent, as well as language and culture (Wæver 2002: 33–6).

Secondly, the relational position of the state/nation *vis-a-vis* Europe is examined. Basically, the constellation of state and nation constrains how Europe can be thought of. Here, then, European identity is not considered a substitute for national identity, as each EU member state's national identity includes a vision of Europe (Wæver 2005: 37). This can be likened to the 'marble cake' concept of European identity discussed in Chapter 2. In the French case, for instance, Europe must be approached in a way that does not threaten the interlocking of state and nation, while the room for manoeuvre is greater in the German case (Wæver 2005: 39).

Thus, political discourse should, in its narrative, present a logic of Europe which is compatible with the state/nation construction. Here, very general concepts of the EU are examined, such as whether the EU is primarily constructed as an intergovernmental organisation composed of sovereign states, a single market or a supranational entity (Wæver 2002: 37–8). The three 'ideal' conceptions of the EU, discussed in the previous chapter, may also shed light on this. In this view, the EU may be seen primarily as a simple problem solving entity, as a value-based community underscored by a European 'we-feeling' based on a common cultural identity or, finally, as a rights-based post-national union, based on broader, 'universal' rights such as democracy and human rights.

The third level of analysis focuses on concrete policies pursued by specific groups of actors, particularly political parties, who argue their positions with reference to levels 1 and 2. Thus, actors might contest each other at level 1 by arguing that their opponents do not offer an appropriate construction of state and nation, or at level 2 by arguing that their construction of Europe will pose a threat to the state/nation constellation, or by pointing out that they have fundamentally misunderstood the realities of the European integration project. This, then, is not static; changes in European integration itself provoke adjustments in the political debate; it became much more difficult following the Maastricht Treaty, for instance, to represent the EU as an organisation based on 'normal' interstate co-operation (Wæver 2002: 37–41).

The sources consulted are similar to those used in more traditional foreign policy analysis (Larsen 1997: 29). Regarding the question of the formation of state and nation, however, historical studies using a similar perspective can be drawn on (Waever 2002: 40). Generally, the focus is on the discourse of the political elite rather than the broader national discourse as the aim of the analysis is to discover the structures through which 'one' must talk about Europe rather than to examine the opinions of the general public. Thus, the main sources will be parliamentary debates, speeches by ministers and party manifestoes and position papers. However, in a broader sense, intellectuals, researchers and newspaper editorials also contribute to the national political discourse and these may also be taken into consideration (Waever 2002: 41–2) (Larsen 1997: 29).

Case Study 1: Britain

Concepts of State and Nation in British Discourse

The United Kingdom (UK) is a multinational state in that the English, Irish, Scots and Welsh came together in a process lasting from around 1400–1800 as a result of English conquest and political pressure facilitated by royal unions with Wales and later Scotland. As a result, the UK includes a number of distinct geographical, cultural and political entities: England, Scotland, Wales and Northern Ireland. Thus, there have always been distinct cultural communities or 'indigenous minorities' in Britain, that is social groups that can be distinguished by reference to criteria such as ethnicity, religion or race. In addition to the inhabitants of the 'Celtic fringe', well established social groups in this category have included Jews, whose presence has been attested since the eleventh century, and the Roma. There is also some evidence for Muslim settlement in Britain in Tudor times (Malik 2010: 34–5). It can be argued, then, that Britain has long been multicultural; as Crick notes,'Who are we British? For a long time the UK has been a multicultural state composed of England, Northern Ireland, Scotland and Wales, and also a multicultural society … made up of a diverse range of cultures and identities' (Crick 2003: 10).

Thus, although the British state has traditionally been a unitary one with few federal features, the physical and political unity of Britain did not eliminate cultural diversity (Malik 2010: 34). More recently, following some challenges to this unitary structure, particularly in the 'Celtic fringe' countries (Larsen 1997: 34–5), the devolution carried out by the Labour government in the late 1990s as a result of referenda in Scotland and Wales has modified the unitary nature of the British state to some extent.

There has therefore traditionally been little use of the term 'British nation', although the 'British people' has tended to be used more, as there is no ethnic base for British nationalism. Instead, British nationalism appears to be primarily political in nature. Indeed, the British tend to hold dual identities, such as British and English, British and Scottish and British and Welsh (Delanty and Rumford 2005: 72). In addition, British identity tends to be perceived differently in England on the one hand and in the 'Celtic fringe' on the other. The English have tended to see Britain as England writ large, often in a great power context while in Wales or Scotland a 'cultural' Welsh or Scottish identity co-exists with a British identity (Larsen 1997: 36–7).

The dominant discourse on the creation and development of the English, and later British, state is based on the so-called Whig discourse. In the Whig interpretation of the creation of the English state, a great emphasis is placed on the uniqueness of English, and later British, history. In this discourse, every Englishman is 'born free' and inherits certain inherited liberties as rights. However, the liberties once enjoyed by the Anglo-Saxons were withdrawn following the Norman Conquest. Despite some victories, notably the signing of the Magna Carta, the resistance of the English people to absolute rule and tyranny erupted during the Civil War. Eventually, it was argued, the settlement of 1688, the so-called 'Glorious Revolution', inaugurated a new age of English liberty (Larsen 1997: 38). Moreover, according to Wallace, the Whig interpretation of history is inseparable from the British commitment to a non-interventionist state, an open market and a free international economy (1986: 383).

According to this discourse, the main vehicle for the resistance to absolute power and for harmonising and balancing interests was seen as the English, and later British, Parliament, an institution whose sovereignty was paramount and independence unquestioned, without reference to the British state, people or nation.[1] The monarchy has also played an important role; while Parliament represents internal sovereignty, the monarchy represents external sovereignty, in particular independence from Rome and the Pope and from the European continent since 1066 (Risse 2010: 82).

Thus, in the dominant discourse politics has traditionally been seen as centred on Westminster (Larsen 1997: 39). However, while the British state was a unitary one, at least until the devolution of the late 1990s, cultural variety has traditionally been accepted. When compared to France, for instance, there has been little attempt to create a uniform culture across the UK. It is within this context that the Labour Party, in particular, has been able to champion the idea of a 'multicultural Britain', in which the cultures and religious beliefs both of the indigenous British nations and of immigrants and their descendants should be respected. Using a culinary metaphor for multiculturalism, Labour MP Keith Vaz, himself of Indian origin, argued in 2001 that for many, British identity is 'not just fish and chips, but also sweet and sour pork and chicken tikka masala' (cited in Condor 2006: 13). However, cultural individuality should not conflict with the UK's 'essential values'. As former Labour Prime Minister Tony Blair argues;

> Christians, Jews, Muslims, Hindus, Sikhs and other faiths have a perfect right to their own identity and religion, to practise their faith and to conform to their culture. This is what multicultural, multi-faith Britain is about. That is what is legitimately distinctive … But when it comes to our essential values – belief in democracy, the value of law, tolerance, equal treatment for all, respect for this country and its shared heritage then that is where we come together, it is what we hold in common; it is what gives us the right to call ourselves British. At

---

1   Liberal Party discourse challenged this view of parliamentary sovereignty; for them it was something that 'was flexible and could be adapted to circumstances' (Larsen 1997: 47). In consequence, at the next level of discourse there is much less fear of a European 'superstate' in Liberal, and later Liberal Democrat discourse.

that point no distinctive culture or religion supersedes our duty to be part of an integrated United Kingdom. (Blair 2006)

However, such discourse in fact has much older roots. Much of the rhetoric of British Imperialism also emphasised the advantages of a culturally and racially diverse Empire (Condor 2006: 33). As a 1923 school primer proclaims, 'The British Empire is one of the marvels of the world [...] a dominion composed of widely scattered parts, separated by [...] differences of religion, customs, traditions, race and colour; and yet united under one king, one flag and one empire' (cited in Condor 2006: 34).

Constructions of the EU in British Discourse

Britain has, notoriously, been 'semi-detached' from Europe and is often considered the 'awkward partner' in the EU (George 1994). As Risse points out, in contrast to French or German discourse, the stability of British arguments regarding European integration since the end of World War II is remarkable (Risse 2010: 81). Notable in the dominant British discourse is a rejection of the development of a European 'superstate' which is seen as threatening national sovereignty, identity and democracy, while European economic policies, it is feared, reduce flexibility thereby threatening British competitiveness (Schmidt 2006: 18). The major exception is the Liberal party, which having traditionally had a more federalist outlook, has provided an alternative to the dominant discourse on Europe. This section, then, seeks the influence of the British discourse on state and nation on its attitudes towards Europe, and explores whether there are significant challenges to this Eurosceptic discourse among the British elite.

Britain has historically not seen itself as an 'organic' part of Europe, its self-image in the dominant discourse rather being that of a world power focused on its empire and, later, the Commonwealth. In contrast to the focus of British foreign policy on 'the open sea', the empire and later the Commonwealth, the dominant discourse has therefore tended to downplay the importance of Britain's place in Europe. Since the sixteenth century England tended to view Europe as backward politically and economically, and, in the dominant discourse, there was no sense of belonging 'organically' to Europe (Larsen 1997: 52). Indeed, the terms 'Europe' and 'European' began to be used in the English language to define an outside, even alien entity, and the English began to define themselves in contrast to Europeans (Spiering 2004: 144).

It is thus perhaps not surprising that, post-World War II, Europe has continued to be constructed in the discourse of both Labour and the Conservatives as Britain's Other, albeit a usually friendly Other. As Schmidt argues, the British political elite has, from the very beginning, 'defined EU identity in opposition to national identity' (2012: 174). While the British political elite saw co-operation among the Continental powers as a 'dire necessity', they saw the UK as different in that it could pursue other options, including continuing its association with the Commonwealth and cultivating the 'special relationship' with the USA (Spiering 2004: 137). The following view put forward by the Labour Party in 1950 is indicative:

> Finally, the Labour Party cannot see European unity as an overriding end in itself. Britain is not just a small crowded island off the Western coast of Continental Europe. She is the nerve centre of a world-wide Commonwealth which extends into every continent. In every respect except distance we in Britain are closer to our kinsmen in Australia and New Zealand on the far side of the world, than we are to Europe. We are closer in language and in origins, in social habits and institutions, in political outlook and in economic interest. The economies of the Commonwealth countries are complementary to that of Britain to a degree which those of Western Europe could never equal. Furthermore Britain is also the banker of the sterling area. (Labour Party 1950)

Therefore, Britain's commercial, political and emotional links to the Commonwealth were seen as incompatible with participation in a potential 'United States of Europe'; as a result, Britain preferred to be part of the European Free Trade Area (EFTA), which it valued for its 'economic and commercial freedom' in contrast to the 'political straitjacket' of the EEC (Watts and Pilkington 2005: 23). However, it was becoming increasingly clear that Britain was in economic decline, in contrast to the booming economies of the EEC, and was running out of viable trading partners (Leonard 1998: 257). Moreover, as a result of the Suez crisis in 1956, there was increasing consciousness in Britain that its days as a world power were at an end (Watts and Pilkington 2005: 23).

The decision of the Macmillan government to make an (ultimately unsuccessful) bid for EEC membership in 1961 was thus an overwhelmingly pragmatic one; he presented it as a 'commercial move to protect national economic interest'; in contrast, the Labour leader of the time, Hugh Gaitskell, proclaimed that EEC membership would herald the end of both the Commonwealth and of 'a thousand years of history' (Schmidt 2011: 174). Following the second, successful application for membership, however, Gaitskell presented it in terms of the necessity of 'defending the national interest from interfering foreigners' (George 1994: 55). Despite these dominant pragmatic and Eurosceptic discourses, a minority, including Roy Jenkins in the Labour Party, did argue that Britain should join Europe for cultural reasons (Larsen 1997: 53).

The dominant discourse on Europe in Britain has continued to be primarily pragmatic in nature; it presents Europe in terms of the concrete interests it can fulfill. Thus, Europe is presented in 'non-mythical' terms, with little emotional pull, rather than as a natural, organic entity. There is, then, little sense of Europe being based on a common cultural and ethnic foundation. This is perhaps understandable in Britain, where, due to its multinational nature, the concept of 'the British nation' itself is often largely divorced from ethnicity or culture.

As mentioned above, parliamentary sovereignty has been a central feature of British political identity; in the absence of a strong ethnic base parliamentary sovereignty is, together with the monarchy, the central element of the unity of the UK. Thus, the issue of sovereignty has also been central to British discourse on Europe. The justification for British objections to transferring sovereignty to supranational European institutions is often that the latter are undemocratic in that they lack parliamentary scrutiny (Risse 2010: 82). Moreover, in British discourse sovereignty is seen as absolutist and unitary (Larsen 1997: 40). As sovereignty tends to be seen as a 'zero-sum game', then, the EC/EU has frequently been regarded as a threat to Britain as it tends to be represented as a loss of British parliamentary sovereignty. In this discourse, then, fears of a 'federal' Europe or a European 'superstate' are particularly notable.[2]

The dominant discourse in Britain regarding European integration has therefore been primarily intergovernmental in nature. Concern in both the Labour and Conservative parties over a potential European 'superstate', threatening the 'sacred cow' of British parliamentary sovereignty has not changed fundamentally since the 1950s. This attitude is perhaps clearest in the discourse of Margaret Thatcher, although, as Watts and Pilkington point out, it is not substantially different from the views expressed by her predecessors Wilson and Callaghan (2005: 45). In her 1988 Bruges speech, for instance, she argued that;

> Willing and active cooperation between independent sovereign states is the best way to build a successful European community…Europe will be stronger precisely because it has France as France, Spain as Spain, Britain as Britain, each with its own customs, traditions and identity. It would be folly to try to fit them into some sort of identikit European personality. (Thatcher 1988)

This view has thus been most associated with, although not limited to, the Conservative Party, in particular during the Thatcher era and since the Conservatives' defeat in the 1997 general elections. The British opt-out of European Monetary Union (EMU) negotiated by Thatcher's successor John Major had the aim of ensuring that Britain would maintain its monetary independence and, above all, the pound, the 'identity enhancing symbol of the lost Empire' (Schmidt 2012: 175).

William Hague, the first new Conservative leader following their 1997 electoral defeat, exposed fears of a European superstate in his 2000 'elephant test' speech, for instance. Arguing that if it looks, smells and sounds like an elephant it probably is one, he discerned the future shape of a European superstate in the draft Constitutional Treaty, including a proposed president, a parliament, a

---

2   In contrast, the Liberal Party and the Social Democrats, which later merged to form the Liberal Democrats, were both solidly pro-European from the beginning, and were often accused of being 'starry eyed' about European integration. However, in line with its increasing electoral success, the party's discourse on the EU appears to have hardened in recent years; at least it has become less vocal in its support for the EU (Watts and Pilkington 2005: 218–19).

court and a single currency (cited in Watts and Pilkington 2005). The subsequent Conservative leaders, Iain Duncan Smith and Michael Howard, were also sceptical of uncontrolled European political integration. In Howard's view, for instance, the EU should not be 'a one way street to closer integration to which all must subscribe… Forcing common standards upon them will mean that Europe as a whole falls further and further behind as each member state tries to put its own costs onto its neighbours' (Howard 2004).

According to David Cameron, leader of the current Conservative/Liberal Democrat coalition government, with the Lisbon Treaty ratified by all 27 Member States, the Conservative Party now seeks to limit what it views as future federalist damage by implementing laws to 'protect Britain's sovereignty'. These would include a 'Sovereignty Bill', according to which ultimate authority would remain with the British Parliament, which would also have to approve so-called 'ratchet clauses' and a 'referendum lock' intended to prevent further power being handed to the EU without a referendum (Cameron 2009). Such Euroscepticism has also been apparent in the media, including 'quality' broadsheets such as the *Times* and the *Telegraph,* both of which have tended to portray the EU as a potential federalist superstate and as a threat to British sovereignty (Anderson 2004: 160–66). According to Hawkins, two principal images of the EU emerge in the British media; that of the EU as a foreign power, and that of the EU as a forum for interstate bargaining. Although these images may seem contradictory, they are both centred around the idea of Britain being somehow excluded from the EU mainstream, and its interests undermined by the EU integration process (Hawkins 2012: 57).

While the Labour party, especially since the late 1990s, has been much more supportive of EU integration than the Conservatives, the views of the two parties still have much in common. With the modernising of the Labour party under Tony Blair, the Labour party (or New Labour as it was now known) became overwhelmingly pro-European, arguing that, although it would continue to defend vital British interests, it would adopt a much more positive attitude to the EU than its predecessors. Indeed, it proved itself to be a far less 'awkward partner' in the EU than the Conservative governments of Margaret Thatcher and John Major. Blair's Labour government joined the Social Chapter, which Britain had opted out of under the Conservatives, and showed a more conciliatory attitude to the negotiations for the Amsterdam and Nice Treaties, in which he was willing to incorporate extensions to supranational decision making (Leonard 1998: 260).

However, Labour's attitude to the EU was still largely pragmatic; although its discourse has been more pro-EU than that of the Conservatives it has generally used interest rather than identity based arguments to justify its support of the EU (Risse 2010: 83). Moreover, despite its comparatively 'pro-European' stance it continued to prefer an intergovernmental rather than a federal EU, and to promote flexible labour markets rather than the social welfare model supported by some continental socialists (Watts and Pilkington 2005: 232–3). In addition, Blair continued to stress the importance of the 'Special Relationship' with the USA, and viewed Britain as a kind of 'bridge' between Europe and the USA, although the split between these UK and other EU supporters of the Iraq war on the one hand and the majority of the EU leaders on the other exposed the difficulty of upholding this situation (Watts and Pilkington 2005: 230–31).

Despite this, however, Blair saw active involvement in the EU as vital for Britain's interests: 'If we want to stand up for Britain then we have to be in Europe, active, constructive, involved all the time. We have to negotiate tough and get our way, not stand aside and let other European countries make the decisions that matter to us' (Blair 2000). However, as Bale points out, the policies of the two dominant parties still continue to have more similarities than differences;

> The Conservatives, for example, will not be joining the euro. Nor, insofar as it is possible to predict these things, will Labour. The Conservatives want to reform but not to scrap the CAP, decoupling payments from production, making tariff reductions and moving towards co-financing. So does Labour. The Conservatives believe liberalisation is the way forward for 'old Europe' and elide the fact that it is the national governments of France and Germany rather than the EU itself that can deliver it. So does Labour. The Conservatives are determined to prevent, in as much as it is possible, the ECJ making policy and making things awkward for member states. So is Labour. Broadly speaking, the Conservatives are in favour of EU enlargement, partly because it represents an injection of economic dynamism, partly because 'widening' is thought to make 'deepening' more difficult. So is Labour. The Conservatives do not want a common foreign and security policy that endangers or tries to replace the Atlantic alliance. Nor does Labour. (Bale 2006: 9)

Thus, both parties continue to favour a primarily intergovernmental EU. Neither party sees EU integration as a question of cultural identity. However, the lack of emotional identification with Europe does not mean that, in British discourse, 'Europe' should not defend certain values, although those values, including freedom, democracy and the rights of man are seen as 'universal' or 'Western' in nature, rather than specifically 'European'. Even Margaret Thatcher proposed the idea of a 'Magna Carta for the whole of Europe'. Thus, in British discourse, Europe has been seen as an integral part of the West, including the USA, with which it shares values, and is invested with a mission to spread these values (Larsen 1997: 57).

As Schmidt points out, then, 'despite the fact that British leaders have in mind primarily a borderless problem-solving free market when they speak of Europe, they have increasingly referred to the EU's common values, its importance of human rights, and its role as a global actor' (2009: 5). Blair, for instance, in a speech following the French and Dutch rejection of the Constitutional Treaty stated that the EU was a;

> union of values, of solidarity between nations and people, of not just a common market in which we trade but a common political space in which we live as

citizens ... I believe in Europe as a political project. I believe in Europe with a strong and caring social dimension. I would never accept a Europe that was simply an economic market. (BBC 2005)

Such views are not confined to Labour and Liberal Democrat politicians. Conservative Foreign Secretary William Hague, for instance, also indicates that that the Conservative Party sees the EU as somewhat more than a mere problem-solving entity. In his view, the Conservatives 'have always argued that it is in all our common interests that the nations of the European Union use their collective weight in the world to our mutual advantage and in the promotion of our shared values' (Hague 2010).

British Discourse on EU Enlargement to Turkey

The British are generally considered to be among the staunchest supporters of enlargement, including enlargement to Turkey, and the dominant discourses on Turkish accession are inclusionary (Walter and Albert 2009: 241). All the major political parties have declared themselves to be in favour of Turkish accession, and studies of the quality British press also reveal widespread support for (or at least neutral attitudes towards) Turkey's bid for EU membership (Wimmel 2006: 6) (Negrine et al. 2008: 57) (Walter and Albert 2009).

This pro-enlargement attitude has often been put down, in the French and German press for instance (Wimmel 2006:26), to a desire to 'widen' the EU in order to delay or undermine the 'deepening' of integration. There is indeed evidence of this in the discourse, particularly in the more Eurosceptic discourse which has been dominant in the Conservative party since the Thatcher era. Notably, Margaret Thatcher herself saw enlargement as a weapon to combat a 'federal Europe'. In her famous 1988 anti-federalist 'Bruges Speech' she called for a wider European community that stretched from 'the Atlantic to the Urals' rather than one based on deeper integration, arguing that a more tightly integrated EC would be less able to accommodate newcomers (Thatcher 1993: 744).

This view is still put forward by some prominent Conservative politicians. Conservative MP and former candidate for party leadership Liam Fox, for instance, recounts how when a French politician complained to him that Turkey's entry would weaken European integration, Fox had to stifle a 'three cheers to that' (Fox 2006). This brings us back to the 'sovereignty' issue; in this view Turkey's accession would protect British sovereignty by hindering the development of a European 'superstate'.[3]

---

3   This view can also be seen, for instance, among the 'hard' Eurosceptic Independence Party. As EPP Independence member Wise succinctly argues, 'I do not have a vision of the EU. I want Turkey in the EU, because if Turkey enters the EU will collapse' (cited in Öner 2011: 151).

However, an examination of the discourse in both dominant parties reveals that this is far from the only reason put forward for support of Turkey's EU accession bid. As has been argued above, the multinational and multicultural features of the British state, coupled with a traditional lack of emotional connection with and even distrust of Europe mean that the 'value-based' discourse of the EU is a minority one, particularly in the two main political parties. Thus, in a Europe which is not perceived as an organic community based on a shared culture or ethnicity, it is easier to accept the inclusion of a Muslim majority country such as Turkey. Turkey's cultural (or civilizational) Otherness as an obstacle to its EU accession is basically not an issue in the dominant British discourse and such arguments tend to be treated with dismay and incomprehension. As Labour MP Shaun Woodward commented, for instance, 'President Giscard d'Estaing's question about whether Turkey is European is simply the wrong question to ask today'(Woodward 2002).

Similarly, such interpretations of Europe as a 'Christian club' tend to be treated as 'ugly prejudices' in the British press (Wimmel 2006: 19 and 21). Instead, although Turkey's accession would perhaps weaken the EU, given the traditional British distrust of 'excessive' European integration this is not necessarily considered a bad thing, as Timothy Garton Ash, for instance, argues in *The Guardian*;

> But a EU including Turkey would be somewhat less European and somewhat less of a union. It might more accurately be described as a community of contiguous democracies. Is that necessarily a worse thing? It's quite possible to conclude that Turkey is not a European country and should join the European Union. (Garton Ash 2002)

There are, however, exceptions to the dominant discourse in the British quality press, albeit rare ones. John Casey echoes a view more typically found in the dominant French discourse in a *Daily Telegraph* article in response to the question of whether Turkey should join the EU. In his view, Turkey should not be granted full membership due to differences in culture and religious background; 'You can only think this does not matter profoundly if you fail to see how culture overwhelmingly makes us what we are, and does give us a sense of European identity despite the manifold differences … ' (Casey 2002).

There has been an important pragmatic element to both Labour and Conservative discourse in favour of Turkish accession, in line with the dominant British discourse of the EU as primarily a problem-solving entity. In particular, according to this discourse Turkey's entry into the EU would be beneficial for Britain's strategic, political and economic interests, as well as those of the EU and, indeed, the world. This has been clearly emphasised by former Prime Minister Tony Blair, who argued that the EU's decision to open accession negotiations with Turkey was important for the world's future 'peace and prosperity'(BBC 2004b). More recently, former UK foreign secretary David Miliband argued that, '.at the moment, the standoff in the accession process is blighting co-operation with

Turkey across a wider range of policy. And it is Europe that suffers the strategic loss, not Turkey' (Public Service Europe 2011).

Prime Minister David Cameron echoes this support of enlargement; 'We will press to keep the doors of the European Union open to new member states, especially to entrench stability in the Western Balkans where so much European blood has flowed, and also to Turkey' (2009: 6). Conservative politician William Hague expands on this when he states that 'We will uphold the view that the widening of the European Union, including Turkey, is in Europe's collective interest' (Hague 2010). Moreover, in a 2010 speech in Turkey, Cameron himself appears enthusiastic in his support of Turkish accession. When asked the reasons for his visit to Turkey so soon after becoming Prime Minister he argued that 'Turkey is vital for our economy, vital for our security and vital for our politics and our diplomacy'(Cameron 2010).

More specifically, one of the arguments that the Labour party has used in favour of Turkish accession is that, with its predominantly Muslim population, a Turkey anchored in the EU could contribute to avoiding a 'clash of civilizations' within and beyond Europe, an argument that has also frequently been put forward by members of the European Commission (Aydın 2006). This view was reinforced following the September 11 events and, particularly, following the Al-Qaida terrorist attacks on two synagogues and two British targets in Istanbul in November 2003. In this way, then, Turkish inclusion into Europe is often justified in a negative fashion; a rejection of Turkey might have serious consequences for 'the West' (Walter and Albert 2009: 242).

This has also been echoed in Conservative discourse. Fox, for instance, argues that EU membership will protect Turkey from those in the 'fundamentalist shadows'. In this way, then, he attempts to pose the failure to include Turkey in the EU as a security threat by implying that it will force Turkey into the hands of Islamic fundamentalists, thus turning Europe into a 'much more dangerous and destabilised continent' (Fox 2006). More recently, David Cameron emphasised that '…it's the opportunity to unite East and West that gives Turkey such an important role with countries in the region helping to deliver improved security for us all' (Cameron 2010). Such attitudes are also reflected in the quality British press. According to *The Times* Turkey in the EU would be the 'bulwark against the rise of radical Islam' (Kaletsky 2004) and a 'bridge between the Judaeo-Christian and Muslim cultures which is so badly needed' (Whitney 2004) while, according to the same newspaper, 'without Turkey there will never be peace and unity in Europe' (*The Times* 2005). This has also been linked to discussions of Muslim immigration and multiculturalism in Europe. As an article in the *Guardian* argues;

> If there was a secular, democratic, economically successful Muslim state [in the EU] it would kill off intense arguments about the incompatibility of Islam with democracy or Islam with human rights and modernity … finally … it would strengthen the claim of Europe's 15 million-strong Muslim minority to a home in Europe. (Bunting 2005)

Thus, as Schmidt notes, many supporters of enlargement in the UK legitimise the 'no-borders' argument not so much on a pragmatic basis as in the context of a vision of the EU as a rights-based post-national union (2012: 183). In a speech by Jack Straw, for instance, Turkish membership of the EU would be a 'demonstration that Islam is compatible with the values of liberal democracy which form the bedrock of the EU' (Straw 2005). As Aksoy argues;

> The argument that was consistently pointed out by the [Labour] government was that EU membership would help to consolidate democracy and secularism in Turkey, which was overwhelmingly a Muslim nation, and this would, apart from sending all the right messages to other Muslim nations which were similarly trying to democratize, help repair the relations between the West and the Muslim world that were significantly damaged by the September 11 attacks and the subsequent War on Terror. (Aksoy 2009: 476)

In general, then, the fact that Turkey is a Muslim-majority country is generally not seen in itself as an obstacle to adopting 'universal values'. This can be seen, for instance, in Conservative discourse. As Prime Minister Cameron points out, 'I will always argue that the values of real Islam are not incompatible with the values of Europe' (2010).[4] Indeed, particularly in Labour discourse, discourse on Turkey's place in Europe echoes that on a 'multicultural Britain'. As Blair argued in 2004; 'The accession of Turkey would be a proof that Europe is committed not just in word but in deed to a Europe of diverse races, cultures and religions all bound together by common rules and a sense of human solidarity and mutual respect' (BBC 2004b).

As Aksoy notes, some members of the Labour Cabinet stressed the long interaction and cultural links between the Judeo-Christian and Islamic traditions, and the shared values between them (2009: 489). Here, then, the former Labour government's argument appeared to nod towards the value-based community approach, although here this imagined community is not an exclusively Christian one. Dennis MacShane, the former Labour Minister for Europe, for instance, has stressed the medieval Islamic world's contribution to the humanities, sciences and arts, and its role as a shelter for the persecuted minorities of Europe. Thus, in his view, the EU's encouragement of Turkey's accession process would be a way both of recognising the Islamic influence on Europe's cultural heritage and supporting the development of democracy in a predominantly Muslim nation (MacShane 2002).

---

4   This can be contrasted with centre/right political discourse in some other European countries. As former Belgian prime minister and current permanent President of the European Council Herman van Rompuy argues, for instance, 'The universal values which are in force in Europe, and which are also fundamental values of Christianity, will lose vigour with the entry of a large Islamic country such as Turkey' (cited in Cronin 2010).

Case Study 2: France

Concepts of State and Nation in French Discourse

The basic tenets of contemporary French discourse on state and nation have their origins in the French Revolution of 1789. The Revolution, an uprising of the nation against the royal state resulting in the transfer of sovereignty from the monarch to the nation, remains the source of French ideas about the organising principles of democracy in France in the Fifth Republic although these ideas have evolved and been contested over time (Schmidt 2006: 997). Amiraux identifies the four elements which structure the republican project as follows; the unmediated relation between the citizen and the state, secular public education, the belief in France's international mission and a strong, activist state (2010: 65).

Following the Revolution, popular sovereignty replaced the monarchy; the people thus assumed the role of nation, which was elevated to the condition of statehood. In this context, the nation was seen as an abstract term rather than the material people itself; it was perceived as a body of citizens (Holm 2002: 1). Thus, in the French case, the nation seems more like a political concept than an expression of ethnicity; it is an expression of political choice, will and mobilisation (Larsen 1997: 87). Citizenship is therefore not established by birth but is based on socialisation into a shared political community and commitment to French civic culture (Schmidt 2006: 997). As a result, every individual can potentially become a citizen in France if he/she agrees to enter into this political and social contract. Thus, the 'ethnic' citizen does not exist; instead the citizen is 'emancipated' from his/her primary ties and is freely willing to become part of the French nation (Amiraux 2010: 70). The dominant French concept of the political nation is nicely summed up in a 1988 article by the then Socialist Minister for Defence, Jean-Pierre Chevènement;

> The revolution, and the republic which grew out of 1789, shed light upon the French concept of the nation. This is a political notion because the nation perceives of itself as a body of citizens. The concept of nation is based on the idea of the social contract between the individual citizen and the state-nation, where every citizen is part of a whole in a universal perspective. This means that every individual can become a citizen in France, or elsewhere, if he agrees to enter into this political and social contract. A nation that bases its existence on a contractual and universal concept is a political nation. Only the political nation is able to create the political identity of one people, thus preventing the interests of the individual from controlling society. Without a common will, there is no nation. Without a voluntary contract, there is no nation. The nation is open to all those who wish to join this political project and the French nation respects similar projects of other nations. Together with those nations, the French nation will build up the universal principle of freedom (cited in Holm 2002: 1–2).

Thus, in the Republican model citizens are considered to be equal political actors independent of specificities such as culture, ethnicity or religion (Amiraux 2010: 69). France is proud of its ability to turn foreigners, immigrants and 'ethnic minorities' such as the Bretons or Basques into citizens (Holm 2002: 1–2). In this way, integration within the emerging nation was, from the beginning, based on an individual project of equality disconnected from any claims for rights justified on the basis of distinction (Amiraux 2010: 69).

In consequence, France, despite being a country of migration, does not think of itself as a pluralistic society (Amiraux 2010: 65). Multiculturalism is 'un-French' in that the indivisible Republic stands as a countermodel to multicultural communalism (Amiraux 2010: 66–70). In both left and right Republican discourse, then, multiculturalism is a negative word as it is placed in opposition to integration into the political nation, and is seen as promoting the 'ghettoisation' of the nation (Holm 2002: 5–6) by putting culture before politics and groups before individuals (Amiraux 2010: 66).

In republican discourse, religion, like cultural differences, is relegated to the private sphere in order to achieve an egalitarian treatment of all citizens in the public space. Thus, secularism (*laicité*) is another important aspect of French discourse on state and nation, and implies the freedom of belief and equality of all citizens independent of their religious orientation (Amiraux 2010: 72). Indeed, France was the first European nation to put in place the dissociation between citizenship and confession, and from 1905 religion became juridically a private rather than a public matter. As secularism is seen as representing faith in the people and, by extension, the republican norms on which the French nation-state is based, it is perceived as untouchable in French discourse (Holm 2002: 13). Schools, in particular, are responsible for the civic education of individual citizens in a secular system, and, more generally, are expected to act as guarantors of access to universalism and emancipatory values (Amiraux 2010: 74). According to a 2008 survey, France is the most secularised country in the EU; only 10 per cent of French respondents said that religion was 'very important' in their lives, and 60 per cent claimed that they never pray (Amiraux 2010: 96). Indeed, Holm (2002: 15) argues that secularism has become increasingly securitised in the context, for instance, of discussions over the exclusion of three Muslim girls from school for wearing the headscarf.

In French political discourse the state was assigned a strong role in creating the French nation as well as in defending the Republican values it is based on, a task assigned to it by the nation. As Larsen notes, this view of the state as a 'strong and legitimate defender of the people' emanated from the Jacobin victory over the Girondins during the Revolution. While the Girondins were more sceptical about the need for a strong state, the Jacobin view prevailed despite some challenges in the nineteenth century (Larsen 1997: 88). The function of the French state, then, is to express the sovereign will of the nation, to act as the guarantor of national unity and as the protector of the 'rights of man' and to act as carrier of universal revolutionary values (Schmidt 2006: 997). In this case, therefore, the fusion of state and nation implies that the citizens constitute a uniform mass as they endorse the same set of political values; the state thus becomes the guarantor of the national political identity (Holm 2002: 2). For this reason, then, the state had to be strong and interventionist to defend these values from their ever-present enemies. Thus, in contrast to the British case, it can be argued that there was a consensus on the need for a strong state with a role in the economy. Similarly, the centralised nature of the French state is also a legacy of the Jacobins. As politics was considered to be something which took place primarily between the state and nation, political levels between the state and the individual were seen as threatening to the state/ nation (Larsen 1997: 90).

Regarding France's place in the world, there is a consensus in French discourse that France has a *mission civilisatrice* or civilising mission, and should thus play a leading role in the world, particularly in Europe (Risse 2010: 71); as Larsen notes, there is almost no equivalent of 'little Englanders' in France (Larsen 1997: 89). Instead, the message inherited from 1789 was that all mankind should follow the 'universal French message' (Holm 2004: 472). This is connected to the concept that, due to its revolutionary history, France is seen as the birthplace of human rights and democracy, and that modernity, secularism and enlightenment have been identified with the French nation state (Risse 2010: 71–2). This heritage is thus seen as giving France a *mission civilisatrice* to spread its Republican values of *liberté, égalité, fraternité* and the rights of man and the citizen on a global scale (Larsen 1997: 91). This can be seen, for instance, in a 2012 speech by President François Hollande; 'We are not just any country on the planet, not just any of the world's nations … everything that I do will be in the name of [spreading] Republican values around the world' (Hollande 2012).

If there is any concept in French political discourse which relates to ethnicity it is that of *patrie*, the old France of the regions. The concept of *patrie* is, then, a culturally defined one, and relates to the 'non-institutionalised affiliation of a particular group to a defined territory on the basis of common history, language, culture and habits' (Holm 2004: 472). Therefore, the *patrie* is in opposition to the political concept of nation but linked to it, in that the political ideal of the republican nation is translated into a love of one's own culture, language and religion. While the *patrie* and nation are, thus, connected, and the state and nation are inseparable, the state and *patrie* have nothing to do with each other (Holm 2002: 2–3).

Although the regime tried to eradicate the *patrie* following the Revolution on the basis that it was a threat to the values and structures of the French state, the attempt was never entirely successful. As Larsen notes, it was a necessary part of the discourse as the pure political values related to the nation did not provide the emotional warmth necessary to create cohesion (Larsen 1997: 88). However, in French discourse, although the two are bound together, keeping a balance between the political nation and the ethnic *patrie* is important, with the political nation being the core concept and the *patrie* the sub-concept. In this way, in republican discourse, the subordinate role of the *patrie* to the political nation ensures that French identity is not defined solely on the basis of culture (Holm 2002: 3). As is discussed further below, the concept of *patrie* may be in flux, with *patrie* increasingly challenging the position of the political nation as the core concept in national discourse. In fact, Holm refers to *patrie* as a 'time-bomb' (Holm 2002: 2–4).

According to Holm, discourses in favour of the 'right to [ethnic] difference' have placed the concept of *patrie* in a central position and, thus, contributed to its destabilisation (2002: 2–4). This is, then, in the context of an increasing criticism of 'integration' and a new focus on antidiscrimination, notably by the children of first-generation immigrants (Amiraux 2010: 77–8). In particular, events such as the March 2004 banning of visible religious symbols from public schools, and the November 2005 urban riots have led to increased questioning of the limits of the French republican model of integration and citizenship (Amiraux 2010: 81).

In addition, again contrasting with the secularism which underlies the concept of state/nation, and perhaps in reaction to the migrant discourses discussed above, Christianity has been increasingly construed as an element of *patrie,* principally in right-wing discourse, thus potentially excluding Muslims from being assimilable on religious grounds (Holm 2002: 7). However, the re-introduction of Christianity into the right-wing definition of *patrie* potentially endangers the secular concept of the state-nation. The far-right gets around this problem by arguing that, as the republic is secular, it has to guarantee that Christianity is a constitutive feature of *patrie* as Islam is securitised as a threat to the secular nature of the republic (Holm 2002: 13), as well as to French identity in more general terms. According to *Front National* discourse, then; 'French identity is under threat of extinction. If we continue to fill our country with mosques and if our children become like those monotonous Arabs and Africans who lack cultural richness, how can we believe that France will remain the same?' (Front National, cited in Yeğenoğlu 2006: 253).

Moreover, particularly since the 2007 elections and the subsequent beginning of Sarkozy's presidency, the question of national identity has become even more contested at the national level. As Risse notes (2010: 76), the fact that France, under Sarkozy, founded a national ministry of Immigration, Integration, National Identity and Supportive Development in itself suggests a national identity crisis; more specifically, it established a link between immigrants (as a problem) and the need to reaffirm and strengthen the national identity (Amiraux 2010: 77).

Concepts of Europe/the EU in French Discourse

In line with FPDA, the basic codes that frame and constrain the visions of Europe that make discursive sense in France are constituted by the discourses on state, nation and *patrie* (Holm 2004: 473) discussed above, which 'trap' French elites in their discourse on Europe (Schmidt 2007: 992). In contrast to the British case, 'Europe' has played a key role in the construction of the French Self, as it occupies a central place in France's national identity narrative, while there is also a strong belief that France can have a decision-making role in Europe (Wæver 2005: 42–60). As Drake notes, 'French tales of Europe have congealed into a seemingly impermeable discourse because they are so tightly bound to conceptions of French national identity, which itself turns on the republican values of *liberté, égalité and fraternité*' (2010: 19).

Notably, Europe has played a prominent role in French foreign policy since the Enlightenment. France has tended to view itself as Europe's natural leader, with certain obligations to fulfill and a special role to play; it was thus seen as imperative for France to put forward *grands projets* in order to disseminate its Enlightenment values to the rest of the continent (Larsen 1997: 86). Therefore, unlike in Britain, there has traditionally been a strong emotional identification with Europe in French discourse (Tekin 2008: 729).

However, at least until the 1980s, French attitudes to European integration were complex. As Schmidt notes, as ideas about French citizenship and identity tend to be intertwined, any undermining of the French state is perceived as an attack on identity; any form of supranational institution thus challenges and undermines national identity constructions (Schmidt 2006: 998).

Although there was a consensus on the need for European integration in 1945, two different discourses on Europe could be discerned in France by the 1950s. The first of these saw Europe as a political entity that had to be built up as a prerequisite for any French policy, a view which was dominant in the centre parties and on the centre-right of the Socialist Party (PS – *Parti Socialiste*). In the second view, Europe was primarily an instrument for French policy or for furthering particular ideologies. This view was held primarily by the Communists and left wing of the PS, as well as by the Gaullists on the right (Larsen 1997: 96). Thus, as Holm notes, the French political elite has two ways of 'imagining' Europe; as a Europe of states and as a state-like Europe (2004: 471). However, both discourses emphasise the uniqueness of France's role, duty and destiny in what has become the EU (Drake 2010: 5).

According to the Gaullist identity construction, which was heavily critical of European supranationalism, little need was seen to Europeanise French identity; instead the focus was on *l'Europe des nations*. In De Gaulle's view, the state could not be subsumed by Europe because it was sovereign *pour la nation et par la nation* – for and through the nation-and was there to defend Republican values (Schmidt 2006: 998), although opposition became pragmatic acceptance of French EEC membership after De Gaulle's accession to power (Hainsworth, O'Brien and Mitchell 2004: 38). Thus, in Gaullist discourse Europe was not ascribed the qualities of a state in terms of the functions it was to perform; instead, it was seen as a composite of sovereign states of which France was 'first among equals' (Larsen 1997: 97).

In this way, then, the realist view prevailed among Gaullists that French-led European integration, coupled with a strong Franco-German alliance, was the best way to strengthen France's political and economic position (Hainsworth, O'Brien and Mitchell 2004: 38). In other words, Europe was seen as an arena which would allow France to increase its own power in the world; it was, in other words, a *multiplicateur de puissance,* or multiplier of power (Schmidt 2006: 998). Following from this, the idea of *l'Europe puissance,* or 'power Europe' also became an important aspect of Gaullist discourse on Europe. In this view, Europe must exist as a power within the international system in its own right, implying military as well as 'soft' power (Drake 2010: 11–12). However, de Gaulle's ideas continued to be centred around 'a certain idea of France', stressing national independence, grandeur and unity, and continued to incorporate anti-federalist, as well as anti-Atlanticist, ideas. Thus, French independence was not to be compromised; de Gaulle's favourite *modus operandi* continued to be intergovernmental, eventually leading to the so-called 'Empty Chair crisis' of 1965–66, which was finally resolved by the Luxembourg Compromise which established the right of veto (Hainsworth, O'Brien and Mitchell 2004: 39).

Presidents Pompidou and Giscard d'Estaing also used de Gaulle's language on European integration to a great extent. While the Socialists shared this instrumental discourse on Europe in the 1970s (Larsen 1997: 97–8), it was challenged by the late 1970s in conjunction with two crises; the failure of François Mitterand's economic policies, based on Keynesian ideas, which resulted in a crisis in the PS in the early 1980s and the end of the Cold War later in the same decade (Risse 2010: 73). This resulted in a new discourse on Europe in which Europe became depicted as necessary for France and where France and Europe became increasingly conflated in the political language (Larsen 1997: 100).

Following the crisis in the PS after the failure of Mitterand's economic policies, the party moved towards Social Democracy, while it also began to show a more favourable attitude towards European integration. Thus, the French socialists began to highlight the common European historical and cultural heritage. However, this was based on the notion of a 'European France', according to which Europe itself was 'France writ large', in that it was seen as a child of the values of the French Revolution, including enlightenment, democracy and Republicanism (Risse 2010: 74). In this way, then, this discourse took traditional understandings of Frenchness and the French nation state, including sovereignty understood as enlightenment and republicanism, and the French *mission civilisatrice,* and Europeanised them (Marcussen et al. 1999: 621). As Mitterand himself argued in 1986, for instance; 'We are at the moment where everybody unites, our fatherland, our Europe – Europe our fatherland – the ambition to support one with the other, the excitement of our land and of the people it produces, and the certainty of a new dimension is awaiting them' (Mitterand 1986: 104).

In this way, then, in 1983/4 the dominant discourse on the EU in France changed significantly to that of a 'symbiosis' between France and Europe (Larsen 1997: 103–4). Thus, in this discourse, the EC had to become a *Europe puissance,* or 'power-Europe' according to the French model (Holm 2004: 47); in other words, it had to become a political actor in French terms. In this view, the qualities of a political actor should include political features which create common identity, including the following:

- The ability to act. In this view, technical arrangements alone are insufficient for political action; instead, it is based on political will.
- A political actor has a strong internal and external identity. Thus, Europe cannot be a mere free-trade area as loyalty to the actor must be strong and the actor must be able to project itself internationally.
- A political actor must have clearly defined boundaries if its identity is not to be threatened (Larsen 1997: 103–4).

A similar change took place on the French right in the Gaullist party *Rassemblement pour la République* (RPR), leading to a *degaullizing* of the party under Jacques Chirac's leadership and a move towards a tacit acceptance of pooled sovereignty in spite of continued rhetoric on the primacy of the nation state. This was evidenced, for instance, by Chirac's 1984 agreement to a joint list with the pro-European UDF, and the party's 1986 agreement to the Single European Act and the ensuing qualified majority voting (QMV) (Hainsworth, O'Brien and Mitchell 2004: 39–40).

This change in discourse was further entrenched by an identity crisis that appeared with the end of the Cold War provoked by the realisation that France – *la grande nation* – had been left on the sidelines in the post-Cold War security order following the fall of the Berlin Wall and the reunification of Germany. Thus, due to this geo-political shift towards Germany, France had lost its claim to political leadership in an enlarged EU (Schmidt 2007: 995). In addition, there was a general perception of comparative economic decline *vis à vis* the Japanese, South-East Asians and Americans, and of cultural erosion by American consumerist values (Larsen 1997: 102–3). In this context, a new, more active role in Europe was seen as the antidote to France's decline; French European identity was again seen as an extension of French republicanism into Europe and the EU (Risse 2010: 74–5).

French right-wing discourse under Chirac combined the two dominant French discourses on Europe; that of a state-like Europe and a Gaullist Europe of states; thus, Chirac's vision was that of 'a strong France in a strong Europe' (Holm 2004: 476–8). As Drake notes, both Chirac and Lionel Jospin, his Socialist Prime Minister, campaigned in the 2002 presidential elections in favour of an oxymoronic 'European Federation of Nation States' (Drake 2010: 16). This vision thus combined the concept of *l'Europe puissance* with an emphasis on France's leadership role in Europe. As Chirac noted in a speech to the EP in 2002, 'To build and perfect Europe in the twenty-first century is to pursue France's great adventure … to make the great voice of France heard: it will spread afar these high standards and these republican values to which our compatriots are so deeply attached' (cited in Schmidt 2007: 1002).

These two concepts were balanced by support for flexible enhanced co-operation, which would allow further integration for the 'front runners' while allowing looser co-operation for new or reluctant member states (Holm 2004: 476–8). However, Chirac's vision was challenged by a minority of RPR Eurosceptics, who stuck to a traditional Gaullist understanding of sovereignty, and also by the extreme right and the Communists and others on the left (Holm 2004: 476). The split within the RPR became more evident in the context of the Maastricht Treaty and the ensuing referendum, when half of the RPR deputies supported Philippe Séguin's move to reject the ratification of the TEU and declare it unconstitutional. As Séguin argued in 1992; 'Europe buries the concept of national sovereignty and the grand principles of the Revolution: 1992 is literally the anti-1789' (cited in Risse 2010: 75).[5] The issue of the TEU also provoked a split in the PS, when Jean-Pierre Chévènement and his allies formed a separate party, the *Mouvement des Citoyens* (MDC), in opposition to the TEU and the Gulf War (Milner 2004: 64).

Chirac's discourse on Europe as a 'federation of nation states' also, however, became the dominant discourse of the PS as of 1999. In practice, this largely implied an acceptance of the *status quo* in European governance on the part of the PS, although its concern over the democratic deficit is apparent in its support for a European constitution and greater co-legislation powers for the EP. Another concern of the PS has been that of reconciling market forces with the 'European social model', and the concept of a *Europe puissance* to rival the USA, a 'typically French obsession' (Milner 2004: 63).

Under President Sarkozy, France's leadership role in Europe was emphasised, and there was a return to 'a pro-European communicative discourse it had not seen since Mitterand' (Schmidt 2012: 181). The concept of a *Europe puissance* with the features of a French political actor is again notable in President Sarkozy's discourse. It is a Europe which takes actions based on political will, has a strong internal and external identity and possesses clear borders. As Sarkozy remarks in his book *Testimony,*

> Europe cannot simply be a place you come from. To count in the world Europe must be ambitious. Andre Malraux was right to say that 'Europe must be ambitious or it will die'. The EU's founding fathers – Jean Monnet, Robert Schuman, Alcide de Gaspari – had this ambition... These people and governments wanted a Europe that could act, not a passive Europe. They wanted a Europe that would multiply their power ... They wanted a Europe in which they could recognise themselves – a European Europe. They didn't want a Europe with no fixed borders, expanding infinitely, diluting its institutions, policies and will in an ever-wider, heterogenous and loose grouping. (Sarkozy 2007b: 188–9)

In line with the dominant French discourse on the 'strong state', Sarkozy has also emphasised the 'protective' role that the EU should play, in terms of protecting its citizens from forces such as climate change and unlimited immigration, as well

---

5   Later, in the 1999 general election, this *souverainiste* faction of the party eventually broke away to set up a new party with the concepts of national sovereignty and a strong state at its core, the *Rassemblement pour la France et l'Independance de l'Europe* (RPF-IE) under the leadership of Charles Pasqua and Philippe de Villiers (Hainsworth, O'Brien and Mitchell 2004: 40–41) .

as the global financial crisis (Drake 2010: 20). Moreover, Sarkozy's discourse forms a continuity with that of his predecessors in that he emphasises France's decisive role in this Europe; despite the French people's 2005 rejection of the Constitutional Treaty, he argues that 'France, which has always been a motor for Europe, must remain faithful to its vocation as a leader in the process of building the European Union' (2007b: xv). In addition, he emphasises France's *mission civilisatrice* in its foreign policy; 'France is France only when it defends universal values, human rights and individual freedom' (2007b: xiv). In these ways, then, Sarkozy's discourse on Europe is consistent with the dominant French discourse on state, nation and *patrie* (Holm 2009: 9).

Sarkozy's discourse combines Mitterand's concept of a 'state-like Europe' with a traditional Gaullist vision of a 'Europe of the States'. Compared to his predecessors, though, Sarkozy's proposals indicate less focus on unanimity and increased support for QMV and 'super-majorities' in the Council (Drake 2010: 21). This, then, reflects Sarkozy's promotion of a *directoire* of the big EU member states, namely France, Germany, Italy, Spain, Poland and the UK (Drake 2010: 21) (Holm 2009: 23), as in the context of Justice and Home Affairs, for instance, the 'big countries had the same problems to overcome and the same urgency about doing so' (2007b: 53). While in 2007 Sarkozy argued that 'The French and German points of view no longer come close to covering the full spectrum of views, especially compared with Britain and the Central and Eastern European countries' (2007b: 53), more recent speeches indicate that he has increasingly tended to revert to more traditional French ideas of a Franco/German motor for Europe, particularly in the context of the current financial and economic crisis. In a 2011 speech he declared that, 'We will make French-German propositions to guarantee the future of Europe' and that it would be 'unpardonable' to turn back on close co-operation between France and Germany (Scally 2011).

Current President François Hollande has questioned the exclusivity of the Franco-German relationship, while recognising the importance of that relationship;

As much as I believe in the Franco-German partnership, I question the idea of a duopoly. European construction is based on a well-balanced and respectful partnership between France and Germany. The partnerships between Schmidt and Giscard, Kohl and Mitterand, and even between Chirac and Schroeder, have proved that political differences do not mean that we cannot work together. But these heads of state combined an intergovernmental approach with European Union processes. This was the best way to avoid our partners feeling left out, or even worse, subordinate. That balance has changed over the past few years. The Franco–German relationship has been exclusive. European institutions have been neglected and some countries, notably the more fragile ones, have had the unpleasant feeling of facing an executive board. (Hollande 2012)

French Elite Discourse on Turkish EU Accession

As Holm and Drake point out, France has always been reluctant to enlarge the EC/EU as enlargement is viewed as a potential threat to the possibility of strong political actions (Holm 2004: 481) (Drake 2010: 13–14). Although de Gaulle did not use 'Europe' exclusively to refer to the EC (Larsen 1997: 97) instead promoting a wider vision of Europe 'from the Atlantic to the Urals' (Marcussen et al. 1999: 619), enlargement was viewed as potentially weakening *l'Europe puissance,* resulting in de Gaulle's twice vetoing British entry to the EC in the 1960s. As Drake notes, the pursuit of *l'Europe puissance* has meant that every single enlargement of the EC/EU has been resisted and feared to a certain extent by France. Enlargement is seen as 'blurring the edges of Europe' as it implies the introduction of new values, ideas and norms into the existing community (2010: 13–14).

Notably, for the French political elite since the 1980s the geographical and civilizational core of Europe corresponds to the Carolingian area from the Elbe to the Pyrenees; in other words it is a predominantly Franco-German core. In the French view, this core should not be easily accessible to other countries, and membership of the EU should be granted only if the power of the core is not threatened by the accession of the applicant country in question (Holm 2004: 481). As former President Sarkozy argued in 2007, for instance, 'The enlargement of the EU has weakened the common will and placed an insurmountable obstacle before political integration' (Sarkozy 2007b: 189).

The French reaction to the CEE enlargement, although it did not oppose it *a priori,* was consequently much more cautious than the British one, for instance. Prominent French politicians in the early 1990s, including President Mitterand, referred to the CEECs' right to become members of the EC/EU on condition that they fulfilled the political criteria set out in the Treaties for doing so. However, France insisted that enlargement to the CEECs could not be carried out until the EU had itself undergone significant institutional reform, with Mitterand in 1991 stating that enlargement would not take place for 'tens and tens of years' (Sjursen and Romsloe 2006: 142).[6] As Mitterand argued in 1994:

> My worry is that there is too little preoccupation with the institutions. There is nothing solid without institutions. The enlargement of the European Union is necessary; it should not happen to the detriment of its deepening. The Union should have solid, effective institutions that can guarantee further developments with scrupulous respect to democracy. This will be the aim of the 1996 Intergovernental Conference (cited in Sjursen and Romsloe 2006: 156).

---

6   Fear of the CEECs acting as a Trojan Horse for American influence in the EU, particularly in the context of the Iraq crisis, was perhaps another element of French reticence towards the 2004 enlargement, as suggested by former President Chirac's rebuke to the then CEE candidate countries that they had no place airing their views, generally in favour of the UK–USA led alliance, on Iraq (Drake 2010: 13).

As Sjursen and Romsloe point out, the importance granted to institutional reform can be best explained by France's self-perception as a protector of EU political integration. In this view, then, although France's acceptance of the CEECs as potential candidates providing the relevant political criteria were fulfilled suggests a rights-based view of the EU, its insistence that enlargement be accompanied by institutional reform suggests a value-based approach (Sjursen and Romsloe 2006: 155–62).

Turkish accession has proved considerably more controversial in France than the CEE enlargement, and the issue has provoked cleavages on both the left and right. As Göle notes, the issue of a Turkish presence in the EU has hit something hidden, deep-rooted and emotional in French identity in particular (2005). While the right is mostly opposed to Turkish accession, the left is more divided. However, it is only the *Verts* (Greens) and the *Parti Communiste* who are fully supportive of Turkish accession on condition that the Copenhagen criteria are fulfilled (Cautrès and Monceau 2011: 82–4).

On the right, namely the *Union pour un Mouvement Populaire* (UMP), the *Union pour la Democratie Française* (UDF), the centre, and extreme right parties such as the *Front National* (FN) and *Mouvement National Républicaine* (MNR), opposition to Turkish accession predominates, with some exceptions. As Tekin points out, this discourse has had an impact on the French political debate as a whole on the subject of Turkey's EU membership:

> The agenda set by the leading names of the French right such as Valéry Giscard d'Estaing and François Bayrou, and marginal figures of the nationalistic right such as Philippe de Villiers, has contributed much to the spread of Turcoscepticism among political cadres of differing convictions, as well as the general public. (Tekin 2008: 729)

In the neo-Gaullist UMP, the majority is opposed to Turkish full membership although some, including Jacques Chirac, have defended Turkey's European vocation. Even Chirac, however, notably tempered his pro-Turkish position in the run-up to the referendum on the Constitutional Treaty in 2004. The UMP's position became more consolidated in opposition to full membership for Turkey following the election of Nicolas Sarkozy as President of the Republic in 2007 (Cautrès and Monceau 2011: 84–5).

Right-wing opposition to Turkish full membership of the EU is frequently framed in geographical, cultural and religious terms. This is perhaps surprising as, according to the dominant French discourse on state and nation, the idea of the political nation 'does not operate with borders defined by religious, cultural or ethnic criteria' (Holm 2004: 482). Moreover, these essentialist arguments tend to make heavy use of historical stereotypes about the Turks and Muslims (Tekin 2008: 729). This can be explained by the fact that the compatibility of Islam with the republican and secular values of France has been increasingly questioned (Cautrès and Monceau 2011: 84). Thus, a 'Western' civilizational heritage, based on Christian and classical roots, is seen as vital for building a strong Europe in this discourse; the emphasis is on a (European) *patrie* as a foundation for the EU integration project. President of *MoDem* François Bayrou, for instance, argues that Turkey does not form part of European civilization 'because Turkey is not European in geographical, historical or sociological terms. Its anthropology is not the same as ours' (Beylau 2007).

On the left, the PS is divided on the issue of Turkish accession. Many are in favour of Turkish accession in principle provided that Turkey fulfills the Copenhagen criteria, although some are openly against it. As Aydın Düzgit argues, however, although the discourse of the French left, with its rhetoric on multiculturalism and diversity, may at first sight seem substantially different from the more essentialist right-wing discourse, both are heavily constrained by paradigms of the central role of the nation state and modernisation (2009b: 17). Notably, enlargement is supported only on condition that it is not perceived as weakening EU identity. For instance, in the run-up to the elections of 2007, then socialist candidate for President Ségolène Royal, invoking enlargement fatigue, argued that Turkish accession should be postponed until the EU had a stronger identity and its borders were more consolidated;

> I am in favour in principle but not now, as Europe is in decline and, before enlarging it, we must relaunch it ... Europe needs a rest and some time to stabilise its frontiers as, today, most of its inhabitants don't know where Europe starts or where it ends, what it's for or where it's going. (Royal 2007: 309–10)

Thus, opposition to Turkish accession cuts across party lines to unite those who support a *Europe puissance* (Cautrès and Monceau 2011). On both sides of the political spectrum, it is argued that Turkish accession would potentially weaken European political integration through diluting EU identity. As Sarkozy argues, for instance,

> 98 per cent of Turkish territory is not in Europe. In twenty years, Turkey would be the most populous country in the EU, and the Turkish population is majority Muslim ... If Turkey entered the EU, I also wonder on what basis we could exclude Israel, which has such close ties to France and Europe – or even Tunisia, Algeria or Morocco, which were French a half-century ago. Europe would have no more limits. It would become a sub-region of the United Nations. The notion of a politically unified Europe would be finished. (Sarkozy 2007b: 105)

Current President François Hollande, elected in the May 2012 elections, appears to be somewhat more positive towards Turkey's EU accession. He has stated that he would support Turkish accession on condition that it was sufficiently prepared for membership (cited in Köseoğlu 2011), and said that he would lift the veto on the five chapters that are crucial for membership (Flautre

2012). Thus, at first sight, his argument appears to suggest a view of the EU as a rights-based postnational union.

However, Hollande also argues that, while he is not against Turkey's accession in principle, it would not take place during his time in office, and that the negotiations with Turkey would be 'very long' as Turkey 'cannot be easily integrated because of its history, geography, culture and potential influence' (Flautre 2012) (*Le Monde* 2012). More specifically, he cites the Cyprus issue as an obstacle to Turkey's accession, as well as the question of the recognition of the Armenian genocide as a problem in Turkey's accession process, although he has said that he would not use this issue to oppose Turkey (*Le Monde* 2012) (Flautre 2012).

Thus, in France, it appears that both right and left nod towards a value-based Europe with a strong identity. The difference is, however, that while Turkish accession is, on the left, generally portrayed as problematic and a long-term project due to cultural and religious differences it is not usually seen as impossible given adequate EU institutional preparation and sufficient compliance with the Copenhagen criteria on Turkey's part. On the right, however, Turkey's religion and culture are frequently depicted as insurmountable barriers to its full membership of the EU. These views are also broadly reflected in the left and right leaning quality press respectively. The liberal-conservative *Le Figaro,* for instance, has tended to use ethical-political arguments focusing on culture and identity against Turkish accession, while defending a 'Christian Europe'. In contrast, while the *Le Monde* journalists have also been rather sceptical about Turkish accession, they have generally rejected the culture and identity argument. Instead, while not rejecting Turkish accession outright, they have tended to argue that neither Turkey nor the EU is ready for such a move; thus it would potentially weaken European integration (Wimmel 2006: 15–17).

Case Study 3: Turkey

Discourse on State and Nation

Turkish discourse on state and nation has its origins in the foundation of the Turkish Republic in 1923, and has been heavily based on French concepts of state and nation, which, as discussed above, are viewed as an organic whole. According to the doctrine of the Kemalist founders of the Turkish republic, the Turkish nation was 'purified' in several regards. The Ottoman and Islamic past was rejected, non-Muslim elements of society were excluded, while all remaining Muslims were considered 'Turks' (Yanık 2011: 81). In short, then, Kemalism aims at 'state autonomy from domestic and international forces with the goal of creating a modern, secular and homogenous (Turkish) nation state' (Yavuz 2009: 27). Thus, Westernisation for the sake of resisting the West required 'de-Orientalization' (Kösebalaban 2007: 89). The sovereignty of the Turkish Republic was viewed as absolute and indivisible by the Kemalists; Atatürk described sovereignty as a notion that 'does not accept sharing in any meaning, form, colour and appearance' (cited in Kösebalaban 2007: 93).

The state defined its interests in terms of crafting a new nation out of diverse ethnic and religious groups; in pursuit of this goal, ethnic and religious identities were subordinated into a state-determined and regimented Turkish nationalism. In traditional Kemalism, then, there is little room for ethnic diversity; the idea was to 'create Turks' out of the various *millets* of the Ottoman Empire. Therefore, the Lausanne treaty, which replaced the Sèvres treaty, only recognised non-Muslim minorities including Armenians, Greeks and Jews; large Muslim minorities, such as Kurds and Alevis, as well as smaller Christian minorities including Assyrians, Chaldeans, Catholics and Protestants were not granted minority status. Even in the event that the state had to recognise the existence of a minority, however, their demands for recognition and cultural rights were to be resisted as much as possible (Grigoriadis 2009: 138).

Thus, ethnic diversity in the public sphere was Otherised as a threat to the unity of the Turkish state. In particular, ethnic minorities were viewed as potential collaborators with the West in undermining the Turkish state, and such attitudes persist in the discourse of nationalists and the traditional Kemalist elite. As former Turkish President Ahmet Necdet Sezer argued, in the context of the 'Working Group on Minority and Cultural Rights' report in 2005, for instance,

> Promoting – apart from cultural rights – ethnic, religious and confessional differences of communities that live together could harm national unity and disintegrate the nation state … In the unitary state, country, nation and sovereignty are single, indivisible. The founding and real element of the Republic of Turkey is the Turkish nation. (*Radikal* 2004)

Foreign policy, too, was based on the perception of 'external and internal threats' to the sovereignty of the nation. As one Turkish general pointed out; 'You will see that Turkey has the most internal and external enemies of any country of the world' (cited in Bilgin 2005: 184). The military, then, played a core role as defender of the nation state, both in its foreign policy and in domestic politics; Turkey therefore became a 'military nation'. In domestic politics, military service was also ascribed an educational and civilizing role, as it was meant to imbue the young conscripts with the values of the new republic (Jenkins 2007: 340).

Moreover, the Kemalist reforms sought to control religion in order to create a new secular society. Legal reforms ended 'the dualism of the Ottoman era, when cadres and institutions borrowed from Europe co-existed with the Islamic ones', a change which also began to have a 'widespread impact on informal institutions, value orientations and social relations in Turkey' (Tezel 2010: 130). In this context, then, Atatürk carried out a series of Westernising reforms intending to undermine the Islamic presence in the social, as well as the political and legal, sphere (Tezel 2010: 131). Secularism in the Kemalist sense was also based on the French revolution concept of secularism. In this view, instead of being neutral towards religion, the secularist state seeks to remove religion from the public sphere and put it under state control (Yavuz 2009: 25–6). To this end a secular administrative unit, the *Diyanet İşleri Bakanlığı* (Presidency of Religious Affairs) was set up in 1924 in order to carry out the management of places of worship and to enlighten society on the topic of religion (Gözaydın 2008: 160) including supervising mosques and educating and appointing clergy (Rumford and Turunç 2011: 145).

In this way, Islam has been used and reinvented for the furtherance of national and state interests, and has been an important source of legitimacy of the Turkish state. In particular, in the Kemalist view, the Islamic ethos of community is important in shaping the daily lives of Turks (Yavuz 2006: 36–9). If a comparison is to be made with the French situation, then, it can be argued that, just as the Christian heritage underlies the French *patrie* the Turkish equivalent of *patrie* is based on traditional Islamic values. Therefore, for Turkish nationalists, while a non-Muslim Greek, Armenian or Jew may become a Turkish citizen they cannot become a Turk (Yavuz 2009: 39–40).

Thus, in common with the French state, the Kemalist Turkish state also had a *mission civilisatrice*. In this case, its civilizing mission was to raise Turkey itself to the standards of contemporary civilization, which it sought to do by rejecting the Ottoman past, which was blamed by the Kemalist elite for Turkey's backwardness *vis-a-vis* Western civilization (Parlak and Kılıçarslan 2006: 131–2). Therefore, the young country's military, political and legal systems were based on European rather than Ottoman ones, while the ethnic diversity and political Islam which had characterised the Ottoman empire were discarded to create a new ethnically homogenous, secular Turkey. Parker (2009a: 1092), for instance, argues that the archetypal Kemalist citizen is 'someone who is a moderate Sunni, alcohol (raki) drinking, Western dressed and educated, a believer in modernity while deeply patriotic and ever suspicious of both imperialist and separatist intent'.

While Kemalism had been the dominant identity discourse from the founding of the Turkish Republic, its hegemony began to be challenged in the more relaxed atmosphere engendered by Turgut Özal's premiership between 1983 and 1993 and by the end of the Cold War, which resulted in the fostering of neoliberal economic policies and the development of a new political language about human rights, civil society and privatisation (Yavuz 2009: 45). This new atmosphere allowed a series of previously repressed identity discourses to resurface and challenge the dominant Kemalist identity.

One of these was a political Islamic identity. In the late 1990s Islamist forces became more prominent in Turkish politics, with the Islamist Refah (Welfare) party notably playing an important role in the coalition government of the time. Meanwhile, the declaration of the Turkish candidacy for EU accession in 1999 provoked expectations among the general public that a deep, sustained process of democratic reform would begin (Johansson-Nogues and Jonasson 2011: 117). Moreover, Kurdish and Alevi groups also gained confidence and wondered how they could express their identities in the public sphere (Yavuz 2009: 29).

In this context, the victory of the moderate Islamist[7] AKP in the 2002 general elections can be said to have consolidated an alternative national identity discourse to traditional Kemalism, one which is more plural in nature, aiming to balance secular and religious interests, and the ethnic Turkish majority with Kurdish, Armenian and other minority groups (Johansson-Nogues and Jonasson 2011: 117). Inspired by Ottoman legacies (Adib-Moghaddam 2011: 166), the AKP thus seeks to discontinue the Kemalist authoritarian nation-building project and defend the role of Islam in the public sphere while recognising the multiculturalism of the country, including political and cultural rights for the Kurdish minority (Yavuz 2009: 265–6). As İçener and Çağlıyan-İçener argue, then, AKP discourse indicates a search for a harmonious fusion between conservatism and democracy (2011: 24–5). Thus, in the view of Rumford and Turunç, 'Turkey is mutating from a Kemalist state to a state and society of manifold modernities and varying philosophies' (2011: 153). One group that seems to be largely excluded from this new atmosphere of pluralism and freedom, however, is women; as Cizre notes, 'it is important to point out that the boundaries between 'us' and 'them' have increasingly included women' (Cizre 2011b: 102).

In many respects, then, the AKP resembles European Christian Democrat parties in their approaches to moral, educational and liberal matters, their international attitudes and, above all, in their support of liberal democratic values and the rights of the individual *vis à vis* the state (Bardakçı 2010: 32).

Thus, the AKP has sought to redefine the meanings of state, national identity, secularism and political community (Yavuz 2009: 267) and has 'done a great deal in dethroning the players, venues, and areas previously under the control of Turkey's hegemonic Kemalist regime' (Cizre 2011a: iii). These transformations are also economic, ideological and social in nature. In economic terms, the most notable reform is economic liberalisation and the introduction of market conditions (Yavuz 2009: 267) which have resulted in better business opportunities and increased prosperity (Cizre 2011a: iii). While the AKP continues to proclaim a secularist outlook, its vision of secularism differs from the Kemalist one in that, for Erdoğan, secularism separates the state from religion and the state should remain neutral towards all religions while guaranteeing the religious freedom of individual citizens (Parker 2009a: 1090).

Indeed, the AKP has prevailed over the Kemalist establishment in a number of ways, although Kemalists have viewed the AKP as a threat to the secular regime since its 2002 victory. For instance, the AKP successfully resisted the establishment's attempts to prevent it from installing its candidate, Abdullah Gül, as President of the Republic. The first of these attempts took the form of an attempted 'e-coup' on the part of the military, to which the AKP responded

---

7   While some observers characterise the AKP as a 'transformation of a religiously oriented party to a moderate, conservative, democratic and globalist centre right political party', others see them as 'closet Islamists' with a hidden agenda to Islamise the country (İçener and Çağlıyan-İçener, 2011: 24).

by reasserting the subservient position of the armed forces in democracies in a televised press conference. The second was the Constitutional Court's arbitrary redefinition of the quorum in presidential elections, to which the AKP responded by amending the constitution so that the President would be elected by popular vote (Çınar 2011: 112). Moreover, the AKP has gradually consolidated its position in the state apparatus by infiltrating into key institutions and positions that were once the exclusive province of Kemalists, including the top echelons of the judiciary and the presidency of the Higher Education Council. In addition, it has restricted the legal-institutional sphere of the military's influence through a series of reforms, and has rendered the military subject to public scrutiny (Çınar 2011: 112–13).

Perhaps surprisingly, the AKP became the champion of EU membership in contrast to more traditional Islamist parties such as the Refah party and its successor the *Saadet* Party, whose discourse has generally been anti-Western and anti-European (Avcı 2011a: 415) focusing on such issues as traditional morality, family values, religious education and establishing closer links with Muslim countries (Celep 2011: 427). In addition, in a notable departure from the traditional Kemalist Western-oriented attitude to foreign policy, AKP foreign policy has been less uniquely focused on Europe in recent years; it can instead be described as a 'soft Euro-Asianism' (Avcı 2011a: 409), stressing Turkey's hybrid identity as Islamic/Asian in addition to Western/European (Rumelili 2011: 241). Davutoğlu, in particular, has stressed that Turkey should act as a 'central country' in the Middle East, Asia, the Balkans and Transcaucasia, and should become a 'problem solver' contributing to 'global and regional peace' (Hale and Özbudun 2010: 110–20).

In conclusion, Turkish national identity discourse has undergone considerable diversification since the end of the Cold War, which can be seen as a 'critical juncture' for Turkey. While Kemalist discourse is certainly not dead, it is finding itself increasingly challenged at a fundamental level by the new Islamist and multicultural discourse best represented by the AKP. Although the war between these dominant discourses is perhaps not over, the AKP appears to be winning the battle, something which, for Cizre for instance, can be explained by 'the political impotence, lack of ideological vitality, articulation and coherence of the oppositional political actors' (2011a: iv).

Discourse on Europe/the EU

Turkey has always had a complex relationship with Europe (Bardakçı 2010: 27). As has been discussed earlier in this book, Europeanisation attempts in Turkey date back as far as the latter decades of the Ottoman empire, specifically to the *Tanzimat* reforms of the nineteenth century (Mango 2005: 15–16). Atatürk's reforms, carried out in the 1920s and 1930s in the new Turkish republic, put an end to traditional Ottoman institutions while promoting, among other things, secularisation, the emancipation of women, the adoption of the Latin alphabet and the Western calendar, and the adoption of Western dress (Sümer 2009: 125). Although Atatürk generally emphasised that he wanted to modernise his country, thus making his people part of a universal civilization, he recognised that what he was undertaking was in fact Westernisation (Mango 2005: 18) (Sümer 2009: 125), and that he would have to carry it out despite the West rather than with its help. In his own words, 'The West has always been prejudiced against the Turks. But we Turks have consistently moved towards the West … in order to be a civilized nation, there is no alternative' (cited in Morris 2005: 30). Kemalist foreign policy, then, entailed the realisation of a civilizational shift (Yavuz 2009: 208).

Thus, Europe was seen as the final stage of civilization, a model 'against which Ottoman and Turkish modernisers measured their efforts to reform their political, educational and military systems' (Bardakçı 2010: 27). Therefore, Kemalists and the CHP, the main Kemalist party, have supported both Turkey's adaptation to the values and institutions of the West and its economic and political independence from the West; they have been simultaneously pro-Western and anti-imperialist (Celep 2011: 423). A recent examination of Turkish discourse on the EEC between 1967 and 1980 shows that Turkish support for the EEC was expressed in civilizational terms (Dösemeci 2012: 89). In this context, then, in Kemalist discourse Turkey's success in its EU accession bid is perceived as a yardstick of its progress towards civilization;

> Turkey-EU relations give rise to great strain in Turkish society, not only due to the expected economic costs and benefits but also due to an endemic identity crisis. Turks tend to see their relations with Europe as constitutive of their identity. They perceive the treatment of their potential membership of the EU as an indicator of how others see them. (Uğur and Canefe 2004: 2)

While Europe, and thus the EU, is represented as a model of civilization to be emulated, it has also been represented as threatening to Turkish sovereignty; between 1967 and 1980, for instance, 'the Turkish opposition perceived and presented integration as a threat to the Turkish nation, allowing the latter to be conceptualised and imagined in different ways' (Dösemeci 2012: 92). Broadly speaking, in different discourses, the EEC was depicted as a threat to the Turkish nation-state's independence and integrity, as an elitist threat to the Turkish people, and as a cultural threat to the distinct Turkish heritage and traditions (Dösemeci 2012: 95). As Kösebalaban notes, 'the image of the West in the Kemalist mentality continues to represent the Other' (2002: 131). This ambiguity can be largely explained by the historical experiences of the Ottoman Empire, which have resulted in the so-called Sèvres and Tanzimat syndromes, today most strongly represented in the discourse of the nationalist MHP,[8] although these syndromes are also present in the discourse of traditional Kemalists, best represented by the CHP.

---

8   The MHP, whose roots can be traced to the late 1940s, is broadly comparable to radical right-wing parties in Europe in its nationalist and ethnocentric platform, and rests on a romantic and racist notion of Turkish history (Avcı 2011:437).

Together, the Sèvres and Tanzimat syndromes result in an image of 'a conspirational West bent on the destruction of Turkish national integrity with the collaboration of 'internal enemies' (Kösebalaban 2002: 131). Specifically, the Tanzimat syndrome results in a delegitimisation of collective and individual rights, while the consequences of the Sèvres syndrome are isolationism in the area of foreign policy and 'Westernization without the West' at home (Yılmaz 2006: 31). Thus, as Kösebalaban argues, 'on one side of the coin lies the perpetual domestic threat, *irtica,* and on the other lies the perpetual external enemy, Europe' (Kösebalaban 2007: .90).

The Sèvres syndrome dates from the treaty of Sèvres, signed by the Ottoman Empire and the Entente powers on August 10, 1920, which effectively carved up and divided the Ottoman Empire among the European powers which had been victorious in World War 1. The Arabian Peninsula and Mesopotamia were granted to Britain, Syria and South-East Anatolia to France, eastern Thrace and Izmir to Greece and the rest of Western Anatolia to Italy. As Yılmaz argues, the memory of Sèvres is often connected to an even deeper historical memory, that of the Crusades:

> There is a route that started with the crusades and reached its peak with the Treaty of Sèvres, which is the hidden agenda of Europe. This hidden agenda is to drive Turks out of Istanbul and Anatolia which supposedly belong to Christians, and give it back to Greeks, Armenians, Kurds and to its real owners, that is the Christian and/or Arian people. (Yılmaz 2006:37)

The *Tanzimat* syndrome, on the other hand, is derived from the nineteenth century reform programme of the same name, discussed in Chapter 3. A major motive for these reforms was to regain the allegiance of the Empire's Christian subjects and to contain their separatist tendencies, as well as to appease the European Great Powers who had put pressure on the Empire to grant the Christians economic, political and cultural liberties. However, the reform process resulted in the weakening of centre-periphery relations within the Ottoman Empire and eventually contributed to its weakening and collapse (Yılmaz 2006: 31).

It can be argued, then, that the Turkish Republic, while aiming for Westernisation, was also based on a deeply ambiguous attitude to the West as a result of the Tanzimat and Sèvres syndromes. While there was an effort to maintain relations with the West at a certain level, then, the Kemalist state pursued a policy of 'Westernization without the West'. As Bardakçı argues,

> the Treaty of Sèvres became the most important symbol of Turkish distrust towards Europe, which is deeply ingrained in Turkish political culture. As a corollary of the perception of Europe as a potential 'enemy', Turkey remains cautious and vigilant towards Europe. (2010: 27)

Both syndromes, then, continue to be present in Turkish political discourse today. As Guida, for instance, argues, 'The Sèvres syndrome as applied to the

Turkish media and to Turkish intellectuals is crucial to an understanding of Turkish politics, shedding light on Turkish foreign relations, policies, and the various positions that are taken' (Guida 2008: 39). Similarly, Kirişçi argues that 'Sèvrephobia' has acted as a 'cultural filter' for perceiving the outside world (2006). In this context the EU, together with the USA and the Catholic Church, has been viewed with scepticism particularly on the nationalist right and the Kemalist left,[9] and such attitudes can also be noted among Eurosceptic Islamists, such as the Saadet (Felicity) Party (MacMillan 2013: 111). The nationalist MHP may be defined as varying between hard and soft Euroscepticism (Bardakçı 2010: 40) in that, while it claims to have no enmity towards Europe, Turkey should strive to preserve its national character, unity and sovereignty which, it is implied, are threatened by the prospect of EU accession. As Yılmaz points out:

> for the MHP, EU demands for minority rights constitute a direct threat to the power of the Turkish state and the unity of the nation by continuing the centuries-old Western strategy of dividing the Turkish nation by creating 'artificial minorities, taking them under Western patronage and provoking them to rebel against the state. (Yılmaz 2011: 5)

In the MHP's view, 'when these conditions [for EU accession] are compared with Sèvres, it's almost as if Sèvres has been resurrected'(MHP 2010: 36–7). The CHP, once supportive of European integration, has also become increasingly Eurosceptic during its time in opposition to the AKP government, criticising the latter's implementation of EU reforms on two counts. As well as arguing that the AKP was using the EU accession process as an instrument to further its socially conservative agenda, it also accuses the AKP government of failing to defend Turkey's national interest (Celeb 2011: 425).

In 2008, for instance, the CHP applied to the Constitutional Court for the cancellation of the Law on Foundations. The Law, which improved the status of the foundations owned by non-Muslim minorities, was meant to replace previous legislation on minority rights which dated back to 1936, and was at least partly the consequence of EU pressure for reform in this area (Bardakçı 2010: 3). The CHP argued that the bill was nothing but an attempt to revive the Sèvres treaty; according to Deniz Baykal, then leader of the party, demands that had been rejected even in the Sèvres treaty had been brought to Parliament (*Hürriyet* 2006). Rahmi Güner, CHP MP for Ordu, argued that the Law on Foundations would 'endanger Turkey's sovereignty, independence, unitary structure and the gains made with

---

9   Bardakçı (2010:28) notes that the descriptions of political parties as 'left' or 'right' in the Turkish context do not correspond with those in Europe as, in Turkey, they are not based on their position on socio-economic policies. Instead the 'right' refers to a commitment to religious, conservative and nationalist values, and is therefore more society-oriented while the 'left', at least the centre-left, is closely associated to the state.

the Lausanne treaty' and that he did not want 'foreigners, via the foundations, to organise political activities in Anatolia again'(Erboz 2008).

Following its election in 2002, the AKP demonstrated a positive attitude to EU accession in contrast to other Islamist parties, which have traditionally maintained that EU membership equals assimilation into 'Western civilization', viewed as incompatible with Islamic cultural values. The Islamist *Saadet* party, for example, sees the EU as a 'Christian club' descended from Crusaders bent on exploiting Turkey. In its view, in contrast, Turkey needs to become the leader of a union of Muslim nations (Yılmaz 2011: 5). In order to explain the AKP's pro-EU stance, Yavuz argues that, following the February 28 process and the politicisation of the judicial system, Islamic groups began to regard the EU as a source of protection from the Kemalist state and a source of external support for democratisation, including a reduction in the power of the military, the institutionalisation of human rights and economic development (Yavuz 2009: 215–16).

In this way, then, the AKP drew on the EU to 'domesticate and force not only the state but also the anti-systemic actors to change their perceptions and strategies and to take on EU norms as the point of reference to create a new social contract in Turkey' (Yavuz 2006: 3). On this basis, the AKP carried out 'momentous' EU-related reforms, touching on previously 'taboo' areas such as the extension of minority rights to the Kurds, the abolishment of the death penalty and a broader definition of freedom of association and expression (Avcı 2011a: 417). As Minister of State Ali Babacan emphasised, for instance, membership in the EU would trigger a 'reform process that will bring universal standards and practices to all areas of daily life' (cited in Duran 2008: 87).

However, the AKP does not take the Kemalist view that EU membership involves Turkey's giving up its traditional identity and legacy in order to assimilate into European culture. Instead, it emphasises cultural differences, particularly those emanating from Turkey's Islamic identity, and talks about entering or integrating into the EU instead of giving up its identity in order to 'become European' (Yavuz 2009: 203) (İçener and Çağlıyan-İçener 2011: 25). In this way, while previous governments had argued that Turkey would, as a result of its EU accession, be integrated into some other civilization, the AKP wants to promote a modern and reformist Islamic identity by emulating successful European ideas and values (Yanık 2009: 542) (Yavuz 2009: 209).

Thus, the AKP regards Turkey's Islamic and European identities as complementary; it tends to depict Turkey as bridging the West and Islam (Yanık 2009: 534). It also represents Turkey as a peacemaker or mediator between East and West, and argues that the West must support a democratic, peaceful and successful Muslim Turkey as, thanks to its combined Western and Islamic nature, it would be the best antidote to Huntington's 'clash of civilizations' thesis (Yavuz 2009: 209–10) (Yanık 2009: 541). As Erdoğan put forward in 2002, for instance, 'When we enter the EU, we are not going to represent the clash of civilizations and cultures, instead Turkey by being the 'bridge' will help to achieve the merger of different cultures and civilizations'(Hürriyet 2002).

Moreover, AKP discourse focuses on Turkey's geopolitical importance by depicting it as a country in transition from middle-sized power status to being a major power (Yanık 2011: 80). In particular, such discourse came to the fore following the launching of the 'Alliance of Civilizations' initiative in 2004, led by Turkish Prime Minister Erdoğan and then Spanish Prime Minister Zapatero (Yanık 2009: 541). As Erdoğan argued in a 2004 interview, for instance;

> a country like Turkey, where the cultures of Islam and democracy have merged together, taking part in such an institution as the EU, will bring harmony of civilizations. That is why we think it is the project of the century. We are there as a guarantee of an entente between the civilisations. The countries that want to exclude us from Europe are not playing their part in history. (Castle 2004)

Here, as Kuzmanovic argues, the AKP, by emphasising the difference yet compatibility of European and Islamic civilizations, seeks to pacify both the EU and those in Turkey who are sceptical of the AKP's 'ulterior motives' on the one hand and Islamists in Turkey on the other (Kuzmanovic 2008: 53). More recently, the AKP's hybrid identity has been evident in its foreign policy towards the Middle East, characterised by a notable increase in activism and in independence from the West. However, the two roles are seen as complementary rather than contradictory in AKP discourse; as AKP foreign minister Davutoğlu stated, for instance, 'if Turkey does not have a solid stance in Asia, it will have very limited chances with the EU' (cited in Önis and Yılmaz 2009: 9). Indeed, Davutoğlu has argued that the Middle East is not an alternative to Europe for Turkey; instead its new activism there has actually brought it closer to Europe (Rumelili 2011: 241–3).

In addition, Turkey has also been depicted as beneficial to the EU in security and, increasingly, economic terms in AKP discourse. Notably, the Orientalist image of the Turk as 'sick man of Europe' has been rejected and, eventually, reversed in recent AKP discourse, which argues that Turkish accession will not be a drain on EU resources but will rather benefit the EU (MacMillan 2013: 114–15). As Erdoğan argued in a 2010 speech in Bosnia Herzegovina, 'Turkey does not want to be a burden on the EU, but rather it wants to help share the difficulties the union has confronted'(*Hürriyet Daily News* 2010). Similarly, Turkey's EU envoy Egemen Bağış stressed in 2009 that 'Turkey will be an honourable member of the EU and not the sick man of Europe' (Bağış 2009).

On the contrary, Turkey is portrayed as being of significant benefit to the EU in economic and security terms; its economic and demographic vitality are juxtaposed with Europe's ageing population and crisis-ridden economy (MacMillan 2013: 114–15). In a recent speech in Denmark, for instance, Bağış portrayed Turkey, with its dynamic economy and large market, as a 'saviour' for crisis-ridden Europe (Karabat 2010). Thus, this can be seen as an inversion of the traditional European metaphor of Turkey as the 'sick man of Europe': in the AKP's discourse, it is Europe itself which is the 'sick man'. Similarly, in another speech Bağış argued that;

> The EU is important for Turkey, but Turkey is much more important for the EU. Today, if we take into account the problems Europe encounters such as the fight against illegal migration, energy crisis, economic crisis, ageing labour force, climate change, the need for new markets, security, terror and the fight against drugs, Europe cannot attain success without Turkey's contribution. As we become aware of our power, they will also become aware of Turkey's power. (Bağış 2009)

In the same vein, in a 2011 article in *Newsweek*, Prime Minister Erdoğan took the 'sick man' metaphor further by describing Europe's employment and social security sectors as being 'comatose', its economy as 'stagnant' and its population as 'near geriatric', in contrast to Turkey, which he dubs 'the Robust Man of Europe'. He argued that the EU had no real alternative to Turkey, and that, due to shifts in world power in politics and economics, it needed Turkey, with its growing geopolitical and economic importance in order to be a 'stronger, richer and safer' Union;

> ...Turkey has been putting its imprint on the global stage with its impressive economic development and political stability. The Turkish economy is Europe's fastest growing sizeable economy, and will continue to be so in 2011...And it's not only economics. Turkey is becoming a global and regional player with its soft power. (Erdoğan 2011)

However, while the AKP still declares itself in favour of EU accession, it has itself become increasingly critical of the EU, and its reform record since 2005 has become much more scanty despite some attempts to tackle diversity issues since 2009, most notably its Kurdish initiative which has sought to extend cultural and linguistic rights to the Kurdish minority (Avcı 2011a: 417). Notably, however, the AKP has been reluctant to abolish the controversial article 301 of the Turkish Penal Code, which provides for intellectuals to be put on trial for insulting the Turkish state and nation, and several leading writers and journalists have been tried under this article, including Orhan Pamuk, Elif Şafak and Hrant Dink. This decline in the AKP's Euro-enthusiasm can be explained by increasing domestic opposition to EU accession, as well as a loss of empowering appeal on the part of the EU, most notably due to opposition to Turkey's full membership on the part of right-wing politicians in Europe, which has damaged the credibility of EU conditionality (Avcı 2011a: 416–19).

In this context, then, Europe has also been constructed as violating universal principles in AKP discourse; this has generally targeted those, most notably on the Franco-German right, who reject full membership for Turkey on the grounds that it does not belong to 'European civilization' and, instead, propose a more limited 'privileged partnership' (MacMillan 2013: 115–16). In particular, AKP discourse has emphasised the unfairness and arbitrariness of the 'privileged partnership' as a substitute for Turkish full membership; in this case it is the EU that is accused of not playing by the rules; in other words it is not living up to the concept of *pacta sunt servanda*. Moreover, opponents of Turkish accession on identity/religious grounds are characterised as backward, uncivilized and 'medieval' in AKP discourse, in contrast to the modern, secular and civilized Turks (MacMillan 2013: 115). Such discourse focuses, in particular, on the criticism that a Europe without Turkey would be a 'Christian club'. As Erdoğan succinctly argued, for instance, 'The idea of 'Christian Europe' belongs to the Middle Ages. It should stay there' (Castle 2004).

In contrast, in AKP discourse, an EU that accepted Turkey would prove that it was not a 'Christian club' and was, instead, a rights-based postnational union. Moreover, for the AKP, Turkish accession would refute the 'Clash of Civilizations' thesis (MacMillan 2013: 116). As Abdüllah Gül has argued, for instance;

> Turkey's EU membership will mean that Europe has achieved such maturity that it can incorporate a major Muslim country into its fold and that the EU stands for common values and institutions rather than a common religion. For Turkey, EU membership will mean anchoring more than a century-old Western vocation in the highest standards of democritisation, good governance and integration. For the world, this would be evidence that civilizations line up in terms of their democratic vocation, and not on the basis of religion. (Gül 2007: 29)

Conclusion

The case studies in this chapter indicate that discourse on state and nation does have a constraining effect on national discourses on Europe and, more specifically, on discourses on Turkey's bid for EU accession. Of the three countries examined, it is Turkey where the dominant discourse on state and nation has been significantly challenged in recent years. It is perhaps premature to argue that the AKP discourse has replaced Kemalist discourse as the dominant one on state and nation; it is, however, certainly an *alternative* dominant discourse. While the dominant discourses on state and nation have remained much more stable in the British and French cases, there have been some perhaps more minor, but still important, changes in recent years. In the British case, the unitary nature of the British state has given way to significant devolution to Scotland and Wales; in the French case, the republican model of immigrant assimilation has been challenged, while on the right the concept of *patrie* has become increasingly identified with Christianity.

According to FPDA, British policy towards the Turkish membership bid can be explained by British discursive attitudes towards Europe which, in turn, are shaped by British discursive constructions of state and nation. British nationhood is a primarily political, rather than ethnic, construction, centred upon Parliament and the monarchy. Both of these traditionally represent national sovereignty, the former by defending individual rights and freedoms, the latter representing British sovereignty from Europe (primarily France) and the Pope. Moreover, in foreign policy, Britain has traditionally viewed itself as a world power rather than a European power.

Thus, regarding European integration, there has been a persistent fear of the development of a European superstate which would threaten the sovereignty of the British Parliament, one of the bastions of British identity. While the Labour Party in recent years has been more pro-European than the Conservatives, it also continues to insist on a primarily intergovernmental EU. Britain thus made the decision to join the EEC in the 1960s for pragmatic reasons rather than through any deeper sense of European identity. Such pragmatism continues to dominate the discourse of both major British parties regarding the EU. However, importantly, the EU is also seen as a guardian of 'universal values' such as democracy or human rights.

These attitudes, then, are reflected in British discourse on Turkish accession to the EU. Turkey's accession is supported for the pragmatic benefits it could bring to the EU due to its growing economy and important geopolitical situation between East and West. Moreover, importance is also given to Turkey's fulfillment of the political accession criteria, reflecting a 'rights-based' understanding of the EU. 'Value-based' arguments rejecting Turkish accession on the basis of its cultural and religious background appear, however, to be almost absent from the discourse. There is little sense that Turkey's Muslim heritage should exclude it from full membership of the EU providing it respects the 'universal values' which, according to the Treaties, underscore the EU. Indeed, rejection of Turkish accession on religious or cultural grounds would be fundamentally alien to British constructions of state and nation, which tend towards the 'multicultural'.

French discourse on Europe is also heavily influenced by the discourse on state and nation, itself shaped by the Republican discourse which developed following the French Revolution. This is characterised by a political rather than an ethnic concept of the nation; thus French nationality is determined by allegiance to the political nation rather than by ethnic or religious characteristics. This is, however, supported by the sub-concept of *patrie,* based on a cultural sense of belonging such as a shared history, language or traditions. Other features of the dominant Republican discourse on state and nation include a strong, centralised state and an international *mission civilisatrice* to spread Republican values around the world.

Regarding Europe, while de Gaulle and his followers argued for a 'Europe of the nations' in which France was seen as playing a dominant role, this was challenged, especially from the 1980s, by a competing discourse according to which Europe was seen as France writ large. This discourse is influenced by the concept, important in French discourse on state and nation, that a successful political actor requires a strong identity and definite borders. Thus, in this view, the EU is primarily conceived of as a value-based community.

For this reason, a cautious attitude towards enlargement is common in French discourse, as it tends to be viewed as a potential threat to EU integration, in that it is seen as possibly weakening Europe's institutional functioning, and therefore its strength as a political actor. Thus, in French discourse, adequate preparation on the part both of the candidate countries and of the EU institutions is seen as a *sine qua non* for enlargement to take place. The question of Turkish full membership of the EU has, however, been particularly controversial and, especially on the right, is rejected on the grounds of culture and religion.

In the Turkish case, the traditional Kemalist discourse on state and nation in Turkey has faced significant challenges since the end of the Cold War, most notably by the AKP, which has now been the governing party for over a decade. In particular, as has been noted, the AKP has challenged Kemalist conceptions of secularism, minorities and the democratic process, and has seen the EU as a potential anchor for its democratising reforms. On this basis, the AKP has also challenged the traditional Kemalist 'love/hate' relationship with Europe. While, in Kemalist discourse, Europe (and hence the EU) tends to be simultaneously represented as a model of civilization to be emulated and as a potential threat, AKP discourse shows a much 'cooler' attitude towards Europe in that it no longer appears as the peak of civilization or as a threat to Turkish sovereignty and unity. Indeed, the EU is often depicted as backward and struggling, in urgent need of fresh Turkish economic and demographic blood. Instead of an example of civilization, the EU is rather represented as a *different* civilization, albeit one which shares certain values with Turkey.

To conclude, of the three cases examined, British and Turkish attitudes to the EU, and consequently to Turkish accession, share many similarities. In both countries, there is a sense that Europe represents Other rather than Self, albeit frequently a friendly Other. Primarily for this reason, the EU tends not to be depicted as a 'value-based community' in either country; it is instead viewed mostly in pragmatic and rights-based terms. It is on this basis, then, that Turkish accession is supported; Turkey is seen as potentially bringing economic and security advantages to the EU, while demonstrating that Islam and 'universal values' are not incompatible. This provides a stark contrast with the French case, where identification with Europe has traditionally been strong. French discourse, then, tends to emphasise the importance of a *Europe puissance,* or powerful Europe, which can only exist if Europe has a strong identity and borders. Thus, the EU is often viewed in value-based terms, and its identity, particularly on the French right, is seen as based on a 'European civilization' understood in cultural terms, with Christianity playing a strong role.

Conclusion

This study has been based on the constructivist premise that political/territorial identities, including EU identity, are fundamentally social constructs rather than primordial in nature. Discourse, especially elite discourse, plays a particularly important part in this identity construction. Another important concept which has underlied this analysis is that identities are constructed *vis à vis* a perceived Other or Others, which may be considered threatening, inferior, aberrant, exotic, neutral or even superior in nature to the Self. Identities may be inclusive or exclusive, potentially open or closed to their Others. EU identity, for instance, tends to be inclusive when faced with CEE applicant countries such as Croatia, but exclusive in regard to applicants perceived as geographically non-European, such as Morocco. The current book concludes that Turkey is depicted both as an inclusive and an exclusive Other, depending largely on the political and national background of the speaker.

On this basis, then, this study has been carried out on the understanding that elite attitudes to Turkey's EU accession, and, specifically, the arguments used in favour of and against Turkey's membership of the EU can shed light on how the EU itself is perceived. In addition, it is put forward that the issue of Turkish accession represents a 'critical juncture', which may provoke both a change in elite discourse and a greater receptiveness on the part of the general public to elite discourse.

The analysis of arguments across the EU indicates that there is a basic division in EU elite discourse between those who support Turkey's accession in principle and those who reject it on the grounds that Turkey is, in cultural and religious terms, fundamentally non-European. Supporters of eventual Turkish full membership tend to depict the EU as a rights-based postnational union, primarily based on 'universal' rights such as democracy and human rights, as well as a problem-solving entity whose legitimacy is based on the benefits, particularly in the areas of security and the economy that it can provide to its members. In other words, the EU is perceived as the bearer of a 'universal' civilization with its roots in Europe but potentially available to all. In this context, Turkish accession is supported on the grounds that it would not only secure liberal democracy in Turkey, but would help to prevent a 'clash of civilizations' by providing a positive example for other Muslim majority states. Moreover, in this view, Turkish accession would boost security and economic growth in the EU.

The contrasting view, particularly prevalent on the European right, is that Turkey should not be granted full membership of the EU as it is not fundamentally 'European'. This, then, indicates an understanding that the EU is a value-based union, based on a 'thicker' cultural identity with its roots in the religious, cultural and historical heritage of Europe. An examination of the discourse suggests that these are seen as based on the heritage of ancient Greece and Rome, historical events such as the Enlightenment and the Industrial Revolution and, above all, Christianity. Importantly, this heritage, particularly that of Christianity, is seen as a condition for the development and full adoption of norms such as democracy, human rights or the rule of law. In other words, these norms are seen as specifically European (or Western) rather than universal. This view is close to that proposed by Huntington in that it tends to perceive the world as divided into several distinct culturally based, and relatively fixed, civilizations, rather than a 'universal civilization' potentially open to all. In this discourse, Islam is portrayed as especially incompatible with 'European civilization' and thus with liberal democracy, and Turkish accession is rejected as it is perceived as weakening the values underpinning the EU and, therefore, the integration project itself.

In fact, as discussed in Chapter 2, this debate is an old one, based on stereotypes of the East as 'barbaric' and 'despotic', which ultimately have their origins in ancient Greek attitudes towards the Persians. In particular, parallels can be drawn between the current debate and the nineteenth century debate over the inclusion of the Ottoman Empire in the Concert of Europe. In nineteenth century European discourse, it was taken for granted that the Ottomans were less 'civilized' than the European powers in terms, for instance, of the rule of law and the protection of individual rights. However, there was a divergence of opinion over whether the Ottomans were inherently 'civilizable' or not; while one school of thought considered that it was the European powers' job to lead the Ottomans along the path to enlightenment, others thought that they were irredeemably barbaric and could never become civilized. Although put in somewhat different terms, a rather similar discussion is taking place today over Turkish accession to the EU. Whether rightly or wrongly, Turkey is frequently depicted as less 'civilized' than the EU in terms of democracy, human rights and the rule of law both by supporters and opponents of its accession. Again, to put it bluntly, the debate continues to be centred on whether Turkey can come up to 'European standards' in these areas with help from the EU, or whether, because of its 'Eastern', Muslim heritage, it is inherently barbaric and despotic to the extent that is can never be brought up to EU 'standards of civilization'.

Thus, the consensus which was reached over CEE enlargement has broken down in the case of Turkish accession. The 'official' line on enlargement to the CEECs put forward, notably, by the European Commission indeed focused, as expected, on the need to extend liberal democracy to CEE. However, it also spoke to those who viewed the EU as a value based community as it discussed the enlargement in terms of the EU's duty to 'reunite the European family'. Even in the discourse of supporters of eventual Turkish accession, Turkey's 'Europeanness' is rarely referred to, while there is little if no discussion of a 'duty' to 'reunite' Europe by allowing Turkish accession. While such discourse may resonate with a view of the EU as a rights-based postnational union, it leaves those who view it in more cultural terms, as a value-based union, rather cold to say the least.

The three case studies in the final chapter indicate that diverging national discourses on state and nation may have an important constraining influence on how the EU is perceived in national discourses, and, consequently, on whether, and how, Turkish accession is predominantly supported or opposed. In both Turkish and British discourse, the EU is seen as Other, albeit a primarily friendly Other. Indeed, in both cases, there are also examples in the discourse where the EU is portrayed as a notably unfriendly, rather threatening Other. In Britain, it tends to be perceived as a threat to the 'sacred cow' of national parliamentary sovereignty; among Turkish nationalists it is, notably, seen as a potential threat to the very unity of the country. Even when the discourse on EU accession is more positive in these countries, it rarely depicts the EU as a value-based union with a strong cultural identity. Instead EU accession is important for pragmatic reasons and in order to spread potentially 'universal' norms associated with liberal democracy.

The French case provides a notable contrast. Here, there is a strong identification of the French nation-state with Europe, which is often portrayed as 'France writ large'; in this discourse, then, the EU should be as strong a political actor as possible. Moreover, in French discourse, a strong political actor requires a strong identity and clear borders. In the case of the EU, enlargement is generally treated with mistrust as it is seen as potentially weakening integration. Particularly in the case of Turkey, this opposition has become much more overt and more culturally based in nature. This is especially true on the right where, along with the rise of the importance of the ethnic *patrie* in national discourse on state and nation, Christianity has become an important identity marker.

Thus, although a comprehensive series of national case-studies would be needed in order to verify this hypothesis, this study tentatively argues that differing national discourses on state and nation and Europe are reflected in differing national positions regarding Turkish accession, which then, to a certain extent, interact with each other in the European public sphere encouraging their refinement into two broad visions of the EU and of Turkey's accession. In this sense, then, the findings of this study tend to concur with Risse's conclusion that 'Two distinct visions of Europe and the EU are on display and are becoming ever more salient in the public spheres', the first a liberal, cosmopolitan Europe, the second a more exclusionary 'nationalist' Europe' (2010: 245).

Another argument, which has occasionally been used together with pragmatic and right-based arguments in support of Turkey's eventual EU accession, also nods towards a value-based understanding of the EU. Unlike the value-based arguments used on the European right, however, these arguments include Turkey in the cultural European family. Indeed, this view of Europe, instead of seeing it as a uniquely Christian cultural area, acknowledges the important role that Muslim culture and science played in the development of European civilization. A similar argument stresses that, through the ages, the territory where Turkey lies today has been a cradle of European culture. Such arguments still imply a cultural identity for the EU, and therefore eventual borders.

However, when compared with arguments for a 'Judeo-Christian' EU, the cultural identity implied is much more inclusive, closer to the vision of Europe as a relatively flexible 'civilizational constellation' than to a comparatively rigid, Huntingtonian-type civilization. It is suggested that, if a compromise is reached between supporters and opponents of Turkish accession, it will be on the basis of such arguments. Here, some common ground could be found between those who would exclude Turkey on cultural grounds and those who would include it on rights-based grounds. Indeed, an EU based on a 'civilizational constellation' understanding of Europe would come close to a Habermasian 'constitutional patriotism', predominantly founded on universal norms but also underscored by some kind of 'we feeling'.

Given that such arguments are relatively rare in the discourse, however, it is perhaps overly optimistic to think that such a consensus can be reached. It is undeniable that, particularly via medieval Al-Andalus, Islamic culture and learning had an important impact on the development of European culture. Indeed, it is perhaps doubtful if many of the milestones of 'European civilization', including medieval scholasticism, the Renaissance, the scientific revolution, the discovery of America or even the Enlightenment, would have occurred without the input of Muslim learning. On the other hand, as has been noted, the old construction of the East, particularly the Muslim East, as Europe's Other, notably as a threatening and/or inferior Other, continues to be deeply entrenched in much European discourse on Turkey's accession. For Turkey to be fully accepted as part of the European family would require an ability to see beyond the stereotypes such as the barbaric, despotic 'Terrible Turk' and the inferior 'Sick Man of Europe'. Similarly, Turkish discourse emphasising Turkey's Islamic identity, or even its role as a bridge between civilizations is unlikely to encourage those in the EU member states or institutions to see Turkey as an inherent part of Europe.

Although the main focus of this book has been on elite discourse, public opinion can also play an important role in the accession process, particularly when referenda are involved. The low level of public support, both across the EU and in Turkey itself can, to a certain extent, be understood in the general context of enlargement fatigue, or even a more general 'Eurofatigue', among the EU public. However, as discussed in Chapter 3, research suggests that a significant part of public opposition to Turkish accession is cultural in nature; it can thus be seen both as a symptom of the extension of nationalism to the EU scale at the grass-roots level and as a consequence of the impact of right-wing elite discourse. The sharp decline in Turkish public support for enlargement, on the other hand, can be largely explained by the mixed messages that Turkey has been receiving from the European elite, by the decline in enthusiasm on the part of the Turkish government and by the fact that the crisis-ridden EU is no longer such a pole of attraction for an increasingly prosperous Turkey.

Bibliography

AB Haber. 2006. *Olli Rehn: AB'nin 'GenişlemePolitikaları' konusundayenibiru zlaşıyaihtiyaçvar* [Online, 20 July]. Available at: www.abhaber.com/haber. php?id12725 [accessed: 10 March 2009].

Abusara, A. 2010. Public Opinion in Turkey on EU Accession: An (Un)desirable Marriage. *Different Dimensions of European Security*, 17, 77–87.

Adib-Moghaddam, A. 2011. *A Metahistory of the Clash of Civilisations*. London: Hurst.

A&G Araştirma. 2008. *AB Raporu 2008* [Online]. Available at: http://agarastirma. com.tr/abye-uyelik-anketipdi [accessed: 18 January 2011].

Agence France Presse. 2004. *Fabius Réitère son Opposition a l'Entrée de la Turquie dans L'UE* [Online, 2 November]. Available at:http://afp.pressedd. com [accessed: 20 September 2010].

Akça, G and Hülür, H. 2004. Osmanlı-Türk Düşüncesindeki Doğu-Batı İmgelerini Küreselleşme Tartşmaları Bağlamında Yeniden Düşünmek. *Türkiyat Araştırmaları Dergisi*, 260–82.

Aksoy, N. 2003. Turks in Elizabethan Drama, in *Historical Image of the Turk in Europe: 15th Century to the Present*, edited by M. Soykut. Istanbul: Isis, 197–210.

Aksoy, S. 2009. The Prospect of Turkey's EU Membership as Represented in the British Newspapers *The Times* and *The Guardian* 2002–2005. *Journal of European Studies*, 39(4), 469–506.

Aktar, C. 2012. The Positive Agenda and Beyond: A New Beginning for EU-Turkey Relations? *Insight Turkey*, 14(3), 35–44.

Alessandri, E. and Sali, S. 2009. Italian Perceptions, in *Turkey Watch: EU Member States' Perceptions on Turkey's Accession to the EU*, edited by S. Akşit, Ö. Şenyuva and Ç. Üstün. Ankara: Middle East Technical University, 58–73.

Amin, S. 1989. *Eurocentricism*.New York: Monthly Review Press.

Amiraux, V. 2010. Crisis and New Challenges? French Republicanism Featuring Multiculturalism, in *European Multiculturalism Revisited*, edited by A. Silj. London: Zed Books, 65–104.

Anderson, P.J. 2004. A Flag of Convenience? Discourse and Motivations of the London-Based Eurosceptic Press, in *Euroscepticism: Party Politics, National Identity and European Integration*, edited by R. Harmsen and M. Spiering. Amsterdam: European Studies, 151–70.

Artemel, S. 2003. View of the Turks from the Perspective of the Humanists in Renaissance England, in *Historical Image of the Turk in Europe: 15th Century to the Present*, edited by M. Soykut. Istanbul: Isis, 149–74.

Asbeek Brusse, W. and Griffiths, R.T. 2004. Good Intentions and Hidden Motives: Turkey/EU Relations in a Historical Perspective, in *Turkey and the EU Enlargement*, edited by R.T. Griffiths and D. Özdemir. Istanbul: Istanbul Bilgi University Press, 13–28.

Avcı, G. 2006.Turkey's EU Politics: Consolidating Democracy Through Enlargement?, in *Questioning EU Enlargement: Europe in Search of Identity*, edited by H. Sjursen. London: Routledge, 62–78.

Avcı, G. 2011a. The Justice and Development Party and the EU: Political Pragmatism in a Changing Environment. *South European Politics and Society*, 16(3), 409–21.

Avcı, G. 2011b. The Nationalist Movement Party's Euroscepticism: Party Ideology Meets Strategy. *South European Politics and Society*, 16(3), 435–47.

Aydın, S. 2006. Seeking Kant in the EU's Relations with Turkey [Online]. Available at: www.tesev.org.tr/etkinlik/seeking_kantf_TR_EU_Relations.pdf [accessed: 3 December 2009].

Aydın-Düzgit, S. 2009a. *Discursive Construction of European Identity in the EU's Relations with Turkey: The Case of the European Commission*, ISA Annual Conference, New York, 15–18 February 2009 [Online]. Available at: http://citation/allacademic.com/meta//p_mla_apa_research__citation/3/1/2/519.pdf [accessed: 12 October 2010].

Aydın-Düzgit, S. 2009b. Constructing Europe through Turkey: French Perceptions on Turkey's Accession to the European Union. *Politique Européene*, 29(3), 47–82.

Bağış, E. 2009. *The Future of Turkey/EU Relations and Expectations* [Online, 15 November]. Available at: http://egemenbagis.com/en/1148 [accessed: 9 March 2011].

Bale, T. 2006. Between a Soft and a Hard Place? The Conservative Party, Valence Politics and the Need for a New Eurorealism. *Parliamentary Affairs*, 59(3), 385–400.

Bardakçı, M. 2010. Turkish Parties' Position Towards the EU: Between Europhilia and Europhobia. *Romanian Journal of European Affairs*, 10(4), 26–41.

Bardakoğlu, A. 2008. Culture of Co-Existence in Islam: The Turkish Case. *Insight Turkey*, 10(3), 111–26.

Barysch, K. 2007. 'What Europeans Think about Turkey and Why'. *Centre for European Reform Essays* [Online, 13 September]. Available at: http://www.cer.org.uk/sites/default/files/publications/attachments/pdf/2011/essay-turkey-barysch-2sept07-1392.pdf [accessed: 3 November 2011].

Baysoy, E. 2011. Modernleşme ve Jeopolitik Ekseninde Doğu Sorunu. *Güvenlik Stratejiler Dergisi*, June, 26–52.

BBC. 2004a. *Have Your Say: Should Turkey Join the EU?* [Online, 22 December] Available at: http://newsvote.bbc.co.uk/mpapps/pagetools/print/news.bbc.co.uk//2/hi/talking_point/3 [accessed: 5 September 2011].

BBC. 2004b. *Blair Hails Turkey-EU Talks Deal* [Online, 17 December]. Available at: http://wwwnews.bbc.co.uk_news/politics/4105731.stm [accessed: 5 May 2010).

BBC. 2005. *Blair's European Speech* [Online, 23 June]. Available at: http://news. bbc.co.uk/2/hi/uk_news/politics/4122288.stm [accessed: 13 November 2009].

BBC. 2006a. *UK Vows to Back Turkey's EU Bid* [Online]. Available at:http://news. bbc.co.uk/2/hi/europe/6980019.stm [accessed: 5 December 2009].

BBC. 2006b. *Sarkozy Avrupa'yı Uyarıyor* [Online, 6 October]. Available at www.bbc.co.uk/turkish/europe/story/2006//10/06100.6_sarkozy_turkey.shtml [accessed: 17 October 2009].

BBC. 2010. Have Your Say: Should Turkey Join the EU? [Online, 27 July]. Available at: http://www.bbc.co.uk/blogs/haveyoursay/2010/07/should_turkey_ join_the_eu [accessed: 23 October 2011].

Beylau, P. 2007. Francois Bayrou: Non a L'Adhésion de la Turquie. *Le Point* [Online, 17 January]. Available at: http://www.lepoint.fr/actualites.monde/2007-01-17/ interview-francois-bayrou-non-a-l-adhesion-de-la-turquie924//01/30358 [accessed: 15 August 2011].

Bilgin, P. 2005. Rethinking Turkey's Security Discourses: The Challenge of Globalization. *European Journal of Political Research*, 44, 175–201.

Blair, T. 2000. *Annual Speech to City Audience at Mansion House* [Online, 30 November]. Available at: http://webarchive.nationalarchives.gov. uk/20050302192710/number10.gov.uk/page1535 [accessed: 20 May 2009].

Blair, T. 2003. *I Want to Solve the Iraq Issue via the United Nations*. Speech at Labour's Local Government, Women's and Youth Conferences. SECC, Glasgow [Online, 15 February]. Available at: http://www.labour.org.uk/ tbglasgow/ [accessed: 18 July 2012].

Blair, T. 2006. Speech delivered to the Runnymede Trust on December 8. *Runnymede Bulletin*, 348, 1–4.

Bogdani, M. 2011. *Turkey and the Dilemma of EU Accession: When Religion Meets Politics*. London: I.B.Tauris.

Boğaziçi University, Autonomous University of Madrid, University of Granada and Avrupa ile Diyalog Derneği. 2009. *Problems of Europeanization and European Perceptions of Turkey as a Future Member State* [Online]. Available at: //http://www.bcces.boun.edu.tr/indexphp/projects/79-problems- of-europeanization-and-european-perceptions-of-turkey-as-a-future- member-state [accessed: 14 November 2010].

Boomgarden, H. and Wüst,A. 2012. Religion and Party Positions Towards Turkish EU Accession. *Comparative European Politics*, 10(2), 180–97.

Bowley, G. 2004. EU Commissioner's Remark on Turkey Raising Eyebrows, *New York Times* [Online, 8 September]. Available at: http://www.nytimes. com/2004/09/08/news/08iht-union_ed3__3.html [accessed: 6 March 2011].

Breakwell, G.M. 2004. Identity Change in the Context of the Growing Influence of European Union Institutions, in *Transnational Identities: Becoming European in the EU*, edited by R.K. Herrmann, T. Risse and M.B. Brewer. Lanham: Rowman and Littlefield, 25–39.

Bruter, M. 2004. Civic and Cultural Components of a European Identity: A Pilot Model of Measurement of Citizens' Levels of European Identity, in *Transnational Identities: Becoming European in the EU*, edited by R.K. Herrmann, T. Risse and M.B. Brewer. Lanham: Rowman and Littlefield, 186–213.

Bunting, M. 2005. Regime Change, European Style is a Measure of Our Civilization: European Self-interest must not be Trumped by the Politics of Identity on the Road to Turkey's Accession to the EU. *The Guardian: Comment and Debate* [Online,26 September]. Available at: http://www.guardian.co.uk/ politics/2005/sep/26/turkey.eu [accessed: 26 June 2011].

Buzan, B., Wæver, O. and De Wilde, J. 1998. *Security: A New Framework for Analysis*. London: Lynne Rienner Publishers.

Çakır, A.E. 2011. Political Dimension: Always in the List of 'Also-Rans': Turkey's Rivals in EU-Turkey Relations, in *Fifty Years of EU-Turkey Relations: A Sisyphean Story*, edited byA.E. Çakır.London: Routledge, 10–45.

Çakır, A.E. and Gergelova, A. 2010. Tug of War or Lifelining? Central European Views on Turkey's Accession to the EU, in *The Politics of EU Accession*, edited by L. Tunkrová and P. Šaradín. London: Routledge, 113–27.

Caldwell, C. 2010. *Reflections on the Revolution in Europe*. London: Allen Lane.

Cameron,D.2009.*A Europe Policy that People can Believe In* [Online,4 November]. Available at: http://www.conservatives.com/News/Speeches/2009/11/David_ Cameron_A_Europe_policy_that_people_can_believe_in.aspx

Cameron, D. 2010. *PM's Speech in Turkey* [Online, 27 July]. Available at: http:// www.number10.gov.uk/news/pms-speech-in-turkey/ [accessed: 5 October 2010].

Carr, M. 2006. You are Now Entering Eurabia. *Race and Class*, 48(1), 1–22.

Casanova, J. 2006. The Long, Difficult and Tortuous Journey of Turkey into Europe and the Dilemmas of European Civilization. *Constellations*, 13(2), 235–47.

Casey, J. 2002. Turkey Must Not Join the Christian EU. *The Telegraph* [Online, 13 December]. Available at: http://www.telegraph.co.uk/comment/personal-view/3585210/Turkey-must-not-join-the-Christian-EU.html [accessed: 15 September 2010].

Cassarino, J.P. 2006. Approaching Borders and Frontiers: Notions and Implications, *Carim Research Report 3*

Castano, E. 2004. European Identity: A Social-Psychological Perspective, in *TransnationalIdentities: Becoming European in the EU*, edited by R.K. Herrmann, T. Risse and M.B. Brewer. Lanham: Rowman and Littlefield, 40–58.

Castiglione, D. 2009. Political Identity in a Community of Strangers, in *European Identity*, edited by Jeffrey Checkel and Peter Katzenstein. Cambridge: Cambridge University Press, 29–51.

Castle, S. 2004. Recep Tayyip Erdogan: 'Taking Part in the EU will Bring Harmony of Civilisations – It Is the Project of the Century'. *The Independent* [Online, 13 December]. Available at: http://www.independent.co.uk/news/people/profiles/recep-tayyip-erdogan-taking-part-in-the-eu-will-bring-harmony-of-civilisations-it-is-the-project-of-the-century685203.htm [accessed: 13 May 2011].

Cautrès, B. and Monceau, N. 2011. *La Turquie en Europe: L'Opinion des Européens et des Turcs.* Paris: Presses de Sciences Po.

Celep, Ö. 2011. The Republican People's Party and Turkey's EU Membership. *South European Society and Politics*, 16(3), 423–34.

Checkel, J. 2001. Social Construction and European Integration, in *The Social Construction of Europe*, edited by T. Christensen, K.E. Jorgensen and A. Wiener. London: Sage, 50–65.

Checkel, J. 2005. It's the Process, Stupid! Process Tracing in the Study of European and International Politics. *ARENA Working Paper*, 26/2005. Oslo:ARENA.

Checkel, J. 2006. Constructivist Approaches to European Integration. *Arena Working Paper*, 06/2006. Oslo: ARENA.

Christiansen, T. 1997. Reconstructing European Space: From Territorial Politics to Multi-Level Governance, in *Reflective Approaches to European Governance*, edited by K.E. Jorgensen. Basingstoke: Macmillan, 51–68.

Christiansen, T., Jorgensen, K.E. and Wiener, A. 2001. Introduction, in *The Social Construction of Europe*, edited by T. Christensen, K.E. Jorgensen and A.Wiener. London: Sage, 1–21.

Çınar, M. 2011. The Electoral Success of the AKP: Source of Hope and Despair. *Insight Turkey*, 13(4), 107–28.

Çırakman, A. 2001. From Tyranny to Despotism: The Enlightenment's Unenlightened Image of the Turks. *International Journal of Middle East Studies*, 33(1), 49–68.

Çırakman, A. 2002. *From the 'Terror of the World' to the 'Sick Man of Europe'.* New York: Peter Lang.

Çırakman, A. 2003. Sir Paul Rycaut and his Influence on the 18th Century Thought of the Turks, in *Historical Image of the Turk in Europe: 15th Century to the Present*, edited by M. Soykut. Istanbul: Isis, 227–46.

Citrin, J. and Sides, J. 2004. More Than Nationals: How Identity Choice Matters in the New Europe, in *Transnational Identities: Becoming European in the EU*, edited by R.K. Herrmann, T. Risse and M.B. Brewer. Lanham: Rowman and Littlefield, 161–85.

Cizre, Ü. 2011a. Guest Editor's Note. *Insight Turkey*, 13(4), iii–v.

Cizre, Ü. 2011b. Turkey at the Crossroads: From 'Change with Politics as Usual' to Politics with Change as Usual. *Insight Turkey*, 13(4), 83–106.

Condor, S. 2006. Representing, Resisting and Reproducing Ethnic Nationalism: Official Labour Party Representations of Multicultural Britain [Online]. Available at: www. reprints.lancs.ac.uk/11178/1/1.pdf [accessed: 28 March 2010].

Conservative Party. 2008. *Should Turkey Join the EU?: Discussion on Conservative Home's Seats and Candidates Blog* [Online, February 29]. Available at: http://conservativehome.blogs.com/goldlist/2008/02/are-you-in-favo.htm [accessed: 15 November 2010].

Cram, L. 2012. Does the EU Need a Navel? Implicit and Explicit Identification with the European Union. *Journal of Common Market Studies*, 50(1), 71–86.

Crick, B. 2003. The New and the Old: The Report of the 'Life In the United Kingdom' Advisory Group. London: Home Office.

Cronin, D. 2010. Keeping Turkey out of Europe. *The Guardian* [Online, 6 January]. Available at: http://www.guardian.co.uk/commentisfree/2010/jan/06/turkey_european_union_membership [accessed: 12 April 2010].

Curley, T.M. 2009. Social Identity Theory and EU Expansion. *International Studies Quarterly*, 53, 649–68.

Cümhüriyet. 2012. European Commissioner says EU sees Turkey as Family Member [Online, 9 February]. Available at: http://en.cumhuriyet.com/?hn=314234 [accessed: 8 May 2012].

De Ravinel, S. 2004. Identifier la Turquie a L'Europe Serait Une Erreur. *Le Figaro* [Online, 13 August]. Available at: http://lefigaro_fr.php?archive=DszTn 8dCK780C8uwiNq9T8Co59GECCSHinCX%2BJurRQwCpEEmWS7hSbbn UXbpK012a [accessed: 28 June 2011].

De Vreese, C.H and Boomgarten, H.G. 2006.Media Effects on Public Opinion about the Enlargement of the European Union. *Journal of Common Market Studies*, 44(2), 419–36.

De Vreese, C.H., Boomgaarden, H.G. and Semetko, H.A. 2008. Hard and Soft: Public Support for Turkish Membership in the EU. *European Union Politics*, 2008(9), 511–30.

Delanty, G. 2003. The Making of Post-Western Europe: A Civilizational Analysis. *Thesis Eleven*, 72(8), 8–25.

Delanty, G. and Rumford, C. 2005. *Rethinking Europe: Social Theory and the Implications of Europeanization.*Oxon: Routledge.

Demossier, M. 2007. The Political Structuring of Cultural Identities in Europe, in *The European Puzzle: The Political Structuring of Cultural Identities at a Time of Transition*, edited by M. Demossier. Oxford: Bergham Books, 49–66.

Den Boer, P. 1995. Europe to 1914: The Making of an Idea, in *The History of the Idea of Europe*, edited by K. Wilson and J. van der Dussen. London: Routledge, 13–82.

Derrida, J. 1994. *The Other Heading: Reflections on Today's Europe*. Bloomington, Indiana: Indiana University Press.

Diez Medrano, J. and Gutierrez, P. 2001. Nested Identities: National and European Identities in Spain. *Ethnic and Racial Studies*, 24, 753–78.

Diez Medrano, J. 2009. The Public Sphere and the European Union's Political Identity, in *European Identity*, edited by J. Checkel and P. Katzenstein. Cambridge: Cambridge University Press, 81–107.

Diez, T. 2004. Europe's Others and the Return of Geopolitics. *Cambridge Review of International Affairs*, 17(2), 319–35.

Diez, T. 2005. Constructing the Self and Changing Others: Reconsidering 'Normative Power Europe'. *Millenum: Journal of International Studies*, 33(3), 613–36.

Diez, T. 2007. Expanding Europe: The Ethics of EU-Turkey Relations. *Ethics and International Affairs*, 21(4), 415–22.

Diez, T. 2011. Ethical Dimension, in *Fifty Years of EU–Turkey Relations: A Sisyphean Story*, edited by A.E. Çakır. London: Routledge, 158–75.

Diez, T. and Steans, J. 2005. A Useful Dialogue? Habermas and International Relations. *Review of International Studies*, 31, 127–40.

Dixon, J.C. 2010. Opposition to Enlargement as a Symbolic Defence of Group Position: Multilevel Analyses of Attitudes toward Candidates' Entries in the EU-25. *British Journal of Sociology*, 61(1), 127–54.

Dodd, C. 2002. Democracy and the European Union, in *Turkish Transformation, New Century, New Challenge*, edited by B.Beeley. Huntington: Eothen Press, 241–83.

Dorronsoro, G. 2004. The EU and Turkey: Between Politics and Social Engineering, in *European Union Foreign and Security Policy: Towards a Neighbourhood Strategy*, edited by R. Dannreuther. London: Routledge, 48–61.

Dösemeci, M. 2012. Turkish Opposition to the Common Market: An Archeology of Nationalist Thought, 1967–1980. *South European Society and Politics*, 17(1), 87–107.

Drake, H. 2010. France, Europe and the Limits of Exceptionalism, in *The End of the French Exception? Decline and Revival of the French Model*, edited by T. Chafer and E. Godin, 187–202.

Duchesne, S. 2008. Waiting for a European Identity … Reflections on the Process of Identification with Europe. *Perspectives on European Politics and Society*, 9(4), 379–410.

Duran, B. 2008. The Justice and Development Party's 'New Politics': Steering Toward Conservative Democracy, a Revised Islamic Agenda or Management of New Crises?, in *Secular and Islamic Politics in Turkey: The Making of the Justice and Development Party*, edited by Ü. Cizre. Oxon: Routledge, 80–106.

Durão Barroso, J.M. 2008. *Winning Hearts and Minds: The EU/Turkey Partnership* [Online, 11 April]. Available at: http://europa.eu/rapid/press-release-SPEECH-08_191-en.htm.locale=en [accessed: 3 June 2010].

Duyulmuş, C. 2008. *Europeanization of Minority Rights in Turkey* [Online]. Available at: http://web.uvic.ca/ecsac/biennial2008/conference%program_files/ Duyulmus [accessed: 23 September 2009].

Economist. 2011. Readers' comments on *Turkey and Europe: An Uncertain Path* [Online 15 October]. Available at: http://www.economist.com/node121532303/ comments [accessed: 19 January 2012].

Erboz, F. 2008. Fesat Yuvası Patrikhane ve Soros Çetesine Karşı MHP ve CHP'den Direniş. *Yeniçag* [Online, 1 February] Available at: http://www.yg.yenicaggazetesi. com.tr/habergoster.php?haber=4933 [accessed: 6 September 2010].

Erdoğan, R.T. 2004. *Why the EU Needs Turkey* [Online, 28 May]. Available at: http://www.sant.ox.ac.uk/areastudies/lectures/Erdogan.pdf [accessed: 15 September 2010].

Erdoğan, R.T. 2011. The Robust Man of Europe: Turkey has the Vigor that the EU Badly Needs, *Newsweek* [Online, 17 January]. Available at: http://www. newsweek.com/2011/01/17/the-robust-man-of-europe.print.html [accessed: 20 July 2011].

Erensu, S. and Adanalı, Y. 2004. Turkey in the Eye of the Beholder: Tracking Perceptions of Turkey in Political Cartoons. *Kontur*, 10, 58–72.

Eriksen, E.O. 2003. Integration and the Quest for Consensus – On the Micro-foundation of Supranationalism, in *European Governance, Deliberation and the Quest for Democratisation*, edited by E.O. Eriksen, C. Joerges and J.Neyer. Oslo:ARENA.

Eriksen, E.O. and Fossum, J.E. 2003. *Understanding Habermas: On Communicative Action and Deliberative Democracy*. London: Continuum.

Eriksen, E.O. and Fossum, J.E. 2004. Europe in Search of Legitimacy: Strategies of Legitimation Assessed. *International Political Science Review*, 25, 435–59.

Euractiv. 2005. Rehn: Turkey is Already a Privileged Partner of the EU [Online, 14 July] Available at: http://euractiv.com/enlargement/rehn-turkey-privileged-partner-e-news-2114418 [accessed: 23 March 2010].

European Commission. 2004. *Recommendation of the European Commission on Turkey's Progress Toward Accession*. Brussels: European Commission.

European Commission. 2005. *Eurobarometer 62, Oct–Nov 2004*. Brussels: European Commission.

European Commission. 2006. *Eurobarometer 64. Public Opinion in the European Union*. Brussels: European Commission.

European Commission. 2007. *Eurobarometer 67. Public Opinion in the European Union*. Brussels: European Commission.

European Commission. 2008. *Eurobarometer 69. Public Opinion in the European Union*. Brussels: European Commission.

European Commission. 2009a. *Eurobarometer 71. Annex for the Future of Europe*. Brussels: European Commission.

European Commission. 2009b. *Flash Eurobarometer 257*. Brussels: European Commission.

European Commission. 2010a. *Eurobarometer 73. Public Opinion in the European Union*. Brussels: European Commission.

European Commission. 2010b. *Eurobarometer 74. Public Opinion in the European Union*. Brussels: European Commission.

European Council. 1993. *Presidency Conclusions of the Copenhagen European Council of 21–22 June*, SN180/1/193, REV 1.

European Elites Survey. 2008. [Online]. Available at: EES08Ingxsit[1]pdf [accessed: 15 September 2011].

European Parliament. 1995. *Report of the Committee on Culture, Youth, Education and the Media*, A3-0072/95.

European Parliament. 2003. *Debate on Turkey's Application for EU Membership* [Online, 4 June]. Available at: http://www.europarl.europa.eu/sides/getDoc. dr.pubRef=//EP//TEXT+CRE+20030604+ITEM+004+DOC+XMLTW/ EN8language=W [accessed: 20 July 2012].

European Parliament. 2004. *Debate on Turkey's Progress towards Accession* [Online, 13 December]. Available at: http://www.europarl.europa.sides/ getDoc.do?type=CRE&reference=20041213&secondRef=ITEM-010&format=XML&language=EN [accessed: 5 September 2011].

European Parliament. 2006. *Debate on Turkey's Progress towards Accession* [Online]. Available at: http://www.europarl.europa.eu/sides/getDoc.do?type= CRE&reference=20060926&secondRef=ITEM-012&format=XML&language=EN [accessed: 13 October 2011]

European Parliament. 2011. [Online: 15 April] Available at: www.europarl.europa. eu/en//headlines/content/20110408STO17340/html/Future [accessed:27 April 2011].

European Parliament. 2012a. *European Parliament Resolution on the 2011 Progress Report on Turkey* (2011/2899) [Online, 20 March]. Available at: www.europarl.europa.eu/sides/getDoc.do?type=MOTION&reference=B7-2012-0189&language=EN [accessed: 23 May 2012].

European Parliament. 2012b. *Debates – Enlargement Report for Turkey* [Online, 28 March]. Available at: www.europarl.europa.eu/sides/getDoc.do?pubRef=-//EP//TEXT+CRE+20120328+ITEM-018+DO… [accessed: 11 April 2012].

European Union. 2007. Treaty of Lisbon. *Official Journal of the European Union* C306, vol. 50.

European Voice. 2008. Markus Ferber (German EPP) – Where's This Relationship Leading? [Online,17 July]. Available at: www.europeanvoice.com [accessed: 14 October 2011].

Evans Prichard, A. 2004. Turkey's Muslim Millions Threaten EU Values, Says Commissioner. *The Telegraph* [Online, 8 September]. Available at: http:// www.telegraph.co.uk/news/worldnews/europe/belgium/1471281/Turkeys-Muslim-millions-threaten-EU-values [accessed: 21 June 2010].

Favell, A. 2009. Immigration, Migration and Free Movement in the Making of Europe, in *European Identity*, edited by J. Checkel and P. Katzenstein. Cambridge: Cambridge University Press, 167–89.

Fearon, J.D. and Laitin, D.D. 2000. Violence and the Social Construction of Ethnic Identity. *International Organization*, 54(4), 845–77.

Flautre, H. 2012. France-Turkey: 'Le Changement, C'est Maintenant'. *Today's Zaman* [Online, 5 June]. Available at: http://www.todayszaman.com/ newsDetail_getNewsById.action?newsId=280359 [accessed: 8 June 2012].

Fligstein, N. 2009. Who are the Europeans and How does this Matter for Politics?, in *European Identity*, edited by J. Checkel and P. Katzenstein. Cambridge: Cambridge University Press, 132–66.

Foucault, M. 1972. *The Archeology of Knowledge*. New York: Harper and Row.

Fox, L. 2006. A Bridge Too Far? *Turkey Could be a Beacon to the Islamic World* [Online]. Available at: wwww.conservatives.com [accessed: 17 December 2009].

Frattini, F. 2010. *The EU and Turkey Need Each Other.* Speech by Minister Frattini at the Ita-Turk Dialogue Forum. Italian Ministry of Foreign Affairs [Online, 9 November]. Available at: www.estei.it/MAE/EN/Sala_Stampa/ ArchivoNotizie/Interventi/2010/11/20101109_ForoItaloTurco.html [accessed: 15 October 2011].

Garton Ash, T. 2002.A Bridge Too Far? *The Guardian* [Online, 14 November]. Available at: http://www.guardian.co.uk/world/2002/nov/eu.turkey [accessed: 23 September 2009].

George, S. 1994. Cultural Diversity and European Integration: The British Political Parties, in *National Cultures and European Integration*, edited by S. Zetterholm. Oxford: Berg, 49–64.

Gerhards, J. and Silke, H. 2011. Why Not Turkey? Attitudes Towards Turkish Membership in the EU among Citizens in 27 European Countries. *Journal of Common Market Studies*, 49(4), 741–66.

Giscard d'Estaing, V. 2004. A Better European Bridge to Turkey. *Financial Times* [Online, 24 November]. Available at: http://www.ft.com/cms/s/1/263d9778-3e4b-11d9-a9d7-00000-e2511c8.html#ax222CUedbkUQ [accessed 8 November 2009].

Gow, D. and MacAskill, E. (2004). Turkish Accession Could Spell End of EU Says Commissioner. *The Guardian* [Online, 8 September]. Available at: www. guardian.co.uk/world/2004/sep/08/turkey.eu [accessed: 15 July 2011].

Göle, N. 1995. Interpénétrations: L'Islam et L'Europe. Paris: La Découverte.

Gözaydın, İ. 2008. Religion, Politics and the Politics of Religion in Turkey, in *Religion, Politics and Turkey's EU Accession*, edited by D. Jung and C. Raudvere. New York: Palgrave Macmillan, 139–58.

Grigoriadis, I.N. 2009. *Trials of Europeanization: Turkish Political Culture and the European Union*. New York: Palgrave Macmillan.

Grillo, R. 2007. European Identity in a Transnational Era, in *The European Puzzle: The Political Structuring of Cultural Identities at a Time of Transition*, edited by Marion Demossier. Oxford: Bergham Books, 67–84.

Guida, M. 2008. The Sèvres Syndrome and '*Komplo*' Theories in the Islamist and Secular Press. *Turkish Studies*, 9(1), 37–52.

Gül, A. 2007. Turkey's Role in a Changing Middle East Environment. *Mediterranean Quarterly*, 15(1), 1–7.

Gül, M. 2009. Orta Çağ Avrupa Tarihi. Istanbul: Bilge Kültür Sanat.

Habermas, J. 1981. *The Structural Transformation of the Public Sphere: An Inquiry Into the Category of Bourgeois Society*. Cambridge: Polity Press.

Habermas, J. 1993. *Justification and Application: Remarks on Discourse Ethics*. Cambridge: Polity Press.

Habermas, J. 1998. *The Inclusion of the Other: Studies in Political Theory*. Cambridge: Polity Press.

Habermas, J. 2001. *The Post National Constellation*. Cambridge: Polity Press.

Habermas, J. 2006. *The Divided West*. Cambridge: Polity Press.

Habermas, J. 2009. *Europe: The Faltering Project*. Cambridge: Polity Press.

Haesly, R. 2001. Euroskeptics, Europhiles and Instrumental Europeans: European Attachment in Scotland and Wales. *European Union Politics*, 2(1), 81–102.

Hague, W. 2010. *The Biggest Risk for Britain is Five More Years of Brown* [Online, 10 March]. Available at: http://www.conservatives.com/News/Speeches/2010/03 [accessed: 12 October 2010].

Hainsworth, P., O'Brien, C. and Mitchell, P. 2004. Defending the Nation: The Politics of Euroscepticism on the French Right, in *Euroscepticism: Party Politics, National Identity and European Integration*, edited by R. Harmsen and M. Spiering. Amsterdam: European Studies, 37–58.

Hale, W. and Özbudun, E. 2010. *Islamism, Democracy and Liberalism in Turkey: The Case of the AKP*. Abingdon: Routledge.

Hall, R.B. 2002. Applying the 'Self/Other' Nexus in International Relations. *International Studies Review*, 3(1), 101–11

Happold, T. 2002. Straw: Turkey is EU's Acid Test. *The Guardian* [Online, 23 March]. Available at: http://www.guardian.co.uk/world/2004/mar/23/turkey.eu [accessed: 12 July 2009].

Havel, V. 1994. Speech to the European Parliament in Strasbourg, 8 March

Hawkins, B. 2012. Nation, Separation and Threat: An Analysis of British Media Discourses on the European Union Treaty Reform Process. *Journal of Common Market Studies*, 50(4), 561–77.

Held, D. 1980. Introduction to Critical Theory: Horkheimer to Habermas. Berkeley: University of California Press.

Herranz-Surralles, A. 2012. Justifying Enlargement in a Multi-Level Policy. A Discourse Institutional Analysis of the Elite-Public Gap over European Union Enlargement. *Journal of Common Market Studies*, 50(3), 385–402.

Hobsbawm, E. 1997. *On History*. London: Weidenfeld and Nicolson.

Hollande, F. 2012. France Isn't Just Any Country. *Slate* [Online, 7 May]. Available at: http://www.slate.com/articles/news-and-politics/foreigners/2012/05/an-interview-with-french-president [accessed: 8 June 2012].

Holm, U. 2002. The Implication of the Concept of the French State-Nation and 'Patrie' for French Discourses on (Mahgrebi) Immigration. *Academy for Migration Studies in Denmark (AMID) Working Paper*, 6/2002.

Holm, U. 2004. The Old France, the New Europe and a Multipolar World. *Perspectives on European Politics and Society*, 5(3), 469–91.

Holm, U. 2009. Sarkozysm: New European and Foreign Policy into Old French Bottles? *DIIS Working Paper* 2009: 30 [Online]. Available at: http://www.diis. dk/graphics/publications/wp2009/wp2009/wp2009-30_sarkozysm_web.pdf [accessed: 20 May 2011].

Hooghe, L. and Marks, G. 2005. Calculation, Community and Cues: Public Opinion on European Integration. *European Union Politics*, 2005/6, 419–43.

Howard, M. 2004. Full Text: Michael Howard's Speech on Europe. *The Guardian* [Online, 12 February]. Available at: //http://www.guardian.co.uk/politics/2004/ feb/12/conservatives.uk [accessed: 5 March 2009].

Huntington, S. 1993. The Clash of Civilizations? *Foreign Affairs*, 72[3].

Huntington, S. 1997. *The Clash of Civilisations and the Remaking of the World Order.* London: Simon and Schuster.

Huysmans, J. 1998. Revisiting Copenhagen or on the Creative Development of a Security Studies Agenda in Europe. *European Journal of International Relations*, 4(4), 479–505.

Huysmans, J. 2000. The European Union and the Securitization of Migration. *Journal of Common Market Studies*, 38(5), 751–71.

Hülsse, R. 2000. Looking Beneath the Surface: Invisible Othering in the German Discourse about Turkey's Possible EU Accession. Ionian Conference, Corfu, Greece, 19–22 May 2000.

Hülsse, R. 2006. Imagine the EU: The Metaphorical Construction of a Supra-Nationalist Identity'. *Journal of International Relations and Development*, 2006(9), 396–421.

Hürriyet. 2006. CHP Launches Salvo against the EU [Online, 6 September]. Available at: www.hurriyetdailynews.com/default.aspx [accessed: 11 November 2011].

Hürriyet Daily News. 2010. Erdoğan: Turkey Does Not Want to be EU Burden [Online, 6 April]. Available at: http://www.hurriyetdailynews.com. default.aspx?pageid=438&n=erdogan-turkey-does-not-want-to-be-eu-burden-2010-04-06.

İçener, E. and Çağlıyan-İçener, Z. 2011. The Justice and Development Party's Identity and its Role in the EU's Decision to Open Accession Negotiations with Turkey. *Southeast European and Black Sea Studies*, 11(1),19–34.

İnalcık, H. 2010. *Osmanlılar: Fütühat, İmparatorluk, Avrupa ile İlişkiler.* Istanbul: Timaş.

Independent Commission on Turkey. 2004. *Turkey in Europe: More than a Promise?* [Online]. Available at: www.independentcommissiononturkey.org [accessed: 8 March 2007].

Jenkins, G. 2007. Continuity and Change: Prospects for Civil-Military Relations in Turkey. *International Affairs*, 83(2), 339–55.

Johansson-Nogues, E. and Jonasson, A.K. 2011. Turkey, Its Changing National Identity and EU Accession: Explaining the Ups and Downs in the Turkish Democratization Reforms. *Journal of Contemporary European Studies*, 19(1), 113–32.

Kaelble, H. 2009. Identification with Europe and Politicization of the EU since the 1980s, in *European Identity*, edited by J. Checkel and P. Katzenstein. Cambridge: Cambridge University Press,193–212.

Kaletsky, A. 2004. Let Turkey Join the EU. *The Times* [Online,7 October]. Available at: http://www.thetimes .co.uk [accessed: 5 May 2010].

Karabat, A. 2010. Bağış: Hold on Europe, Turkey is coming to rescue you. *Today's Zaman* [Online,10 December]. Available at: http://www.todayszaman.com/ newsDetail-getNewsByld.action;jseesionid=534703AA0318E8596DEFB8 [accessed: 13April 2011].

Kirişçi, K. 2006. Turkey's Foreign Policy in Turbulent Times. *Chaillot Paper 92* [Online]. Available at: http://www.europa.eu/uploads/media/cpO92.pdf [accessed: 15 September 2010].

Knutsen, T.L. 1997. *A History of International Relations Theory.* Manchester: Manchester University Press.

Kösebalaban, H. 2002. Turkey's EU Membership: A Clash of Security Cultures. *Middle East Policy*, 10(2),130–46.

Kösebalaban, H. 2007. The Permanent 'Other'? Turkey and the Question of European Identity. *Mediterranean Quarterly*, 18(4), 87–111.

Köseoğlu, F. 2011. Hollande, Türkiye'nin AB Üyeliğine Daha Ilımlı. *Netgazete* [Online, 17 October]. Available at: www.netgazete.com/News/798768/ hollande__turkiyenin_ab_uyeligine_daha_ilimli.aspx [accessed: 28 March 2012].

Kristeva, J. 1991. *Strangers to Ourselves.* New York: Columbia University Press.

Kubicek, P. 2004. Turkey's Place in the New Europe'. *Perceptions*, Summer 2004,

Kučera, P. 2010. Becoming European: Kemalism as an Ideology of Westernism. *The Politics of EU Accession*, edited byL. Tunkrová and P. Šaradín. London: Routledge, 18–33.

Kumrular, Ö. 2005. Kanuni'nin Batı Siyasetinin Bir İzdüşümü Olarak Türk İmaji, in *Dünyada Türk İmgesi*, edited by Ö. Kumrular.Istanbul: Kitap, 109–28.

Kumrular, Ö. 2008. *Türk Korkusu: Avrupa'da Türk Düşmanlığın Kökeni.* Istanbul: Doğan.

Kuran-Burçoğlu, N. 2003. A Glimpse at Various Stages of the Evolution of the Image of the Turk in Europe: 15th to 21st Centuries, in *Historical Image of the Turk in Europe: 15th Century to the Present*, edited by M. Soykut. Istanbul: Isis, 21–44.

Kuran-Burçoğlu, N. 2007. From Vision To Reality: A Socio-Cultural Critique of Turkey's Accession Process, in *Turkey and the European Union: Prospects For a Difficult Encounter*, edited by E. LaGro and K. Jorgensen. Hampshire: Palgrave Macmillan, 147–68.

Kuzmanovic, D. 2008. Civilization and EU-Turkey Relations, in *Religion, Politics and Turkey's EU Accession*, edited by D. Jung and C. Raudvere. New York: Palgrave Macmillan, 41–66.

Kylstad, I. 2010. Turkey and the EU: A 'New' European Identity in the Making?. *LSE 'Europe in Question' Discussion Paper*, 27/2010.

Labour Party. 1950. *European Unity: A Statement by the National Executive Committee of the British Labour Party.* London: Labour Party.

Laclau, E. and Mouffe, C. 1985. *Hegemony and Socialist Strategy: Towards a Radical Democratic Politics.* London: Verso.

Laffan, B. 2004. The European Union and its Institutions as Identity Builders, in *Transnational Identities: Becoming European in the EU*, edited by R.K. Herrmann, T. Risse and M.B. Brewer. Lanham: Rowman and Littlefield, 75–96.

Lahav, G. 2004. *Immigration and Politics in the New Europe: Reinventing Borders.* Cambridge: Cambridge University Press.

Lake, M. 2005. Introduction, in *The EU and Turkey: A Glittering Prize or a Millstone?,* edited by M. Lake. London: Federal Trust for Education and Research, 9–14.

Larsen, H. 1997. *Foreign Policy and Discourse Analysis: France, Britain and Europe.* London: Routledge.

Larsen, H. 1999. British and Danish European Policies in the 1990s: A Discourse Analysis Approach. *European Journal of International Relations*, 1999(5), 451–83.

Le Monde. 2012. La Position de Hollande sur la Turquie: Entre Ouverture et Fermeté [Online, 2 May]. Available at: www. lemonde.fr/election-presidentielle-2012/ article/2012/04/12/ la- position-de-hollande-sur-la-turquie- entre-ouverture-et-fermete [accessed: 28 May 2012].

Leonard, D. 1998. *Guide to the European Union*, London: The Economist in Association with Profile Books.

Leparmentier, A. and Zecchini, L. 2002. Pour ou Contre l'Adhésion de la Turquie à l'Union Européene. *Le Monde*, [Online, 9 November]. Available at: http://lemonde.fr/cgi-bin/ACHATS/acheter.cgi?offre=ARCHIVES&type_ item=ART_ARCH_30J&objet_id=780143 [accessed: 16 October 2009].

Levin, P.T. 2011. *Turkey and the European Union: Christian and Secular Images of Islam.* New York: Palgrave Macmillan.

Lewis, B. 1993. *Islam and the West.* New York: Oxford University Press.

Lilley, K.D. 2002. Imagined Geographies of the 'Celtic Fringe' and the Cultural Construction of the 'Other' in Medieval Wales and Ireland in *Celtic Geographies: Old Culture, New Times.* D.C. Harvey, R. Jones, N. McInroy and C. Milligan (eds). London: Routledge.

Lundgren, A. 2002. The Limits of Enlargement in *Enlargement and the Finality of the EU. ARENA Report* 7/02. Oslo: ARENA, 35–48.

Lundgren, A. 2006. The Case of Turkey: Are Some Candidates More European than Others?, in *Questioning EU Enlargement: Europe in Search of Identity*, edited by H. Sjursen. London: Routledge,121–41.

Machiavelli, N. 1952. *The Prince.* London: Encyclopaedia Britannica.

MacLaren, L. 2002. Public Support for the European Union: Cost/Benefit Analysis or Perceived Cultural Threat?. *The Journal of Politics*, 64(2), 551–66.

MacLaren, L. 2007. Explaining Opposition to Turkish Membership of the EU. *European Union Politics*, 8[2], 251–78.

MacMillan, C. 2010a. Privileged Partnership, Open Ended Accession Negotiations and the Securitisation of Turkey's EU Accession Process. *Journal of Contemporary European Studies*,18(4), 447–62.

MacMillan, C. 2010b. Orientalist Discourse and Major Issues Regarding Turkey's Accession Process, in *From Here to Diversity: Globalization and Intercultural Dialogues*, edited by C. Sarmento. Cambridge:Cambridge Scholars Publishing.

MacMillan, C. 2013. Competing and Co-Existing Constructions of Europe as Turkey's 'Other(s)' in Turkish Political Discourse. *Journal of Contemporary European Studies*, 21(1), 104–21.

MacShane, D. 2002. Europe Must Embrace Islam Too. *The Guardian* [Online, 24 November]. Available at: http://www.guardian.co.uk/world/2002/nov/24/turkey.foreignpolicy [accessed: 24 September 2008].

Malik, M. 2010. Progressive Multiculturalism: The British Experience, in *European Multiculturalism Revisited*, edited by A. Silj.London: Zed Books, 11–64.

Manço, U. 2007. *Turks in Europe: From an Image to the Complexity of Migrant Social Reality* [Online]. Available at: http://www.flwi-ugent.be/cie/umanco/umanco5.htm [accessed: 3 December 2011].

Mango, A. 2005. The Modern History of a Solid Country, in *The EU and Turkey: A Glittering Prize or a Millstone?*, edited by M. Lake. London: Federal Trust for Education and Research, 15–28.

Manners, I. 2002. Normative Power Europe: A Contradiction in Terms? *Journal of Common Market Studies*, 40(2), 235–58.

Manners, I. 2006. The European Union as a Normative Power: A Response to Thomas Diez. *Millenium: Journal of International Studies*, 35(1), 167–80.

Marbeyed, S. 2007. Prime Minister Erdoğan Speaks to FM. *MidEast Views* [Online, 20 November]. Available at: www.mideastviews.com/articleview.php?art=270 [accessed: 30 November 2010].

March, J. and Olsen, J.P. 1989. *Rediscovering Institutions: The Organizational Basis of Politics*. New York: Free Press.

March, J. and Olsen, J.P. 1998. The Institutional Dynamics of International Political Orders. *International Organisation*, 52(4), 943–69.

Marcussen, M., Risse, Engelmann-Martin,D., Kopf, H.J. and Roscher, K. 1999. Constructing Europe? The Evolution of French, British and German Nation State Identities. *Journal of European Public Policy*, 6(4), 614–33.

Mayer, F.C. and Palmowski, J. 2004. European Identities and the EU: The Ties that Bind the Peoples of Europe. *Journal of Common Market Studies*, 42(3), 573–98.

McNair, B. 2000. *Journalism and Democracy: An Evaluation of the Political Public Sphere*. London: Routledge.

Milliyetçi Hareket Partisi (MHP). 2010. *Avrupa Raporu* [Online]. Available at: www.mhp.org.tr/files/raporlar/avrupabirligi/ab_ve_turkiye_aralık_2010.doc [accessed: 25 June 2011].

Milliken, J. 1999. The Study of Discourse in International Relations: A Critique of Works and Methods. *European Journal of International Relations*, 5(2), 225–54.

Milliyet. 2012. AB Üyeliğine İnanç Kalmadı [Online, 23 August]. Available at: http://gundem.milliyet.com.tr/ab-uyeligine-inanç-kalmadi/gundem/gundemdetay/23.08.20121584924/de [accessed: 23 August 2012].

Milner, S. 2004. For an Alternative Europe: Euroscepticism and the French Left Since the Maastricht Treaty, in *Euroscepticism: Party Politics, National Identity and European Integration*, edited by R. Harmsen and M. Spiering. Amsterdam: European Studies, 59–82.

Minkenberg, M. 2012. Christian Identity? European Churches and the Issue of Turkey's EU Membership. *Comparative European Politics*, 10(2), 149–79.

Minkenberg, M., Boomgarten, H., de Vreese, C. and Freire, A. 2012. Introduction: The European Union's Enlargement and Turkish Membership: The Role of Religion. *Comparative European Politics*, 10(2), 133–48.

Mitterand, F. 1986. *Reflexions sur la Politique Exterieure de la France – Introduction a Vignt-Cinq Discours*. Paris: Librerie Artheme Fayard.

Morin, E., Touraine, A., Rufin, J.C. and Sorman, G .2004. *Pourquoi il faut accueillir la Turquie* [Online]. Available at: http://www.info-turc.org/article797.html [accessed: 10 August 2010].

Morozov, V. and Rumelili, B. 2012. The External Constitution of European Identity: Russia and Turkey as Europe-makers. *Cooperation and Conflict*, 47(1), 28–48.

Morris, C. 2005. *The New Turkey: The Quiet Revolution on the Edge of Europe*. London: Granta.

Müezzinler, A. 2009. Greek President: We Cannot Support Turkey's Membership to the EU. *The Journal of Turkish Weekly* [Online, 19 November]. Available at: http://www.turkishweekly.net//news/93107/greek-president-39-we-cannot-support-turkey-39-membership-to-the-eu-39.html [accessed: 30 October 2011].

Müftüler Baç, M. and Taşkın, E. 2007. Turkey's Accession to the European Union: Does Culture and Identity Play a Role? *Ankara Review of European Studies*, 6(2), 31–50.

Müftüler-Baç, M. 2008. Turkey's Accession to the European Union: The Impact of the EU's Internal Dynamics. *International Studies Perspectives*, 9(2), 201–19.

Müller, J.W. 2006. A 'Thick' Constitutional Patriotism for the EU? On Morality, Memory and Militancy, in *Law and Democracy in the Post National Union*, edited by E.O. Eriksen, C. Joerges and F. Rödl. Oslo: ARENA, 375–400.

Mummendey, A. and Waldzus, S. 2004. National Differences and European Plurality: Discrimination or Tolerance between European Countries, in *Transnational Identities: Becoming European in the EU*, edited by R.K. Herrmann, T. Risse and M.B. Brewer. Lanham: Rowman and Littlefield, 59–74.

Nas, T. 2011. Economic Dimension, in *Fifty Years of EU–Turkey Relations: A Sisyphean Story*, edited by A. E. Çakır. London: Routledge, 46–66.

Negrine, R., Kejanlioglu, P., Aissaoui, R. and Papathanassopoulos, S. 2008. An Analysis of How the Press in Four Countries Covered Turkey's Bid for Accession in 2004. *European Journal of Communication*, 23(1), 47–68.

Neumann, I.1999. *Uses of the Other: The East in European Identity Formation*. Minneapolis: University of Minnesota Press.

Neumayer, G. 2004. The River of No Return. *American Spectator* [Online, 17 December]. Available at: http://spectator.org/archives/2004/12/17/the-river-of-no-return [accessed: 13 May 2011].

Nicolaidis, K. 2003. Turkey is European … for Europe's Sake. In *Turkey and the European Union: from Association to Accession*. The Netherlands Ministry of Foreign Affairs [Online]. Available at: //http://users.ox.ac.uk/sstc0041/turkey-european.pdf [accessed: 10 July 2009].

Nicolaidis, K. and Howse, R. 2002. 'This is my EUtopia …' Narrative as Power. *Journal of Common Market Studies*, 40(4), 767–92

Nugent, N. 2007. The EU's Response to Turkey's Membership Application: Not Just a Weighing of Costs and Benefits. *Journal of European Integration*, 29(4), 481–502.

Nuttall, C. and Traynor, I. 1997. Kohl Tries to Cool Row with Ankara. *Guardian*, March 7, 24.

Oğurlu, E. 2010. *European Perceptions on Turkey's Accession to the EU*, İKV Conference on Turkeyand the EU-Opportunities and Challenges in the Accession Process, Istanbul, Turkey, 16–18 June 2010.

Öner, S. 2007. *An Analysis of European Identity Within the Framework of the EU: The Case of Turkey's Membership* [Online]. Available at: http://www.veraznanjemur.bos.rs/materijal/selcen-teblig-pdf. [accessed: 20 April 2010].

Öner, S. 2011. *Turkey and the European Union: The Question of European Identity*. Plymouth: Lexington Books.

Öniş, Z. 2003. Domestic Politics, International Norms and Challenges to the State: Turkey-EU Relations in the post-Helsinki Era, in *Turkey and the European Union: Domestic Politics, Economic Integration and International Dynamics*, edited by A. Çarkoğlu and B. Rubin. London: Frank Cass, 9–34.

Öniş. Z. and Yılmaz, H. 2009. Between Europeanization and Euro-Asianism: Foreign Policy Activism in Turkey during the AKP Era. *Turkish Studies*, 10(1), 7–24.

Ortaylı, İ. 2008. *Avrupa ve Biz: Seçme Eserler 1*. Istanbul: İş Bankası Kültür Yayınları.

Parker, O. 2009a. 'Cosmopolitan Europe' and the EU-Turkey question: The Politics of a 'Common Destiny'. *Journal of European Public Policy*, 16(7), 1085–101.

Parker, O. 2009b. Why EU, Which EU? Habermas and the Ethics of Postnational Politics in Europe. *Constellations*, 16(3),392–409.

Parlak, İ. and Kılıçarslan, Ö. 2006. The West or the EU as 'the Other' from the Perspective of National Pride. *South-East Europe Review*, 3, 123–48.

Paul, A. 2012. Turkey's EU Journey: What Next? *Insight Turkey* 14(3), 25–34

Poettering, H.G. 2004. *Speech from Mr. Hans-Gert Poettering, Chairman of EPP-ED Group*. [Online, 21 July]. Available at: //http://www.epp.group.eu/Activities/pspeech04/Spe0721poettering2_en. Ap [accessed: 15 June 2010].

Poyraz, T. and Arıkan, G. 2003. Avrupa-Türkiye İlişkileri ve Dönemsel Olarak Değisen 'Öteki' Tanımları. *Hacettepe Üniversitesi Edebiyat Fakültesi Dergisi*, 20(2), 61–71.

Public Service Europe. 2011. *Miliband: World Needs a Strong Europe*. [Online, 13 May] Available at: www.publicserviceeurope.com/article/342/milliband-world-needs-a-strong-europe [accessed: 5 June 2012].

Radikal. 2004. Türk Ulusu bir Üstkimliktir, [Online, 29 October]. Available at: http://radikal.com.tr/haber.php?haberno=132639 [accessed: 14 June 2011].

Recchi, E. 2006. From Migrants to Movers: Citizenship and Mobility in the European Union, in *The Human Face of Global Mobility*, edited by M.P. Smith and A. Favell, 53–77.

Redmond, J. 2007. Turkey and the European Union: Troubled European or European Trouble? *International Affairs*, 83(2), 305–17.

Rehn, O. 2007. *Avrupa'nın Gelecek Sınırları: Türkiye bir Köprü Mü, Yoksa Ergime Potası Mı?* Istanbul, 1001 Kitap.

Rehn, O. 2008. *Europe's Smart Power in its Region and the World* [Online, 1 May]. Available at: www.europa.eu/SPEECH-08-222-EN[1].pdf [accessed: 6 May 2011].

Reus-Smit, C. 2009. Constructivism, in *Theories of International Relations*, edited by S. Burchill, A. Linklater, R. Devetak, J. Donnelly, T. Nardin, M. Paterson, C. Reus-Smit and J. True. London: Palgrave Macmillan, 212–36.

Rietbergen, P. 1998. *Europe: A Cultural History*. London: Routledge.

Risse, T. 2000. 'Let's Argue!' Communicative Action in World Politics. *International Organization*, 54(1), 1–39.

Risse, T. 2004. Social Constructivism and European Integration, in *European Integration Theory*, edited by A. Wiener and T. Diez. Oxford: Oxford University Press, 159–75.

Risse, T. 2010. *A Community of Europeans? Transnational Identities and Public Spheres*. New York: Cornell University Press.

Risse, T. and Engelmann-Martin, D. 2007. Identity Politics and European Integration: The Case of Germany, in *The Idea of Europe from Antiquity to the European Union*, edited by A. Pagden. Washington: Woodrow Wilson Centre and Cambridge University Press, 287–316.

Rodríguez-Zapatero, J.L. 2009. Spain Supports Turkey's Candidacy to the EU [Online, 5 April]. Available at: http://www.lamoncloa.gob.es/IDIOMAS/9/Actualidades/05042009_RANTurquia.htm [accessed: 10 March 2010].

Rosamond, B. 2000. *Theories of European Integration*. Basingstoke: Macmillan.

Roy, O. 2004. *Globalised Islam:The Search for a New Ummah*. New York: Columbia University Press.

Royal, S. with Colombani, M.F. 2007. *Maintenant*. Paris: Hachette.

Ruggie, J.G. 1998. *Constructing the World Polity: Essays on International Institutionalization*. New York: Routledge.

Ruiz-Jimenez, A., Gorniak, J.J., Kosic, A., Kiss, P. and Kandula, M. 2004. European and National Identities in EU's Old and New Member States: Ethnic, Civic, Instrumental and Symbolic Components. *European Integration Online Papers*, 8(11) [Online]. Available at: http://eiop.or.at/eiop/texte/2004-Olla.htm [accessed: 7 October 2010].

Ruiz-Jimenez, A. and Torreblanca, J. 2007. European Public Opinion and Turkey's Accession: Making Sense of Arguments For and Against. *European Policy Institutes Network Working Papers*, (16).

Rumelili, B. 2004. Constructing Identity and Relating to Difference: Understanding the EU's Mode of Differentiation. *Review of International Studies* 30, 27–47.

Rumelili, B. 2008. Negotiating Europe: EU/Turkey Relations from an Identity Perspective. *Insight Turkey* 10(1), 97–110.

Rumelili, B. 2011. Turkey: Identity, Foreign Policy, and Socialization in a Post-Enlargement Europe. *European Integration*, 33(2), 236–48.

Rumford, C. and Turunç, H. 2011. Identity Dimension: Postwesternisation. A Framework for Understanding East-West Relations, in *Fifty Years of EU–Turkey Relations: A Sisyphean Story*, edited by A.E. Çakır. London: Routledge, 136–57.

Said, E. 1995. *Orientalism*. London: Penguin.

Salter, M.B. 2002. *Barbarians and Civilization in International Relations*. London: Pluto.

Sarkozy, N. 2007a. *Je Veux Que L'Europe Change*. Official Website of the UMP [Online, 21 February]. Available at: http://wwww.u-m-p.org/site/index.php/ump/s_informer/discours/je_veux_que_l_europe-change [accessed: 12 May 20009].

Sarkozy, N. 2007b. *Testimony*. New York, Harper.

Saz, G. 2009. Turkophobia and Rising Islamophobia in Europe: A Quantification for the Negative Spillover on the EU Membership Quest of Turkey. *European Journal of Social Sciences*, 19(4), 479–91.

Scally, D. 2011. Austerity Alone Will Not Solve Crisis. *Irish Times* [Online, 1 December]. Available at: http://www.irishtimes.com/newspapers/world/2011/1206/1224308621939.html [accessed: 8 June 2012].

Scheipers, S. and Sicurelli, D. 2007 Normative Power Europe: A Credible Utopia?. *Journal of Common Market Studies*, 45(2), 435–57.

Schimmelfenning, F. 2001. The Community Trap: Liberal Norms, Rhetorical Action and the Eastern Enlargement of the European Union. *International Organization*, 55(1), 47–80.

Schmidt, V. 2006. Adapting to Europe: Is It Harder for Britain? *The British Journal of Politics and International Relations*, 8(1), 15–33.

Schmidt, V. 2007. Trapped by their Ideas: French Elites' Discourses of European Integration and Globalization. *Journal of European Public Policy*, 14(7), 992–1009.

Schmidt, V. 2009. Envisioning a Less Fragile, More Liberal Europe. *European Political Science*, 8(2), 212–24.

Schmidt, V. 2012. European Member State Elites' Diverging Visions of the European Union: Diverging Differently since the Economic Crisis and the Libyan Intervention? *Journal of European Integration*, 34(2), 169–90.

Şenyuva, Ö. and Akşit, S. 2009. Turkey Seen from the EU: Conclusions, in *Turkey Watch: EU Member States' Perceptions on Turkey's Accession to the EU*, edited by S. Akşit, Ö.Şcnyuva and Ç. Üstün. Ankara: Middle East Technical University, 176–87.

Serbos, S. 2008. Between the Functional and the Essential: European Perceptions and Domestic Choices in the Framework of Contemporary EU-Turkish Relations. *Research Journal of International Studies*, 7, 4–18.

Shakman Hurd, E. 2006. Negotiating Europe: The Politics of Religion and the Prospects for Turkish Accession. *Review of International Studies*, 32(3), 401–18.

Shore, C. 1993. Inventing the People's Europe: Critical Approaches to European Community Cultural Policy. *Man: New Series*, 28(4), 779–800.

Sjursen, H. 2002. Why Expand? The Question of Legitimacy and Justification in the EU's Enlargement Policy. *Journal of Common Market Studies*, 40(3), 491–513.

Sjursen, H. 2006. The European Union between Values and Rights, in *Questioning EU Enlargement: Europe in Search of Identity*, edited by H. Sjursen. London: Routledge, 203–15.

Sjursen, H. 2008. Enlargement in Perspective: The EU's Quest for Identity. *Arena Working Papers*, 5/2008, Oslo: ARENA, 4–6.

Sjursen, H. and Romsloe, B. 2006. Protecting the Idea of Europe: France and Enlargement, in *Questioning EU Enlargement: Europe in Search of Identity*, edited by H. Sjursen. London: Routledge, 142–64.

Smismans, S. 2010. The European Union's Fundamental Rights Myth. *Journal of Common Market Studies*, 48(1), 45–66.

Smith, S. 2001. Social Constructivisms and European Studies, in *The Social Construction of Europe*, edited by T. Christiansen, K.E. Jorgensen and A. Wiener. London: Sage, 189–98.

Solana, J. 2002. Speech at Organisation Islamic Conference-EU Forum [Online, 12 February]. Available at: http://ue.eu.int/ueDocs/cmsData/docs/pressdata/EN/discours/69428.pdf [accessed: 13 July 2011).

Solana, J. 2011. *Social Europe Journal* [Online, 13 June]. Available at:http://www.social-europe.eu/2011/06/reset http://www.-turkeyeu-relations [accessed: 4 February 2012].

Soler i Lecha, E. 2005. Debating Turkey's Accession: National and Ideological Cleavages in the European Parliament, in *The Role of Parliaments in European Foreign Policy*, edited by E. Barbé and A. Herranz. Barcelona: Office of the European Parliament [Online]. Available at: www.iuee.eu/publications-iuee.asp?parent=18up=49pub=30lid=20 [accessed: 3 May 2010].

Soler i Lecha, E and Garcia, I. 2009. Spanish Perceptions, in *Turkey Watch: EU Member States' Perceptions on Turkey's Accession to the EU*, edited by S. Akşit, Ö. Şenyuva and Ç. Üstün. Ankara, CES-METU.

Soykut, M. 2003. The 'Turk' as the 'Great Enemy of European Civilisation' and the Changing Image in the Aftermath of the Second Siege of Vienna In the Light of Italian Documents Political Literature, in *Historical Image of the Turk in Europe: 15th Century to the Present*, edited by M. Soykut. Istanbul: Isis, 45–116.

Spiegel. 2010. Spiegel interview with Turkey's Prime Minister [Online, 29 March 2010]. Available at:www.spiegel.de/international/world/0,1518,686131-2,00. htm . [accessed: 30 November 2010].

Spiering, M. 2004. British Euroscepticism, in *Euroscepticism: Party Politics, National Identity and European Integration*, edited by R. Harmsen and M. Spiering. Amsterdam: European Studies, 127–50.

Strath, B. 2002. A European Identity: To The Historical Limits of a Concept. *European Journal of Social Theory*, 5(4), 387–401.

Straw, J. 2005. *House of Commons Hansard Debates* [Online, 11 October]. Available at: http://www.publications.parliament.uk [accessed 19 November 2011].

Sümer, F. 2009. Turkey, a Special EU Neighbour Patiently Awaiting a 'Promised Marriage. *Eurolines*, 7, 124–38.

Suvarierol, S. and Aydın-Düzgit, S. 2011. Limits of Cosmopolitanism?: European Commission Officials on the Selves and Others. *Alternatives: Global, Local, Political*, 36(2), 155–68.

Szymanski, A. 2007. Germany and the Question of Turkey's Membership in the European Union. *PISM Research Papers*, 4 [Online]. Available at: www.ceeol. com [accessed: 2 February 2010].

Taggart, P. and Szczerbiak, A. 2004.Contemporary Euroscepticism in the Party Systems of the European Union Candidate States of Central and Eastern Europe. *European Journal of Political Research*, 43(1), 1–27.

Tajfel, H. 1982. *Social Identity and Intergroup Relations*. Cambridge: Cambridge University Press.

Taraktaş, B. 2008. A Comparative Approach to Euroscepticism in Turkey and Eastern European Countries. *Journal of Contemporary European Studies*, 16(2), 249–66.

Taylor, I. 2009. Erdoğan in Brussels as Turkey's EU Ambitions Face Decisive Year. *The Guardian* [Online, 19 January]. Available at: www.guardian.co.uk/ world/2009/jan/19/turkey-eu-erdogan-brussels/print [accessed: 5 December 2010].

Tekin, B.Ç. 2008. The Construction of Turkey's Possible EU Membership in French Political Discourse. *Discourse and Society*, 19(6), 727–63.

Tezel, Y.S. 2010. *Transformation of State and Society in Turkey: From the Ottoman State to the Turkish Republic*. Istanbul: İş Bankası Kültür Yayınları.

Thatcher, M. 1988. *Speech to the College of Europe at Bruges*, September 1988.

Thatcher, M. 1993. *The Downing Street Years*. New York: Harper and Collins.

The Times. 2005. Opinion: Should Turkey Join the EU? [Online, 4 October]. Available at: http://www.thetimes.co.uk/tto/opinion/article2033107.ece [accessed: 14 September 2010].

Tocci, N. 2011. Elite Opinion Dimension: Behind the Scenes of Turkey's Protracted Accession Process: European Elite Debates, in *Fifty Years of EU–Turkey Relations: A Sisyphean Story*, edited by A.E.Çakır. London: Routledge, 83–103.

Today's Zaman. 2013. EU Keeps Membership Bid On Track But Delays Talks Amid Protests Row. [Online, 26 June]. Available at: http://www.zaman.com.tr/todays_eu-keeps-membership-bid-on-track-but-delays-talks-amid-protests-row_2104334.html [accessed: 8 July 2013].

Todorov, T. 1984. *The Conquest of America: The Question of the Other*. New York: Harper and Row.

Togan, S. 2002. Turkey Toward EU Accession. *ERF Working Paper Series* 0202 [Online]. Available at: http/: www.erf.org.eg/uploadpath/pdf/0202.pdf [accessed: 26 August 2005].

Tomkinson, F. 2003. 'For the Satisfaction of All that Desire to Look into the Turkish Vanities': Images of the Turk in Seventeenth Century England, in *Historical Image of the Turk in Europe: 15th Century to the Present*, edited by M. Soykut. Istanbul: Isis, 211–26.

Torreblanca, J.I. 2002. Accommodating Interests and Principles in the European Union: The Case of Eastern Enlargement'. *ARENA Report* 7/02. Oslo: ARENA.

Torreblanca, J.I. 2005. Arguing about Enlargement?, in *Enlargement in Perspective:Arena Report* 2/05, edited by H. Sjursen. Oslo: ARENA, 13–40.

Torreblanca, J.I. and Piedrafita, S. 2005. The Three Logics of Enlargement: Interests, Identities and Arguments. *Politique Européene*, 15(1), 29–59.

Transatlantic Trends. 2006. *Top Line Data 2006* [Online]. Available at: www.transatlantictrends.org. [accessed: 10 November 2009].

Traynor, I. 2004. In 1453 Turkey was the Invader. In 2004 Much of Europe Sees it That Way. *The Guardian* [Online, 22 September]. Available at: http://www.guardian.co.uk/world/2004/sep/22/eu.turkey?INTOMPSCREU [accessed: 15 December 2010].

Uğur, M. 2000. *Avrupa Biliği ve Türkiye: Bir Dayanak/İnandırcılıkİkilemi*. Istanbul: Everest.

Uğur, M. and Canefe, N. 2004. *Turkey and European Integration: Accession Prospects and Issues*. London: Routledge.

Underhill, W. (2009). Why Fears of a Muslim Takeover are all Wrong. *Newsweek* [Online, 10 July]. Available at: http://www.thedailybeast.com/newsweek/2009/07/10/why_fears_of_a_muslim_takeover_are_all_wrong.html [accessed: 11 October 2011].

Van der Veen, A.M. 2002. *Determinants of European Identity: A Preliminary Investigation Using Eurobarometer Data* [Online]. Available at: http://isanet.ccit.arizona.edu/noarchive/vanderveen.html [accessed: 24 July 2010].

Verheugen, G. 2000. *The Enlargement Process and Turkey's Place in this Process.* [Online, 9 March]. Available at: http://sam.gov.tr/wpcontents/uploads/2012/02/ Gunterverheugen.pdf [accessed: 19 March 2010].

Verney, S. 2006. Justifying the Second Enlargement: Promoting Interests, Consolidating Democracy or Returning to the Roots?, in *Questioning EU Enlargement: Europe in Search of Identity*, edited by H. Sjursen. London: Routledge, 19–43.

Villanueva Herrero, J.R. 2009. *Turquía en la Unión Europea: Un Sueño de Modernidad* [Online,9 May 2009]. Available at: www.psoe.es/ambito/ izquierdasocialista/docs/index.do?action=viewlid=335130 [accessed: 3 March 2011].

Vucheva, E. 2009. Sarkozy Cancels Sweden Visit over Turkey [Online, 29 May].

Wæver, O., Buzan, B., Kelstrup, M. and P. Lemaitre. 1993. *Identity, Migration and the New Security Agenda in Europe.* London: Pinter.

Wæver, O. 1995. Securitization and Desecuritization, in *On Security*, edited by R. Lipschutz. New York: Columbia University Press, 46–86.

Wæver, O. 1998. Insecurity, Security and Asecurity in the West European Non-War Community, in *Security Communities*, edited by E. Adler and M. Burnett. Cambridge: Cambridge University Press, 69–118.

Wæver, O. 1999. Securitizing Sectors? Reply to Eriksson. *Cooperation and Conflict*, 34(3), 334–40.

Wæver, O. 2002. Identity, Communities and Foreign Policy: Discourse Analysis as Foreign Policy Theory, in *European Integration and National Identity*, edited by L. Hansen and O. Wæver. London: Routledge, 20–49.

Wæver, O. 2004. Discursive Approaches, in *European Integration Theory*, edited by A. Wiener and T. Diez. Oxford: Oxford University Press, 197–216.

Wæver, O., Buzan, B. and de Wilde, J. 1998. *Security: A New Framework for Analysis.* Colorado: Lynne Reider.

Wæver, O. 2005. European Integration and Security: Analysing French and German Discourses on State, Nation and Europe, in *Discourse Theory in European Politics: Identity, Policy and Governance*, edited by D.R. Howorth and J. Turfing. Basingstoke: St. Martin's Press, 33–67.

Wallace, W. 1986. What Price Independence? Sovereignty and Interdependence in British Politics. *International Affairs*, 67(1), 65–85.

Walter, J and Albert, M. 2009. Turkey on the European Doorstep: British and German Debates about Turkey in the European Community. *Journal of International Relations and Development*, 12, 223–50.

Watts, D. and Pilkington, C. 2005. *Britain in the European Union Today.* Manchester: Manchester University Press.

Wheatcroft, A.1993. *The Ottomans: Dissolving Images.* London: Penguin.

Whitney, R. 2004. Room for Turkey in an Expanded EU. *The Times* [Online, 13 September 2004]. Available at: http://www.thetimes.co.uk/tto/opinion/elites/ article2063971.ece [accessed: 13 June 2010].

Williams, M. 2003. Words, Images, Enemies: Securitization and International Politics. *International Studies Quarterly*, 47, 511–31.

Williamson, H. 2004. CDU Leader Says 'Multiculturalism has Failed', *Financial Times* [Online, 6 December 2004]. Available at: http://www.ft.com/cms/s/0/70442618-47b8-11d9-a0fd-00000e2511c8.html#az222^tgpsF84J [accessed: 4 May 2010].

Willis, A. 2011. Imprisonment of Turkish Journalists draws MEP rebuke. *EU Observer* [Online]. Available at: http://euobserver.com/9/3/951 [accessed: 9 March 2012].

Wimmel, A. 2006. Beyond the Bosphorous? Comparing German, French and British Discourses on Turkey's Application to Join the European Union. *Vienna Institute of Science Political Science Series 111.*

Woodward, S. 2002. *House of Commons Hansard Debates* [Online, 11 December]. Available at: http://www.publications.parliament.uk [accessed: 3 May 2009].

Yanık, L.K. 2009.The Metamorpohosis of Metaphors of Vision: 'Bridging' Turkey's Location, Role and After the End of the Cold War. *Geopolitics*, 14(3), 531–45.

Yanık, L.K. 2011. Constructing Turkish 'Exceptionalism': Discourscs of Liminality and Hybridity in Post-Cold War Turkish Foreign Policy. *Political Geography*, 30(2011), 80–89.

Yavuz, H. 2006. The Role of the New Bourgeoisie in the Transformation of the Turkish Islamic Movement, in *The Emergence of a New Turkey: Islam, Democracy and the AK Parti*, edited by H. Yavuz. Salt Lake City: University of Utah Press, 1–22.

Yavuz, M.H. 2009. *Secularism and Muslim Democracy in Turkey.* Cambridge: Cambridge University Press.

Yeğenoğlu, M. 2006. The Return of the Religious. *Culture and Religion*,7(3), 245–61.

Yeh, A. 2000. *Said's Orientalism* [Online]. Available at: www.eng.fju.edu/tw/Literary_Criticism/postcolonialism/Orientalism.htm [accessed: 5 November 2010].

Yılmaz, H. 2005. Indicators of Euroskepticism in the Turkish Public Opinion by the End of 2003: Basic Findings of a Survey, in *Placing Turkey on the Map of Europe*, edited by H. Yılmaz. Istanbul: Boğaziçi University, 182–6.

Yılmaz, H. 2006. Two Pillars of Nationalist Euroskepticism in Turkey: The Tanzimat and Sèvres Syndromes, in *Turkey, Sweden and the European Union: Experiences and Expectations*, edited by I. Karlsson and A. Strom Melin. Stockholm: Swedish Institute for European Policy Studies, 29–40.

Yılmaz, H. 2007. Turkish Identity on the Road to the EU: Basic Elements of French and German Oppositional Discourses. *Journal of Southern Europe and the Balkans*, 9(3), 293–305.

Yılmaz, H. 2009. Europeanisation and its Discontents: Turkey, 1959–2007, in *Turkey's Accession to the EU: An Unusual Candidacy*, edited by C. Arvantiopoulos. Berlin: Springer-Verlag, 53–64.

Yılmaz, H. 2011. Euroscepticism in Turkey: Parties, Elites and Public Opinion. *South European Society and Politics*, 16(1), 1–24.
Zarakol, A. 2011. *How the East Learned to Live with the West*. Cambridge: Cambridge University Press.
Zürcher, E. and Van der Linden. 2007. Kırılma Hattını Ararken, in *Türkiye ve İslam*, edited by Hollanda Kamu Politikaları Bilimsel Kurulu. Istanbul: Başlık.

Index

Note: page numbers followed by 'n' and another number refer to Notes.